IN FARTHEST BURMA

IN FARTHEST BURMA

THE RECORD OF AN ARDUOUS JOURNEY
OF EXPLORATION AND RESEARCH
THROUGH THE UNKNOWN
FRONTIER TERRITORY
OF BURMA AND
TIBET

Captain F. KINGDON-WARD, B.A., F.R.G.S.
*Late Indian Army Reserve of Officers,
attached 1/116th Mahrattas*

Orchid Press

Frank Kingdon-Ward
IN FARTHEST BURMA: The Record of an Arduous Journey of Exploration
and Research through the Unknown Frontier Territory of Burma and Tibet

First published by Seeley, Service & Co., London, 1921
Second edition, 2005, 2019

ORCHID PRESS
P.O. Box 19,
Yuttitham Post Office,
Bangkok, 10907 Thailand
www.orchidbooks.com

Copyright © Estate of Frank Kingdon-Ward. Protected by copyright under the terms of the International Copyright Union: all rights reserved. No part of this publication may be reproduced in any form or by any means, electronic or mechanical, including photocopying, recording, or by any information storage or retrieval system without prior permission in writing from the publisher.

Frontispiece illustration: Frank Kingdon-Ward

ISBN 978-974-524-062-9

TO
The Hon. W.A. HERTZ., C.S.I.
Late Commissioner, Magwe
Upper Burma

'Then some of us went away and annexed Burma, and some tried to open up by Fuzzies in that cruel scrub outside Suakim...'
Rudyard Kipling

1. MARU MAIDENS
Each wears a short cotton jacket and striped hand-woven skirt, with belt of brass bells. Silver hoops encircle the neck and enormous brass rings hang from their ears.

TABLE OF CONTENTS

Preface		x
Chapter I	In the Jungle	1
Chapter II	Life at a Frontier Fort	11
Chapter III	The Forest of Winds and Waters	21
Chapter IV	Fever Camp	29
Chapter V	Ascent of a Virgin Peak	39
Chapter VI	In the Temperate Rain Forest	48
Chapter VII	In the Land of the Crossbow	56
Chapter VIII	Over the Wulaw Pass	65
Chapter IX	By the Singing River	73
Chapter X	Among the Marus	79
Chapter XI	The Long Trail	89
Chapter XII	Among the Lisus	99
Chapter XIII	A Desperate March	112
Chapter XIV	Infinite Torment of Leeches	120
Chapter XV	The Plains	130
Chapter XVI	Through the Kachin Hills	140
Chapter XVII	Back to Civilisation	149
Chapter XVIII	The North-East Frontier	158
Appendix I		169
Appendix II		170
Index		175
About the Author		181

LIST OF PLATES

Frontispiece	Frank Kingdon-Ward	ii
1.	Maru Maidens	vi
2.	The Mighty Mahseer	6
3.	Cane Bridge over the Ngawchang River	6
4.	A Maru Matron	34
5.	Yawyin Children	43
6.	Imaw Bum in June	43
7.	A Yawyin Lisu Family on the Burma Frontier	57
8.	Maru Women pounding Maize	80
9.	Young Nungs	90
10.	A Black Lisu of the Ahkyang	100
11.	A Black Lisu Girl	101
12.	Nung Maidens	106
13.	An Iron Smelter	106
14.	A Maru Grave	116
15.	A Nung Rope Bridge	116
16.	A Duleng Village	121
17.	Shan Girls, Hkamti Long	121
18.	A Duleng Girl ginning Cotton	127
19.	A Hammock Bridge	132
20.	The Monastery, Putao Village	132
21.	Religious Festival on the Hkamti Plain	138
22.	A Kachin Village on the Burma Frontier	142
23.	Kachin Raft on the Mali Hka	152

Map I	The Burmese Hinterland	x
Map II	Map showing the position of The Triangle	159

PREFACE

Many of the illustrations contained in this volume I owe to the kindness of frontier officers, and my thanks are especially due to Mr P. M. R. Leonard of the Frontier Service, and to Mr T. Hare of the Public Works Department, also to Mr A. W. Porter.

I am much indebted to Major J. E. Cruickshank of the 1/2nd Gurkhas (late of the Burma Military Police) for assistance while I was at Hpimaw; to Mr J. T. O. Barnard, C.I.E., now Deputy Commissioner, Fort Hertz; and to Major J. de L. Conry of the Erimpuras.

Finally, I must record the debt of gratitude I owe to Mr W. A. Hertz, C.S.I., late Commissioner, Magwe, Upper Burma, and to Surgeon Brooks of the Indian Medical Service, who together pulled me through a serious illness at Fort Hertz.

F. K. W.
London, 1920

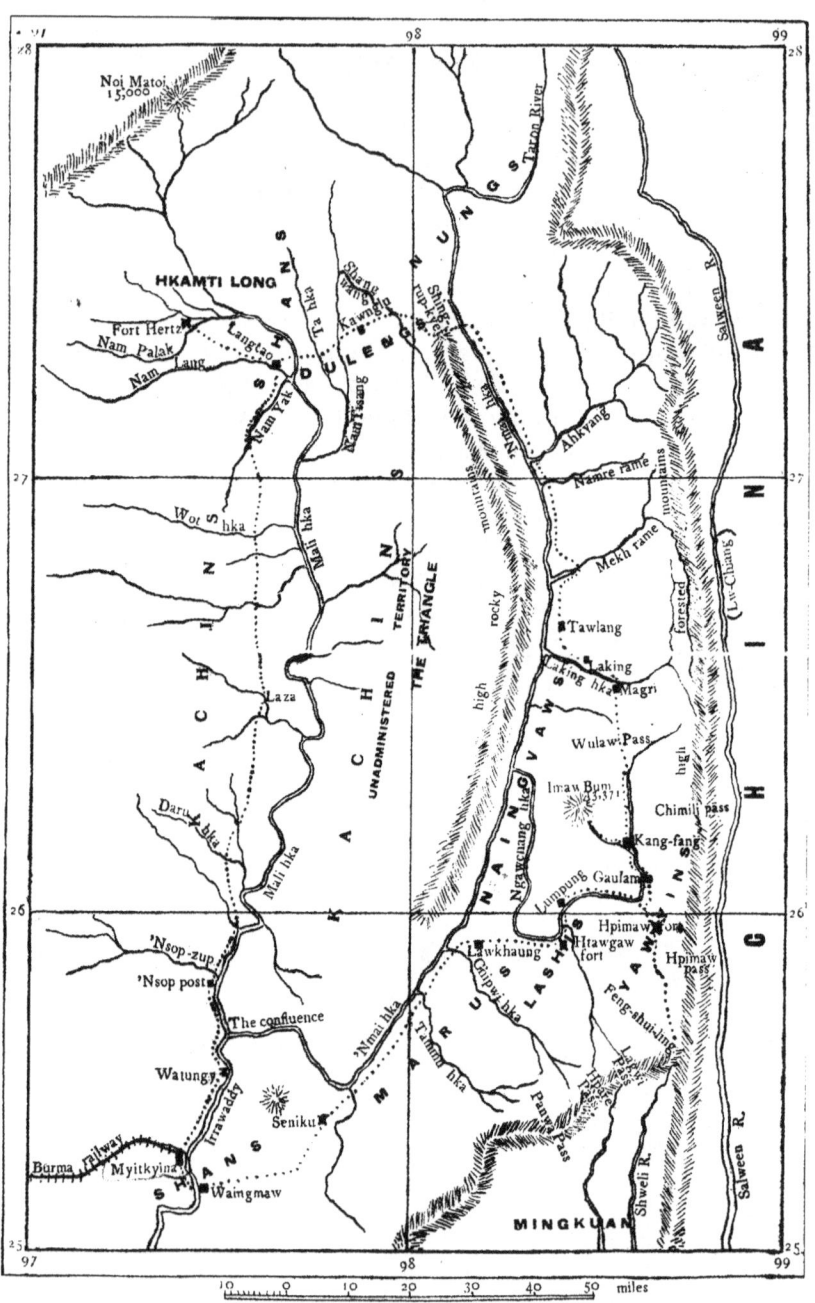

Map I. THE BURMESE HINTERLAND.
Showing the "Triangle", an almost unknown tract between the rivers Mali kha and 'Nmai

CHAPTER I

IN THE JUNGLE

The fateful year 1914 found me back in Burma ready to pursue my botanical researches in another direction.

Throughout 1913 I had continued those investigations, begun in 1911, of the flora of North-West Yun-nan, to which reference is made in a previous work[1]—investigations carried into South-East Tibet on the one hand and as far as the frontiers of remotest Burma on the other. I now determined to see something of the Burmese hinterland from within.

In coming to this decision I was partly influenced by recent events on the North-East Frontier, which besides drawing my attention to a previously unexplored region had made access to it easier than hitherto.

For several years past the nebulous country where Burma, China, Tibet and Assam meet had been the scene of political collisions which threatened to blaze up in the firmament of Indian frontier politics as an incandescent body of uncertain behaviour. When at last out of this growing welter things resolved themselves, the climax was soon reached in the British occupation of Hkamti Long, a small plain surrounded by high mountains some two hundred miles north of Myitkyina.

Here, completely cut off from their relations in the south by savage tribes inhabiting the densely forested mountains which enclose the plain on all sides, have dwelt for centuries an isolated colony of Shans, numbering to-day only a few hundred families. Just previous to this occupation, the more immediate valleys to the east and north-east of Myitkyina on the Burma-Yun-nan frontier had also been brought under the direct control of the Burma Government and the frontier for some distance north delimited; and it was primarily in this direction—namely, up the valley of the 'Nmai hka, or eastern branch of the Irrawaddy and its tributaries—that I proposed to carry on my work.

The ranges of the extreme Burma-Yun-nan frontier, which are crowned by peaks 13,000 feet high, belong to the same mountain system as the Sino-Tibetan ranges farther north, where I had started my explorations, and, as will be subsequently pointed out, may even be in direct communication with them.

I therefore planned a visit to the mountain ranges of the North-East Frontier, on the borders of Yun-nan, to be followed if practicable by an extended reconnaissance up the Burma-China frontier and across to the newly occupied post at Hkamti Long, whence I hoped eventually to reach Assam.

How this programme was only partly carried out in the face of sickness, the

---

[1] *The Land of the Blue Poppy,* by F. Kingdon-Ward. Cambridge University Press, 1913.

unimaginable difficulties of this terrible country and the crowning thunderbolt which fell on Europe in August, 1914—of which, however, I knew nothing until 23rd September, when I was yet twenty-four marches from the railway—is related in the following chapters.

Towards the end of April I left Rangoon for Myitkyina, the northern terminus of the Burma railway, 720 miles distant, whence I had started for China in 1913.

Although Bhamo, 600 miles from the sea, is considered the head of steam navigation on the Irrawaddy, small launches can and do ascend the famous first defile above Bhamo in the dry season, when the water is low; and from Myitkyina, where the river broadens out again, it is possible to ascend another twenty miles to the confluence of the Mali hka and the 'Nmai hka, nearly 1000 miles from the sea. Beyond the confluence, however, steam navigation is impossible either up the 'Nmai hka, the eastern branch and true source stream of the Irrawaddy, or up the western branch, called the Mali hka; but whereas the former is an enormously tempestuous river rushing along at the bottom of a deep cleft in the mountains, comparable in all respects with the great Tibetan rivers such as the Mekong and Salween, and hence unnavigable for any kind of craft, the latter is navigable for shallow draught country boats at least as far north as 'Nsop-zup, and for Kachin rafts a good deal farther.

Little did I realise that some of the military police officers I now met in the Myitkyina club would, ere a year had passed, lie dead in France with the glorious epitaph, "Killed in Action", inscribed over their graves, while others, still happily living, would be veterans in war.

We crossed the Irrawaddy, whose waters had risen suddenly in the course of a night, to Waingmaw on 30th April, but on the following afternoon I returned to Myitkyina, leaving my caravan waiting for me at Waingmaw, and did not get back again till nearly midnight. Leaving Myitkyina after dinner, I hired a country boat and by the light of a crescent moon we dropped down with the current. It was cool and restful out here on the bosom of the great river. In the west the setting moon hung poised over the ebony mountain ranges, throwing a band of silver across the water which danced and frolicked under the bluff where the current ran swiftly. The stars, reflected deep down in the placid stream of mid-river, twinkled brilliantly, and the warm scent of the jungle filled the air. There was no sound save now and again the slapping of saucy waves against the side of the boat and the crooning song of the Burman perched in the stern steering—the boatman forward, who completed the crew, had dropped off to sleep as soon as he had paddled us out into mid-river.

So I lay back and drank in the beauties of the night. How wonderful it would be to go on drifting, drifting down the stream always; but the thought was momentary, there was stern work ahead. I could not afford to live in a dream world, and when the boat grated on sand under the high bank at Waingmaw I came out of my reverie.

On 2nd May we started down the straight road through the half-leafless monsoon jungle to the Shan village of Wauhsaung, where the road branches. I had with me twelve mules, looked after by three Chinese muleteers, hired in Myitkyina, who would take me as far as Hpimaw; and two Chinese servants of my own, one from distant Li-kiang, who had accompanied me to Burma on my return from Yun-nan a month before, and one from Myitkyina, who spoke a little Burmese and might, I thought, be useful on the frontier for that reason, though as a matter of fact we were very soon beyond the range of any Burman-speaking people. The name of the former was T'ung ch'ien, that of the latter Lao-niu, or "old cow", to translate it.

At Wauhsaung we turned aside from the main road via Sadon to T'eng-yueh, for my destination was not Yun-nan, but the frontier region itself, and I intended to follow the frontier northwards, keeping on the Burma side, till I reached mountains of sufficient altitude to support a true alpine flora. Two years before we should, after leaving Wauhsaung, have found ourselves on a jungle path, with unbridged rivers; but in 1912 a good mule road had been made by the Public Works Department as far as Hpimaw, the last occupied post on the frontier, fourteen stages from Waingmaw.

The journey divides itself very naturally into two parts.

For the first seven stages the road keeps to the low-lying country and foot-hills in the valley of the 'Nmai hka, closely following the river, which is generally visible, or at least audible; then it leaves the main river and, crossing a high ridge, winds up and down amongst the tangled jungle-clad mountains lying between the 'Nmai hka and the Salween-Irrawaddy watershed, whose crest marks the frontier, eventually following the valley of the Ngawchang hka a big tributary of the 'Nmai hka.[2]

On 3rd May we marched seventeen miles to a small Shan village, where I slept in the local Buddhist temple, a plain bamboo hut thatched with palm leaves, and distinguished from the residential huts chiefly by several umbrellas suspended from the roof over an altar adorned with two wooden Buddhas. The road through the forest was monotonously level all the way, and I saw few flowers save one or two orchids in the grass by the wayside, and a sturdy pyramidal Curcuma with lemon-yellow flowers concealed beneath a scale armour of pink-tipped bracts which grows commonly is open forest glades throughout Upper Burma.

It was only a few miles to the military police post of Seniku, perched on a hill above the Tumpang hka, where we arrived at midday on the 4th. Here I was only too glad to rest in the excellent bungalow provided, for the heat

---

[2] The word *hka*, which is of frequent occurrence, is the Kachin word for river.

was oppressive. In the afternoon a breeze sprang up, and through the growing mistiness vast clouds could be seen taking shape.

The view from the bungalow over the Kachin hills, with the silver streak of the 'Nmai hka gleaming below, is very fine; in the distance the faint outline of mountains can be discerned. Huge columns of black smoke rose into the air from the burning jungle, which roared and crackled all round us; it was being burnt for clearings, and though it seems a sin to destroy in a few hours what it has taken perhaps centuries to build up, still man must be served.

On 5th May, after crossing the Tumpang hka, a continuous roar filled our ears, and at last we glimpsed the 'Nmai hka through a screen of bamboos; later on we came right down to it, a powerful river, rushing swiftly amongst the rocks.

In the distance high mountains were beginning to lift up their heads. The monsoon jungle was full of strange noises, which ceased mysteriously as soon as one stopped to listen. A rustling of dry leaves—lizards scampering about under the bamboos; a deprecating cough overhead—monkeys are watching our every movement.

It is a most eerie sensation to feel that you are being watched by scores of half-human creatures hidden in the trees and quite invisible. If you stand still a moment there will gradually steal over the jungle a dead silence, broken presently by a little purr; if you are quick you may catch sight of a monkey playing peep-bo with you in a tree, but as soon as he feels he is spotted the head is withdrawn behind a branch and a moment later poked carefully round the other side. Suddenly the silent trees are alive with baboons coughing, grunting like pigs and plunging off into the jungle; they seem to spring out of the violently agitated foliage, where a moment before was nothing, as crowds spring from the paving-stones in big cities. I suppose a monkey's first thought is self-preservation; his second is undoubtedly an insatiable curiosity.

We passed more fires, the bamboos crackling like musketry, interrupted now and again by louder explosions. The echo thrown back from the forest was extraordinary, no less than were the sheets of flame which leapt into the air and sank down again immediately.

I had a swim in the Shingaw hka at sundown, which refreshed me after a fourteen-mile march, and another on the following morning, when we marched only ten miles; but we were well into the foot-hills by this time and the road was nowhere level.

There were plenty of jungle fowl strutting about; in the early morning they came out into the open a good deal, but though noisy they were very wary.

The scenery was daily growing wilder, and pouring rain all through the night of 6th May and half the next day, with wind and lightning, had warned us to hasten if we would reach Hpimaw ahead of the monsoon.

A heavy thunderstorm by night in the hill jungle is an awesome sight.

Flashes follow each other with great rapidity all round the hills, like gun-fire, and peering through the driving rain you see the maddened trees suddenly lit up, and then blotted out; a moment later they are lit up again, fainter this time, as the flash is farther away; then darkness again. Very faintly do they show up yet a third time within the space of a minute—now the flash is miles and miles away and there is no answering roll of thunder. But all the time the wind is howling and the rain drumming on the hard, leathery leaves, till gradually the noise dies down and presently the stars are sparkling in a limpid sky.

May 8th was a day of continuous drizzle. It was our last day by the 'Nmai hka, and we covered fifteen miles. On the following day we crossed the Chipwi River, now very low, and began the ascent of the Lawkhaung ridge.

At the head of the Chipwi valley is the low Panwa Pass into China.

The junction of the Chipwi with the 'Nmai is one of the best mahseer[3] fishing pools on this road, which abounds with famous spots. In every bungalow is kept a fishing record-book wherein you read entries like the following, written up by officers passing through, or on duty down the road:—

"*April 10th.*—Started fishing in the pool at the junction of the Chipwi hka with the 'Nmai. After half-an-hour hooked a big fish, which fought for twenty minutes, when he got away, the line breaking on a rock."

Or again: "We began at the lower rapid opposite the Tammu hka bungalow, and hooked the first fish in fifteen minutes, with seventy-five yards of line out. He fought hard at first, but was landed and killed in half-an-hour. Weight 60½ lbs."

The Lawkhaung ridge divides the basin of the Chipwi hka from that of the Ngawchang hka, and is a separating line between the monsoon forests of Burma and the temperate forests of the mountainous North-East Frontier.

It was a stiff climb up to the military police post of Lawkhaung, and we were caught in a very heavy rainstorm before we got there; the monsoon was indeed close behind us, dogging our footsteps.

There is a considerable Maru village at Lawkhaung, almost the first we had seen, for they occupy spurs well back from the river, and are carefully hidden; the Shans of the Irrawaddy valley we had already left far behind.

The home of the Marus is the valley of the 'Nmai hka, so we scarcely saw them till we reached that river farther north in September.

Lawkhaung is about 4000 feet above sea-level, and continuing the ascent next day, we marched by a road cut in the mountain-side through the forest to Peopat, keeping from 7000 to 8000 feet above sea-level. The vegetation had changed bewilderingly, and the trees, with their heads in the chill mist, wept softly; water gushed and gurgled down all the scuppers of the mountain. Gone were the familiar tattered sheets of the banana; gone too the clumps

---

[3] Mahseer—the big carp, *Barbus tor*, of Indian rivers.

2 & 3. THE MIGHTY MAHSEER AND THE MONASTRY, PUTAO VILLAGE, HAMTIPLAIN. The fish was one of Mr P.M.R. Leonard's sixty pounders caught in the Mali hka. The men supporting it are Kachins. *Photo by P.M.R. Leonard, Esq.* The Nam Hkamti in the foreground. *Photo by T. Hare, Esq.*

of giant bamboo, the fig-trees and graceful palms, their place usurped by the sturdier oaks, magnolias and rhododendrons of a bleaker clime. On the ground lay, spending their fragrance, the large milk-white corollas of a splendid rhododendron. Here they had drifted like snowflakes, but we looked in vain for any tree from which they might have fallen; had they been wafted hither on the breeze, or spread as a couch for some Diana of the forest? At last the problem was solved—the rhododendron was epiphytic,[4] growing at great heights on the biggest trees, generally quite invisible from below.

On the glistening purple slates of the mountain runnels, down which slid thin streams of water, grew violets and patches of a lovely primula (*P. obconica* var.) cooled by the spray. The latter has white flowers with a canary-yellow eye, borne in loose umbels at the summit of long stems, which rise from amongst the rough leaves.

Emerging momentarily from the forest above Piopat—which name is attached to nothing but a bungalow—we stood on the brink of things, and spanning the intervening valley with a *coup d'œil* saw, two stages distant by road, the white speck of Htawgaw fort crowning the hill-top, a lonely rock washed by a sea of forest.

On the 12th we reached Htawgaw, descending two or three thousand feet by a break-neck path almost to the Ngawchang River, and then climbing up again to the fort, which, from an altitude of 6000 feet, commands the whole valley.

Here the country is drier, the vegetation again changing; for the high Lawkhaung ridge takes the first rush of the monsoon on its southern face. Pine-trees, alders and bracken clothe the intermediate slopes, and there are bush rhododendrons and Pieris with beaded spikes of milk-white flowers; but the vegetation of the deep valley is sub-tropical, and of the high mountains northern.

At Htawgaw I met Mr Lowis[5] of the P.W.D., who had built the Hpimaw road[6]—he was now engaged on the fort, a compact little building of stone commanding a splendid view of the Ngawchang valley and the roads to China by the Hpare and Lagwi passes, both under 10,000 feet; also Captain Enriquez, in command of the Gurkha military police. Lowis was going up to Hpimaw in a day or two, so I waited for him.

Once more attention must be drawn to the physical barrier maintained by such a mountain range as the Lawkhaung ridge, actually the watershed between two big tributaries of the 'Nmai hka—the Chipwi to the south, the Ngawchang to the north—for after crossing it we lost sight of the Marus. From Htawgaw

---

[4] *R. dendricola*, sp. nov.
[5] Mr C. C. Lowis, C.I.E., Public Works Department.
[6] Since this was written a cart-road has been built. It follows a different alignment between Seniku and Htawgaw, via the Chipwi valley.

onwards the valley is occupied by Lashis below, by Yawyins (or Lisus) above.

It is three stages from Htawgaw fort to Hpimaw, the road lying up the valley of the Ngawchang hka. For the first half of the journey the valley is comparatively broad and open, but after Lumpung village the river gnaws its way through a fine gorge, and it was here we met with our first cane suspension bridge.

The main supporting cables of rattan, or climbing palm, which grows in the jungle, are securely spliced to trees or to a stout scaffolding on either bank; loops of cane connect the main cables together, forming a hammock framework, like the rigging of a ship, and the slender flooring is composed of canes laid lengthwise along the bottom. Thus in section the bridge resembles the letter V, while a side view of it spanning a broad river is almost a U; and though simple in idea and doubtless easily constructed, it is in appearance a somewhat elaborate structure, chiefly owing to the complicated supporting tackle at either end.

The bridge, of course, sags tremendously. Sliding one foot cautiously before the other and clutching the side cables for support, you start down a steep decline and having reached the bottom in mid-stream, made giddy by the unrhythmical swaying of the structure, and by the rush of water below, ascend the other. Thus in fear and trembling the perilous passage is effected; but, like all such ordeals, familiarity soon robs it of its terrors—the reality, too, is less alarming than the appearance—and gripping the side cables with each hand, one may presently execute an exhilarating *pas seul* over mid-river, springing to the elastic recoil.

The worst bit is always along the naked spar bridging the gap between the bank and the beginning of the hammock, through the gaping jaws of the supporting masts, where it is too wide to admit of holding on to both sides at once.

Very similar cane bridges built by many different tribes are met with throughout the hill jungles of the North-East Frontier and Assam and in the Himalayan foot-hills, at least as far west as Sikkim. The Abor tubular cane bridge is perhaps the most remarkable of all.

From Htawgaw fort the road dips steeply to the Ngawchang and continues up the left bank, finally crossing the river by an excellent wire suspension bridge to the village of Lumpung, the first stage. Just below Htawgaw the Hpare hka, up which lies the path to the Hpare and Lagwi passes into China, is crossed.

The valley is crowded with villages dotting the terraced slopes where rice is grown, and above are steep hills covered with fern brake and crested with dark pine-trees, open to the winds.

On the granite rocks in the river bed many scrubby bushes were in flower, including a small wiry crimson-flowered rhododendron (*R. indicum*), now nearly over, a Pyrus and *Hypericum patulum* with large golden flowers.

Far more remarkable was the number and variety of orchids which grew on the trees, especially on oaks and alders. They were of the most quaint and varied description, more grotesque than beautiful, and of all degrees of blotchiness and colour. I was astonished to see masses of Dendrobium growing even on the pine-trees, whose ascetic-looking branches seemed to afford them neither water, refuge nor adequate support.

The wayside rocks too were thatched with purple and white Dendrobium. Orchids were most abundant between about 3000 and 6000 feet altitude.

On 17th May, in sunny weather, we continued up the right bank of the river a long stage of fifteen miles to Black Rock bungalow, situated where the Ngawchang suddenly changes direction from south to west and enters the gorge. For miles the road is cut out of the sheer cliff face, overhanging the river, and it was here that during the first expedition to Hpimaw, in 1911-1912, several hundred clumsy Government mules fell, or had to be pushed, over the precipice, for they either could not or would not advance and were holding up those behind. A broader road has been blasted now.

It was only the Yun-nan mules which saved the first Hpimaw expedition from being an expensive farce; as it was, comedy is the word.

From Black Rock bungalow Hpimaw fort is just visible at the head of the valley, a speck in the mountainous distance. On 18th May we crossed the Ngawchang again by another P.W.D. bridge, and entered the fertile little Hpimaw valley, whose streams spread out over a floor of rice-fields, and cascade from terrace to terrace—the valley that had been the cause of so much heart-burning in Yun-nan-fu, and of so much irresolution in Simla. It seemed an unattractive place—it was raining now as usual—and an insignificant, to claim so much attention. But it is by such Tom Tiddler's grounds that empires stand or fall.

Lashi women were at work in the paddy swamps—they did not look a prepossessing lot.

Riding slowly up the winding valley, which narrows rapidly, we came to the meeting of the waters, one stream flowing down from the Feng-shui-ling, the other from the Hpimaw Pass.

A short distance up the latter valley lay the village whence the armed might of the Indian Empire had driven the village pedagogue; but the Government of India has ever shown itself dilatory and cowardly in its dealings with the neighbouring power of China, and astonishingly ignorant.

Had it not been for the Imperialist Hertz,[7] a real driving force on the spot, the mandarins of Simla would assuredly have been bluffed by the mandarins of Yun-nan-seng over the Hpimaw valley.

What a delicious scene! The force that had cautiously felt its way for two months from Burma, fearful of meeting resistance, desperately resolved, advancing in battle formation into Hpimaw, to be confronted after all the

---

[7] Mr W. A. Hertz, C.S.I. (see Chapter XVIII.).

rumours of war that are so prolific along the China frontier by a courteous old Chinese schoolmaster! But the Chinaman was in no hurry. He kept the staff waiting half-an-hour. At last he appeared.

"Now," says the O.C., very stern, "you must leave this village."

"I shall be charmed," replies the courtly old man, bowing as only a well-bred Chinaman can; whereupon he packs his bedding and marches over the Hpimaw Pass back into China.

So Hpimaw was occupied by the British, immediately abandoned, and permanently reoccupied the following year, when the fort was built.

From the meeting waters, fringed with blue irises, we climbed two thousand feet up the hill to the fort, perched on a ridge overlooking the village, 8000 feet above sea-level, passing from spring almost into winter, and were welcomed by the commandant[8] to an excellent midday breakfast.

And so I settled down in the commandant's bungalow at Hpimaw fort. It was 18th May of the wonderful year 1914.

---

[8] Captain (now Major) J.E. Cruickshank.

CHAPTER II

LIFE AT A FRONTIER FORT

Grey granite, knotted and corrugated, pleated and crumpled into bewildering tangles, and again hacked through and through by destructive storm waters; stark cliffs of limestone overshadowing the valleys; slopes here clad with rain-drenched forest, elsewhere so steep and rocky that nothing but rank grass and desperate grapple-rooted trees find foot-hold in the short soil; and on a bleak, windy shoulder where a spur, sweeping down from the crest of the range, has broken its back and tumbled away in agony to the deep valley of the brawling Ngawchang hka, blocking the path to China, stands Hpimaw fort.[1]

From the commandant's bungalow just below the fort itself you look across the marble-clouded valley, where invisible villages are snugly tucked away in the folds, to the grey-blue mountain ranges of the 'Nmai hka, crowned by the gaunt mass of Imaw Bum, white-furrowed where the snow-choked couloirs spread fingerwise into the valley. Behind the bungalow the darkly forested slopes of the main range rise abruptly.

The path to China follows the spur from the fort, climbing sometimes steeply, sometimes gently, now perched on the crest, now slipping over and traversing one or the other flank.

The day after my arrival at the fort the commandant and I set out for the pass.

Tearing our way through thickets of silver-leafed and waxen-stemmed raspberries, which cover the mountains in astonishing variety, we soon plunged into a forest of rhododendron, laden with heavy trusses of crimson, scarlet, pink, white and yellow flowers, like huge coloured balls. Here in the depth of the jungle massive-stemmed conifers shoot upwards in all the pride of their great strength and, outstripping every rival, spread protecting arms over all the forest. Strapping smooth-trunked trees from whose bases radiate thin upstanding buttress roots like planks on edge, bracing them for the struggle, bear aloft crowns of foliage like fighting tops; hideous ropes and ribands of crumpled wood, disfigured with loathsome-looking warts, lie coiled like snakes in the gloom, and shouldering their way rudely through the dense foliage, burst into flower far overhead. Everything is bearded with moss, which has felted the wooden pillars and hangs in delicate festoons from the heavy-laden boughs. Orchids cling to niches in the trees, their milk-white, blunt-nosed roots creeping out in all directions, flattened against the trunk like scared lizards and probing ever moisturewards into the darkest

---

[1] There is no fort there now; it has been pulled down.

crevices. Ferns too, apple-green, malachite and olive, with delicately cut fronds, or strap-shaped and erect, help to weigh down the groaning branches buried beneath alien vegetation.

A rank undergrowth surges waist-high round the trees, where pale green butterfly orchids (Calanthe sp.), ferns and Urticaceæ contest the ground with striped cuckoo-pint hiding beneath enormous leaves.[2] Also let us add this fact: these quaint chocolate, pink and green striped cuckoo-pints are provided with lids, the tip of the lid being drawn out into a delicate lash which trails on the ground; and the more rainy the climate, the darker and damper the forest wherein these plants grow, the longer and slenderer this thread. Of what use is this strange appendage? Is it a fishing-line hung over the edge of the great cup into the wilderness below to catch something? Is it a guide rope for guests bidden to the cup? Is it, perhaps, of no use—now—its use long since lost, or one of nature's failures, abandoned? Whatever it is, nothing could be more curious.

Presently we emerged from the dim forest into sunlit meadow where grew mauve primulas with clusters of little tubular flowers like grape hyacinths (*P. limnoica*). Along the fringe of the forest twining plants with ropy yellow stems scrambled over the trees—here were white clematis and cherry-red Schizandra and fragrant honeysuckle. Far below, floating like water-lilies on the sea-green foliage, the milk-washed flowers of a magnolia gleamed.

But it is the rhododendrons which, chequering the forested slopes with splashes of colour, charm one to silence, while the heart seems to cry out with delight.

Here at 9000 feet they are great red-barked trees with tangled branches, and from the fat pointed buds immense bunches of scented flowers, thrusting aside the sticky scales, are pushing out—it seems wonderful enough how all these perfectly shaped and delicately coloured corollas can be packed away inside those closely clasping scales, without injury. But here they are nevertheless, welling honey and flooding the atmosphere with fragrance, while the bees, going mad, tumble over each other in their eagerness to take toll of the passive blossoms.

One species had leaves of frosted silver and fat trusses of citron-yellow flowers, thus resembling *R. argenteum.*

Here too grow species of Schima, Bucklandia, oak, Ficus, Acer and many other trees.

Up and up, still climbing steeply, at one time enveloped in a forest of bamboos so thick that one could not see twenty yards into the brake, and all clothed in green moss; at another, out on the open ridge again, brushing through stiff bunches of Pieris, like white heather. Far down the steeply shelving hillside lies the network of tree-girt veins which gather water from ten thousand

---

[2] *Arisama Wallichianum.*

hidden springs and, overflowing, fling it into the pulsing arteries roaring out of sight.

Grass and bracken grow on this rock-strewn slope, with bushes of blue-washed Hydrangea, golden-leafed Buddleia[3] and willow. Conspicuous too were slender trees of Ekinanthus, from every twig of which hung bunches of striped red cups. In the long grass there sprang up in June—it was but May when the rhododendrons blotched the mountains with colour—a beautiful Nomocharis with rosy flowers speckled with purple at the base, pink geranium, gaudy louse-worts and other flowers.

Suddenly in the forest we came upon a shady bank blue with the lovely *Primula sonchifolia* growing in careless luxury, as primroses do in a Kent copse. The path was strewn with fallen corollas, scattered like jewels. It is a charming plant, with rather the habit of an English primrose, a hemispherical umbel of azure-blue flowers, each yellow-eyed, springing from a thickly clustered rosette of dark green leaves.

Up here it really was still winter—there was snow in one of the gullies.

And now the cold air of the pass itself chilled us, while borne of the wings of the wind came rushing up on every side from invisible valleys the rain-clouds, melting about us as they wrapped round the trees, twisting and whirling through the branches like smoke.

Drip! Drip! Drip! It was the only sound which greeted us, for the torrent was out of earshot in the depths below, and birds are rare and subdued in these gloomy forests—we saw only some long-tailed jays and gaudy woodpeckers. Perhaps even their spirits are oppressed by the ceaseless patter of the rain and the sour smell rising from the sodden leaves whence in a night spring strange and sickly speckled pilei, spawn of perpetual twilight.

A deep gash in the mountain ridge—the pass itself, dipping steeply over into the warm blueness of the Salween valley, across which the sun shone brightly on the wall of mountains opposite, twenty miles away; and across *those* mountains too, deep down in the bowels of the earth, rumbled the red Mekong, another warrior river of Tibet.

We stood now on the rim of the Burmese hinterland, looking into the fair land of China, the threshold of Yun-nan, which means "Southern Cloudland".

On the other side a stony track leads steeply down towards the Salween. Mules might, with difficulty, be taken to the top of the pass on our side, but it is doubtful if they could be taken into China; anyhow, I never saw any cross. I was in the Salween valley, not far south of the Hpimaw Pass, in 1911. It is inhabited chiefly by Shans, and there are no mule-roads there.

The Hpimaw Pass is the most southerly pass leading direct to the Salween valley from Burmese territory, till that river itself enters Burma in the far south.

---

[3] *B. limitanea*, sp. nov.

Above the pass, which is a gap bitten out of the ridge, bushes of crimson-flowered rhododendron, growing amidst a wilderness of rocks and coarse grass, dotted the mountain-side.

The splash of torrents far below, blended into one continuous murmur, came up faintly on the breeze, and but for the wind frisking in the grass a great quiet brooded over these high solitudes.

Gusts of dense cloud boiled silently up from the white cauldron and shut out everything; its clammy breath clung to us, and wetted us through, and passed over, allowing another glimpse into the blue valley of the Salween, while the dull murmur of the torrents rose momentarily to a roar, before dying away into silence again as the next heavy curtain of vapour rushed up. And far away in sunny China puffs of silver cumulus rested lightly on the rocky Mekong divide.

Below the fort are steep slopes covered with high bracken, where grow stately lilies, yellow and white (*Lilium Wallichianum* and *L. nepalense*), purple willow-herb, royal fern (*Osmunda regalis*) and hundreds of sticky wee sundew plants, their glistening leaves outspread to entrap flies, which, when entangled, this murderous little plant innocently sucks to death.[4] Here too grows a tall Hedychium with yellow and white flowers. But the most lovely species of this genus sends up a great candelabrum of cinnabar-red flowers. It is found in shady thickets, but is not common. In the wet, shady gullies, where water is ever dripping, are masses of brightly coloured, glassy-stemmed balsam in great variety, orange, white and violet. And everywhere grow trees.

Standing on the flat shoulder of the spur at sunset, looking down into the vast pit of the valley where the Ngawchang river flows wrathfully, one could follow the changeful air currents, traced in condensing and dissolving vapour as the clouds waxed and waned.

The rainfall in the low valleys on the other side of Lawkhaung range is much heavier than it is to the north in the Htawgaw and Hpimaw valleys, and the clouds from the Burma plains do not at first easily pass over that range, precipitating themselves against it instead.

Thus looking south to the mountain wall standing up between the Chipwi and Ngawchang rivers one saw tall slate-coloured pillars of cloud with cauliflower tops mounting skyward, then flinging off grotesquely shaped puffs which mounted still higher, and melted away even as they rose, in a vain endeavour to cross the barrier.

Day after day they beat impetuously against that rocky shore, filling the air with broken cloud spray, which rushing up on us, fell in drenching showers, leaving blue sky down the valley; while to the south-west those slate-coloured pillars still towered over the distant range in ominous threat, and on the plains of Burma the rain fell in torrents.

---

[4] *Drosera peltata.*

Listen—hardly a sound to be heard! It is the hush of a June night at home; bats, flitting by like shadows, pass and repass, a fire-fly glimmers against the trees and a barking deer cries sharply, once, twice, from the bracken-clad hill-side. A few stars twinkle in the blue vault, and the mountains are dimpled into fantastic forms by light and shadow. But away behind that barrier pitiless drenching rain.

Not that it never rained at Hpimaw! Far from it! Rather was it raining *always* in a persistent, maddening drizzle, with breaks of a few days, or a week, now and then.

It was mid-June when the heavy summer rains began. Then the mountains were hidden, swathed in white bandages of cloud; and at night dense, impenetrable mists enveloped the whole world, it seemed. So I stood one time, a tiny atom on the brink of the last great precipice of all, with the waters roaring louder and louder all round me as the growing torrent lifted up its voice, and all the world weeping quietly—the most melancholy drip! drip! drip!—with a horrible inevitableness. And I struggled to tear aside the grey veil and look out upon the dangers which beset my soul on every hand, but could not; for a moment vague trees and cliffs leered from the other world like giants, and disappeared silently, mysteriously, as they had come, when the heavy white mists boiled over again, while I stood there on the shoulder of the spur, peering into the cauldron below; peering till my eyeballs cracked, afraid to move, and still could see nothing, so that a great fear was upon me, gripping me.

That was fever. But they passed, these wild fancies, born of the racking fever which came to us all in turn. Throughout those days the rain poured through the roof of the bungalow, and the puddles swelled to pools on the floor. But the rain passed too, and after the middle of June came a break.

Hpimaw village lies scattered up the shelving valley 2000 feet below the fort, and is finally pinched out by converging spurs of the main range.

There are moderate-sized, grass-thatched huts raised on stilts, with a deep porch in front, surrounded by little fenced-in patches of opium—such brilliant colours, purple, dusky crimson (the colour of port wine when the lamplight shines through it) and white! The glaucous green poppy heads were being scratched now, and fat tears of sticky fluid were oozing from the wounds and rolling slowly down the side of the globular capsule, ready to be collected. The opium is used locally as a prophylactic against fever, not smoked as in China, but wiped off on a rag, which is then sucked, or soaked in water to make a beverage! Opium pellets are also chewed.

Little stony paths, sunk between hedges of raspberry and St John's-wort, by purling streams, lead from hut to hut. By the water are beds of blue iris and Acacia trees, and in the paddy-fields brilliant blue and gold Tradescantia, with its furry stamens, and the arrow-shaped leaves of Sagittaria, familiar to lovers of East Anglia.

The Lashis are allied to the Maru, Chingpaw, Nung, and others of the

Chingpaw or Kachin family inhabiting the Burmese hinterland. There is a tradition that this particular tribe originated as a cross between a Chinaman and a Maru woman, but however that may be, there is no doubt of their close relationship to the latter.

They occupy the lower land up the Ngawchang hka and its tributaries, their rivals the Yawyins occupying the dourer stony land above them; the villages of the latter are perched on the hill-tops. Perhaps a day will come when the sturdier, hard-working Yawyin will drive out the lazy, opium-ridden Lashi from the more fertile lands, even as he himself was originally dispossessed by the more numerous Lashi.

The Chinese call the Lashi Ch'a-shan and the Marus Lan-su; both tribes are included under the general Chinese designation, *Hsiao-shan-jen*, which means simply, "men of the small hills"; while the *Ta-shan-jen*, "men of the big hills", includes Kachins, Yawyins and some smaller tribes living higher up. The ordinary Yun-nan name for the Kachins is *Shan-t'ou*—*i.e.* "hill-top" (men). There is great confusion of names in a region like this, crowded with different tribes speaking totally different languages and calling themselves by different names, while each in turn is differently named by neighbouring tribes. Moreover, the distribution of tribes such as the Lashi and Yawyin along the Burma-China frontier being discontinuous, some living well inside Yun-nan, others far away down in the Shan states and Burma, they have adopted the dress, habits and to some extent language of their dominant neighbour, Chinese or Burmese; thus we get a further complication in people of the same tribe calling themselves by different names in different parts of the country.

All the familiar tribal names on the North-East Frontier, such as Lashi, Maru, Kachin and Yawyin—the only ones we need concern ourselves with— are either so used by the majority of the tribes themselves, or else are of Kachin or Chinese origin.[5]

I have mentioned tribes as living at distinct levels, one above the other. The explanation is simple.

Speaking generally, the valleys will be more fertile and have more cultivable land than the hills; they will naturally, therefore, be occupied in the first instance by the more powerful tribes, who will remain until driven out.

Hence we would expect to find that the tribes occupying the valleys are the most powerful, while those occupying the highest spurs are the weakest.

The once all-powerful Shans originally occupied the fertile plains and valleys of western Yun-nan, and a large part of Upper Burma, being gradually dispossessed in the former province by the Chinese; but they still occupy the Salween valley, and much of Upper Burma, and the question naturally arises:

---

[5] See Appendix II.

why has not this degenerate remnant been long since driven out of the fertile Salween valley?

The answer is, that the Salween valley is extremely malarious and the Chinaman cannot live there; the thoroughly acclimatised Shans, on the other hand, thrive; hence they are left alone. The same argument applies to other parts of the North-East Frontier. A formerly powerful tribe took possession of the fertile lowland valleys, and became acclimatised and, in spite of degeneration, is now left in possession by more vigorous tribes, who are relegated to the less fertile but healthier hill-tops.

It is said that when the Lashis first came into the Hpimaw valley they found the Yawyins there and drove them out by sheer weight of numbers; however that may be, the Yawyins are now in a fair way to drive out the Lashis in their turn.

Possibly, if we had not occupied Hpimaw, Chinese from beyond the Salween valley would have gradually come over and squeezed out the Lashis, or at least obliterated them as a tribe in their own inimitable way, by absorption.

As to the reputed origin of the Lashis, it is not indeed a very romantic union anyway—a hard-headed, practical Chinaman and a half-wild Maru maid from the jungle. And truly it is difficult to say a good word for the Lashis.

The cynical callousness with which a well-favoured girl—she was only twenty—related the following story of love, intrigue and murder makes one's blood run cold.

A man from another village wished to take her to wife, she said, but she refused the offer. Again and again he had asked her, and still she refused, for she had another lover. At last, tired of importuning her, which is not the way of these hill tribes, the man came to her hut one night and, tying her up, carried her off, with the help of some friends, to his own village.

When she was untied, instead of simply running away, she plotted revenge, determined to rid herself forever of this tedious lover whom she loathed. Therefore she tried to poison him, putting aconite in his food, but failing in this, and growing steadfast in her resolve, she cast aside all subterfuge and sought surer means.

Then in the dead of night she crept to the sleeping form and drawing his own *dah* from its wooden sheath almost severed the hated head from the trunk with a ferocious blow. The man uttered never a groan, but died as he slept, swimming in blood, and she threw the body from the hut. Next morning, she tells us, she walked calmly to her own village and resumed her old life.

One can picture the dreadful scene in the lonely hut—the moonlight glistening on the wet rice-fields all round and shining through chinks in the mat wall, the glowing embers in the square hearth, then the drawing of the keen blade, the measured distance for the stroke, the wrapped figure lying on the split bamboo floor—how that floor must have swayed and cracked under her effort—and the deep breathing of the sleeper. And finally the flash in the moonlight, and the blow dimly aimed in the gloom, but struck well, cutting through helpless flesh and bone, while the blood welled out silently, staining the slippery bamboo, the cold, calculating hand which struck again and again in blind hate, to make certain, chipping the floor.

"And what did you do with the corpse?" she was asked.

"I threw it outside; it was no use in the hut."

And she was strong enough to have done it, not a doubt of that.

The unaffected surprise of the savage girl when arrested and charged with murder because she had legitimately rid herself of a man who was repugnant to her would have been comic in other circumstances. The ingenuous recital of her wrongs, and the awful means adopted in order to safeguard her rights, revealed the primitive law in its ugliest aspect.

More picturesque in his recital of love and intrigue was the fort interpreter, a wizened but agile old Chinaman, yet a very Don Juan, who sometimes came across to the bungalow in the evenings to teach me Burmese.

His home had been in Momien, now called T'eng-yueh, over the border in the Yun-nan mountains, but when he was yet a little child, in the long-forgotten days of the great Mohammedan rebellion, while Sultan Suliman ruled half a province by the blue lake of Tali-fu, the city of T'eng-yueh had been sacked by the victorious Panthays, and his house with many others burnt to the ground, so that his mother was forced to flee over the mountains to Bhamo, carrying him on her back.

Settled in Hsin-kai—that is, New Market, as the Chinese inaptly call Bhamo—for this sleepy town on the banks of the mile-broad Irrawaddy ill recalls the bracing chalk hills and pine woods of Cambridgeshire—he had grown to man's estate, and when the English deposed Thibaw and ruled in Bhamo he returned to his first home to marry.

They are restless folk, these Chinamen of the far west, and after a few years of domestic life in T'eng-yueh he had come to Burma.

There, in old Bhamo, he had met his second love and married her—not that he had grown weary of his first, but simply that business having called him to Burma it was necessary to have a *ménage* there. He recounted his conquests in the field of Eros, and his dull eyes glistened. "I suppose you like your Burma girl best," I suggested confidently, thinking of the dainty butterfly creatures one sees in that charming land, but he answered warmly:

"No! *Ta-jen*. My wife at T'eng-yueh is a very good wife. She is always at home, sewing and doing the housework; she never wants things, nor makes a fuss. But my Burmese girl is sinfully vain. She wants new silk *lone-gyi* always and gold bangles more numerous than Ma-E-Hla next door, and if I won't give them to her, threatens to run away. She is very restless and expensive," he continued sadly, "and does no work in the house; she wants to live like a princess." And the poor old man sighed.

That is so like a Chinaman—always coldly practical, with no room for sentiment.

Yet was he not satisfied with his experiences, but going to the jade mines, which lie far away in the Kachin hills, must needs take a third wife of the country, this time a Kachin.

No great troubles seem to have ruffled their married life till he came to Hpimaw, and fearful of falling amongst even worse barbarians—here he spat significantly—wished to take his latest wife with him.

But she flatly refused to go—for Hpimaw is a foreign land, eighteen days' journey from the jade mines, and so to his chagrin our Don Juan had to make a settlement on her and come away alone.

Whether he had since contracted any temporary alliances at Hpimaw he did not divulge, but he spoke so disparagingly of the Lashis, for whom he had the bitterest contempt, that I think it unlikely. Nor was it tactful to inquire too closely. Poor lonely old man! He had wives all over the country-side, but they were none of them near him; and like a true patriot he thought first of his ancestral home in T'eng-yueh!

The Chinaman has the greatest contempt for all the highland tribesmen; but I sometimes wondered whether my friend had contracted a temporary alliance with a Yawyin maid in the Hpimaw hills. They are nice-looking girls.

As to the fort itself—the reader must not suppose that a fort on the North-East Frontier is a concrete structure mounting guns. How could it be! Nor are such defences required. It is simply a small building, of stone perhaps, or of wood strengthened by walls of brushwood and grass sods, which will stop bullets. The walls are loopholed for rifle and machine-gun fire, and there is an open yard in the middle where, in case of an attack on the post, the mules can be tethered, and any extra people taken inside the fort.

Such frontier forts are always built on prominent spurs, well away from villages, commanding a pass or road, the first object being to secure a clear field of fire, jungle being felled and, if necessary, hill-sides cut away to ensure this.

In the event of trouble on the frontier they are the refuge for everybody in the post, civil and military, and it then devolves upon the garrison to hold the fort, and if possible the road, till help can arrive—which may be a matter of days. The garrison of Hpimaw was then about half a company (100 men), with a couple of machine guns.

These forts, though fulfilling their object, are naturally more imposing than alarming; they are quite strong enough to withstand such troubles as brew on this frontier, and are meant neither for war on the European scale, which is obviously impossible in such a country, nor for prolonged resistance. They would act as centres of resistance against the rebellions and sudden outburst which from time to time flash up on our Indian frontiers, and die away as suddenly and mysteriously as comets come out of the unknown and disappear whence they came. They also serve to impress and overawe the more truculent tribesmen—to prevent rather than to meet trouble.

As regards food we were quite comfortably situated, for though we could procure little in the Hpimaw valley itself, yet, owing to our proximity to the fertile regions of Yun-nan, it was a simple matter to send men over the pass for fowls, eggs, rice and potatoes. In fine weather Chinamen used to come over with supplies for sale, but in the summer they came more rarely, and then I would from time to time send a couple of Lashis across with orders to get what they could; and after a week's absence they would return with perhaps a hundred eggs and a dozen fowls, bought for a few rupees.

Eggs seemed to keep indefinitely at Hpimaw—certainly I often kept them ten days or a fortnight, only a small percentage going bad; and they may have been ancient to start with.

So hard up is the North-East Frontier for food, the villages even in the most favoured districts raising barely enough for their own subsistence, that my Lashi collectors always asked me to supply them with rice. It may be remarked here that the Hpimaw valley and the Hkamti plain are the only places in the whole vast area of the Burmese hinterland where lowland paddy can be grown. Elsewhere mountain rice, buckwheat and maize are universally cultivated.

We kept a number of fowls at the fort, but they were sadly decimated from time to time by wild cats, eagles and perhaps owls, though it may be that the alleged wild cats sometimes had only two legs.

Jungle rats were another pest; they swarmed into our store-rooms at night, and got at anything that was not tightly shut up in a tin, sometimes even opening biscuit tins by pushing them off the shelf on to the floor. They were wily too, and would not look at traps or poison, however carefully concealed; they really seemed to reason on such matters.

The fort commandant also kept up a garden, of which he was pardonably proud, cut out of the steep side of the *khud*; and from this garden he supplied our table with excellent cabbages, radishes, cauliflowers, globe artichokes and other succulent vegetables, all raised from seed. They really did very well considering the vileness of the climate—or perhaps because of it, for did it not in some ways resemble the English climate?

From time to time the fort commandant went on tour and I was left alone. These tours, lasting anything from a week to a fortnight, were confined to such paths as existed, while my goal was rather off those paths into the remoter mountains.

But in the first week of June I decided to accompany him on a trip to the Feng-shui-ling, a pass into China south of Hpimaw, of which he spoke enthusiastically.

And an account of that journey deserves a chapter to itself.

CHAPTER III

THE FOREST OF WINDS AND WATERS

On a fine June morning we set out for the Feng-shui-ling, going straight down the precipitous hill-side below the fort, through tall bracken, 2000 feet to a stream, and then up a narrowing valley; but the mules had to keep to the road.

It was rather lucky for me that the commandant had some mules, as it was difficult to get Lashi porters now, this being just the time when they were busy planting their *taungya*;[1] and though that is really the women's job, the men also have plenty to do for a short time.

This *taungya* are simply hill-sides cleared of jungle. The jungle is cut after the rains and lies for a few months. About March, when it is fairly dry, it is set on fire and the undergrowth burnt out; but the stumps and big tree trunks are only charred, and the latter lie about in all directions, making progress across a steep *taungya* extremely arduous. In the spring the maize is dibbled into the soil, and ripens in the autumn.

After the first year the soil is exhausted and the *taungya* abandoned to the jungle which quickly springs up, covering the place with a dense tangle of herbs and bushes, amongst which small trees soon begin to appear; while a new *taungya* is cleared elsewhere—a complete change of soil instead of a rotation of crops.

It is obviously a very wasteful method of cultivation, but one well suited to such a country.

Down here the air was clammy and oppressive, but the water clear and cool. Strapping leafy herbs clothed the banks, with beds of yellow monkey-flower (*Mimulus nepalensis*) and purple-spotted bugle and balsams.

Certain species of the last-named have curiously swollen nodes, like glass beads, in each of which I found a tiny grub; these swellings occur only at the points where the leaves spring from the stem—that is, at the nodes.

The path, though steep, and in the forest muddy, presented no difficulty to the mules; and early in the afternoon, after crossing a low pass, we emerged into an open bracken-clad meadow and camped by the stream.

Nor far distant, where a boisterous torrent rushed down from the mountains and disappeared into a gorge, stood a small village occupied by half-a-dozen Minchia families from Li-Kiang, in Yun-nan.

As usual in these open sunny spaces we were attended by swarms of persistent blood-sucking flies—horse-flies, blood-blister flies and sand-flies, against which there is no sovereign remedy; one must resign oneself to their

---

[1] *Taungya*—a Burmese word, meaning unirrigated hill-side cultivation.

attentions and forget the irritation in other interests.

The blood-blister flies in particular are pernicious insects, rather smaller than the common house-fly, yellow and black like a wasp. Their bite raises a blood blister the size of a pin's head, which irritates for a long time, though relief is obtained by pricking it and letting out the fluid. The bare legs and arms of the natives are speckled with small black dots, caused by the punctures of this fly. No doubt the blister-fly, like the mosquito, carries one of the many forms of fever suffered in these parts.

Along the stream-side several kinds of raspberry bore fruit, but many of them were more striking for their handsome foliage or habit, or for the soft bloom of wax which whitened their smooth stems, than for the merit of their fruit; yet some too were luscious, and a genus well worth study, and no doubt capable of great things under cultivation. They seem to prefer granite to limestone—nearly all I found were growing on granite.

There was a shrub growing here nearly every leaf of which bore a small rosy spike on the upper surface, somewhat resembling a looper caterpillar standing up; each spike, which was hollow and entered from the under surface of the leaf, contained a small insect, the originator of the disfigurement—as it was from the leaf's point of view. The resemblance to a caterpillar was really striking, but otherwise there was nothing to distinguish the sick leaf from a dozen similarly disfigured met with in England.

With sunset came a relief from the dripping heat, but an immense halo round the moon presaged rain on the morrow.

In order to allow ample daylight for settling into camp, it was our habit to start early, make a single march and halt finally about two o'clock. Consequently we were up at five o'clock and, after a quick meal, away into the forest at an hour when most folks at home are coming down to breakfast.

Our path lay up the big torrent in rich, yet not dense, forest throughout, for there was no bamboo brake to choke it here. Ferns, orchids and strange cuckoo-pints carpeted the ground, or hung from trees, with sometimes blue iris and giant lilies in open dells. But trees and shrubs were in greatest variety, including several rhododendrons, one with white flowers smelling sweetly of nutmeg (*R. megacalyx*, sp. nov.); another, and this, as previously related, a small shrub, always growing epiphytically high up on big trees, whose large white flowers, blotched with lemon-yellow at the base, were the sweetest scented in the world (*R. dendricola*).

There were also Deutzia, smothered in soft pink blossom like Japanese silk, and ropes of snowy-white clematis hanging over the bushes. The lovely *Luculia gratissima* also flourished here.

In the gloomiest depths of the forest we came upon a primula, since called *P. seclusa*, which from a cluster of large rugged dark green leaves sends up tall scapes bearing several tiers of crimson flowers.

At one place in the forest there was a clay bank overhanging a stream—we were crossing a high spur at the time and must have been nearly 9000 feet up then—covered with a mosaic of rough-leafed primulas bearing umbels of little cups filled with seed. They were allied to *P. sonchifolia*, and, like it, blue-flowered, the commandant told me; he had seen them in bloom as early as February, when snow still lay on the ground. One could imagine what that bank looked like, sheeted with blue while the sluggish forest was still half asleep under its snowy blanket, and every stream tumbling and frothing down its muddy channel as the gleaming ice melted.

Here too flourished *Beesia cordata*, a novel genus of Ranunculaceæ.

Immense trees towered all round us. Some were draped with long streamers of moss, others richly covered with ferns and orchids; a few supported small bushes of the most fragrant rhododendrons, whose handsome corollas dappled the ground.

Having made good progress through the forest, we camped at a spot selected by the Lashis who had been sent on ahead to clear the track—a small knoll overlooking the now shrunken stream. Emerging next day from an oak forest interspersed with rhododendrons and holly, we reached a big stream, its banks so thickly overgrown with bamboo that we had to wade knee-deep through the chilly water of the stream itself. The mules enjoyed this, splashing lustily, and when the sun broke through the clouds, and sparkled on the chattering water, it was delightful, save for the leeches which we collected.

Paddling thus slowly up the stream, we came from time to time into the most enchanting meads, where the valley broadened. Here the grass was purple with *Primula Beesiana*, and the shallow waters dotted with tall yellow cowslips, which were not cowslips in fact, but *Primula helodoxa*, growing on the banks, on gravel islands, on fallen tree trunks, in careless profusion. And there were flowering bushes all round us instead of forest, thickets of buckthorn and rose, wayfaring-tree, barberry and honeysuckle, amongst which sprang up white lilies, tall as grenadiers (*L. giganteum*), marsh marigolds and grasping coils of yellow-flowered Codonopsis, sunning itself as it sprawled carelessly over the surrounding plants like a rich exquisite.

Most lovely of all, hiding shyly within the dark bamboo groves, was a meadow-rue, its large white flowers borne singly, half nodding amongst the maidenhair leaves, so that in the gloom of the brake they looked like snowflakes floating through a forest of ferns. I called it the snowflake meadow-rue—there is none more beautiful.

"Why, what a paradise of flowers!" I said to my companion. "Who would have thought that these sorrowful mountains and dim, dripping forests held such treasures!"

"It is pretty," he replied. "I thought you might find something interesting at the Feng-shui-ling."

"Feng-shui-ling! Is that what they call it? Why, that may well mean 'the pass of the winds and waters.'[2] Certainly there is water enough" (we were still paddling up-stream). "Better did they call it 'Hua-shui-lin'—the forest of flowers and waters."

It was indeed a watery valley, full of wet meadows, rank forest and rushing streams.

After a mile or two we left the water and broke through the bamboo lining by a muddy path which ascended sharply to an open meadow, and here we camped amidst the flowers. Close around us on every side rose densely wooded mountains which poured ten thousand tributary rills down into the bamboo-choked streams; and I wondered how we should get back here in August when the waters rose in flood. Not far above us a bare limestone cliff overhung the pass.

It had taken us only three hours, travelling slowly, to reach this spot—altitude about 8000 feet—and after lunch we set out to climb the last 1000 feet to the pass.

Crossing several swamps, where yellow primulas clustered, we entered forest again, ascending steeply by an execrable path. A big rhododendron with enormous leaves (*R. sino-grande*) and a giant conifer[3] were conspicuous trees here, and, as usual, there was a hanging garden between earth and sky, chiefly of a lovely white orchid. An Aristolochia with quaintly bent yellow flowers like a Dutchman's pipe lolled over a bush. Presently we met a party of Yawyins from China, amongst whom was a remarkably pretty little girl; but they were very shy.

The summit of the pass is flat, overshadowed by the high cliff seen from below, which rears itself straight up from a bog at its foot. Many plants were coming on here, but there was scarcely anything in flower yet, and I waded through it with an eye open for snakes, of which we had seen several venomous-looking ones in the marshes round our camp.

The path down the other side leads to Ming-kuan, a fertile and populous valley north of T'eng-yueh, at the source of the Shweli river in Yun-nan. Again we stood on the edge of the Burmese hinterland looking into the fair land of China.

It is by this route that the coolies carry the coffin planks from the upper Ngawchang valley to Yun-nan (see Chapter VII.).

The Feng-shui-ling, though immediately south of Hpimaw, is not, as a matter of fact, on the main watershed, which throws off a long spur here; from the angle formed by this spur with the main divide rises the Shweli, a big

---

[2] It is impossible to tell from the *sound* of Chinese words what they mean, so many different words having the same sound. But the written characters at once distinguish them.

[3] Pseudotsuga sp.

tributary of the Irrawaddy. Descending into China from the Feng-shui-ling, the travellers, after crossing the western branch of the Shweli, finds a range of hills between him and the eastern branch of that river, and then a range of high mountains, the main divide in fact, between the eastern branch of the Shweli and the Salween.

The Shweli thus divides into two branches, exactly as does the Irrawaddy.

Returning to camp, we found that the orderly had bagged a brace of bamboo partridge for dinner, while the servants had collected a basketful of deliciously flavoured little strawberries[4] for our tea. The meadow in which we were camped—an irregular-shaped knoll with outcrops of bush-clad rocks, saved only by its slight elevation from being a marsh—was indeed studded with this fruit, offering us an ample supply daily.

There is plenty of game in these forests, but the jungle is too thick for *shikaring*, at least in the summer, and conditions are all against it. Tree bear used to come in quite close to the fort sometimes, and there were plenty of barking deer about. Serow are not rare either. Early winter would probably be the best time, when the leaves are off some of the trees and the weather set fine for a month or two.

As at all moderate elevations on the North-East Frontier, insect pests were legion—here it was the common fly and the horse-fly by day, and the inevitable sand-fly by night. Add to these the onslaught of ticks and leeches as soon as one stirred out of camp, and it will be realised that there are very real discomforts to be faced on the North-East Frontier during the rainy summer months. Two days spent here enabled me to climb one of the surrounding limestone peaks which reared its head almost directly above us, so near that from its summit it seemed one might toss a pebble amongst the tents, yet separated by a deep belt of that accursed bamboo brake, through which it was necessary to find a passage.

At the first attempt I charged boldly into the obstacle, but after getting covered with leeches, which crept into my boots and lodged in my hair, I accomplished nothing; for losing my bearings as I crawled this way and that, I eventually surmounted the brake, only to climb—the wrong peak!

But at the second attempt, my route being more carefully worked out beforehand, I crossed the belt of bamboo without difficulty and found myself on the flanks of the mountain.

Thence to the summit was easy going, for on the steeper slopes the undergrowth was no hindrance, the forest being open. One face of the mountain comprised a step-like series of precipices, separated by narrow tree-clad ledges, along which it was possible to scramble; and in these mossy nooks grew many interesting plants, including *Primula fragilis*, *Androsace*

---

[4] Two species of Fragaria are found here. One has scarlet fruit, almost tasteless, the other, *F. nhilgarenses*, has white sweetly flavoured fruit.

axillaris and a grotesque chocolate-red slipper orchid (Cypripedium sp.), springing stemless from between a pair of broad heart-shaped glistening leaves which hugged the ground.

It was a Dwarf in stature, it was full-grown in the size of its leaves and flowers, appearing, therefore, deformed. Towards the top of the peak were small rhododendron-trees massed with white flowers of large size, and the summit itself was covered with compact wiry shrubs, amongst which I noticed species of Cotoneaster, yellow jasmine and Weigelia.

I got back to camp drenched and tired; but the Lashis were happy as ever, sitting in camp combing out their black locks, with great deliberation—a favourite and superior performance of theirs, evidently learnt from the Chinese.

I was itching all over from leech bites that night, and though we warned off the sand-flies to some extent with a cigarette smoke screen, it was long before sleep came, and then it was but an uneasy slumber.

Starting homewards next day, we soon reached our first forest camp. Outside in the meadow was bright sunshine, but only a ray here and there pierced the foliage to greet us.

June 9th too was a sunny day, and we travelled slowly, as I wanted to collect seed of the early flowering primulas which covered the clay bank. We found a glorious crimson rhododendron[5] in full bloom, and the "nutmeg" rhododendron scented the path with its delicate fragrance.

Arrived at the Minchia village, we were soon visited in camp by our Chinese friends, and later I went with them to see what I could buy, returning with a goat (price, three rupees twelve annas) and a side of bacon (price, three rupees).

A woman who was amongst the visitors wore a pair of those tasselled silver earring that you see in parts of Yun-nan, which caused the commandant to break the Tenth Commandment. He asked me to open negotiations with the good lady, and there upon began one of those interminable discussions in which the Chinese, so expert, revel; not, it would seem, solely with the idea of scoring off a rival, since John will sell you an article for three ounces of silver, after prolonged argument, which he would not think of parting with for *taels*[6] 3.10 before you had discussed the weather; presumably then, partly for the sheer love of argument.

Of course I was no match for the matron with the earrings, but I played the game as it is played in China.

"That's pretty!" I said, fingering the bauble. "Where did you get it?"

"In Li-kiang, *ta-jen*."

---

[5] *R. facetum*, sp. nov.
[6] A *tael*, written Tl., is a Chinese ounce of silver. In the interior of China lump silver is weighed out in payment for things.

"Li-kiang! I know Li-kiang. I was there last year for the great fair at the temple of the water dragon."

It is considered diplomatic in negotiations of this sort not to talk of the matter in hand; you refer to it casually later, as a postscript. Europeans have earned an unenviable reputation for bluntness with polite Chinamen, owing to their fatal habit of coming straight to the point. We talk "all of a heap", as the mandarins say.

"Ah yes! Many people come to the fair from all parts."

"Even so! I bought a horse from a Tibetan there for Tls. 40. Do you want to sell these earrings?"

"These? I will sell this bangle for four rupees."

"I do not want the bangle, and I have not got four rupees. It is a pretty bangle nevertheless, and I will give you three rupees. How much did you say for the earrings?"

"Four rupees"—taking one off.

"It is too much. I am a poor man, but I will give you two. Why did you leave Li-kiang?"

"It was arranged that I was to marry a neighbour, according to Chinese custom. But I ran away from home with my lover, and we came to Ming-kuan. When the soldiers came to Ming-kuan, at the time of the great rising during the ninth moon three years ago, we crossed the mountains and settled here, under protection of the English."

"China is a beautiful country. The Chinese are peaceful, but the soldiers are wicked men. Next year, at the time of the grain rain [April], I shall return to Li-kiang. How much did you say for the earrings?"

"*Ta-jen* is a Government official, therefore he is rich. You shall have them for three and a half rupees."

"Only Chinese Government officials are rich. Let me see the earrings. They are not very good, and I will not buy them. I have travelled all over China—it is a beautiful country."

"Food is cheap there. How much will *ta-jen* give for the earrings?"

"I will give two rupees for the bangle."

"No, the earrings—how much, *ta-jen*?"

"I do not want them, but I will give two rupees."

"Take them, *ta-jen*; three rupees."

"All right, two rupees eight annas—it is very dear, but what does it matter!"

After that transaction was disposed of the commercial spirit became contagious, and people drifted into camp with all sorts of ridiculous articles for sale, including their clothes and bedding.

The idea was abroad that we were prepared to purchase the entire village, and the simple folk would, I believe, readily have parted with most of it in exchange for our bright rupees. As I had played the distinguished rôle of middleman in such business as was transacted—and no business, from a marriage to a railway contract, is ever conducted in China without that important functionary—the village headman sent me round a stone bottle of that fiery and inebriating Chinese wine called *hsiao-chiu*,[7] made from rice, having both looks and tastes like methylated spirit, and having, as in duty bound, tasted it, I passed it on to the men, with a note of warning.

It being the night of the full moon, a woman whose husband had died a few months previously was sacrificing a small porker and visiting the grave, for it is the Chinese custom, on the 1st and 15th of the moon, to visit the graves of the departed and send imaginary remittances of silver and the commodities of this world to the inhabitants of the spirit world.

By morning all our bread had turned bright green, and it was evident that the rains were approaching. The added burden of a continuous high temperature to places which have a summer rainfall of eighty or ninety inches, as in many parts of Burma, favours a luxuriant growth of mould on articles such as boots, bread, books, and other things, while such articles as are in some measure stuck together—cameras, for instance, and again books—become unstuck.

It was a hot march back, for the sun beat fiercely into the enclosed valley, which exuded water everywhere, turning the atmosphere into a vapour bath, so that we sweated abominably. Even after toiling up out of the steaminess to the fort on the open ridge we found it warm enough on such a day; but the clouds clustered ominously over the Pass of the Winds and Waters.

However, it had been both an enjoyable and successful week, and we got back just before the rain began in earnest.

---

[7] *Hsiao-chiu*—literally "small wine," as we should say small beer.

CHAPTER IV

FEVER CAMP

What so jolly as a bright day after a fortnight's grey skies and ceaseless rain!
In the laughing sunshine, the delicately dressed trees flaunting their flowers and leaves, the proud mountains watching over their first-born valleys throbbing with the rush of new life-giving liquid, the exquisite blue heavens where float a few wads of silver cloud, we perceive God; and the surge of thankfulness for life which rushes up from the depths of our hearts, overwhelming expression, so that we gaze on the scene in a rapture of mute ecstasy—this feeling too is of God. Would that we might continue to live in the glow of that Divine inspiration! At least it is something to have realised, if only for the moment, our own divine nature and our oneness with God.

Thus I mused one fresh morning after weary days of rain as I stood outside the fort, gazing across the gaping valley of the Ngawchang to the rippling forests and snow-smeared screes of Imaw Bum,[1] and be held in those splendid mountains a world of romance, from which the veil must be torn aside. The whole scene was wrapped in a soft blue film, the distance streaked with white snow which stood out in amazing relief; and at sunset long waves of stratus cloud lapped against the indigo rocks, where they projected from the darkness of the valley.

Two days later, therefore, on 22nd June, we set out, making a bee-line for a low col opposite the fort, and thence straight down to the Ngawchang river, rather than follow the long mule-road down the Hpimaw valley to its junction with the main valley, and up the latter again.

In this wise we descended by the zigzag footpath to Hpimaw village, crossed the head of the valley, and so up the opposite slope to the col which separates a sugar-loaf limestone peak, called Laksang Bum, from the main range.

On the far side of the col lay *taungya*—mountain cultivation—with felled giant tree trunks, blackened by fire, confusedly piled in every direction, making the way arduous; but the view of high mountains right before us, framed between gaping spurs, lured us forward. In the June twilight we came on three wooden Yawyin huts, perched on the bleak crest of the ridge which plunged steeply to the valley below, and hired a guide from amongst the inhabitants.

Then on down the steep limestone slope, its crisp turf speckled with stunted bushes of Cotoneaster, oak and white-flowered Bauhinia, till, as night deepened, we reached a splashing torrent in the valley.

---

[1] Height, 13,371 feet.

On again through the leafy darkness of the stream bed to another Yawyin village, where we halted; but our night's slumber was rudely interrupted by the rival cries of dogs and babies.

Besides my two Chinese servants, Yawyin guide and eight Lashi porters, I had with me two hired collectors, odd little fellows, lazy and unenterprising to a degree. Bum-pat in particular was a stumpy-legged, flat-nosed, pudding-faced little rascal, but a pocket Hercules when he chose to exert himself. He loved to pluck flowers by the wayside, not for my pleasure, but to set jauntily in the wide bamboo tubes which were thrust through his ragged ear-lobes; small brass rings hung likewise from these same tubes, and strips of scarlet cloth were threaded through other holes in the upper lobe of each ear. Beside him the tall, lantern-jawed Yawyin, with his plain bag hung over one shoulder and his long *dah* over the other, looked almost simple.

Reaching the Ngawchang next day, we followed a path up-stream by tangled hedges of bramble, climbing fern (Lygodium sp.) and white sprays of Polygonum, through luxuriant meadows, across water-logged rice-fields whence rose the far-away gurgle of invisible streams spilling over from one terrace to the next, into dark, forested gullies full of ferns and blue forget-me-not and velvet-leafed rock plants, to a cane suspension bridge spanning the gorge.

Here the cliffs were hung with a curtain of creepers, dependent from giant trees, and from the wet crevices sprang a wealth of ferns, begonias and clusters of violet, waxen-flowered didissandra.

The swaying bridge, so flimsy in appearance, so strong in fact, is thirty yards long, and seems to swing in an everlasting wind driven through the gorge by the water rushing along below; however, we crossed without incident, and then came a steep climb up the cliff to the open paddy-land above.

Working in the fields, with their already short skirts tucked still higher, were several stout-limbed Lashi girls, who exchanged loud-voiced greeting with my men.

"What savages!" cried T'ung-ch'ien, thinking of the demure matrons of China. "Look at their feet! Look at their hair! They are not dressed!"

And indeed his disparaging remarks were merited, for our Amazons were wading in the mud, and had, besides tucking up their skirts, thrown aside their jackets, displaying ample breasts. Their coarse black hair, which so aroused Tung's derision, was cut in a fringe round the forehead, like a mop, and tied in a knot on top of the head; their feet were bare, number eights, rather a contrast to the "six-inch gold lilies" of Tung's fellow-country women. Through the pendulous lobes of their distorted ears were thrust large bamboo tubes, supporting in turn heavy brass rings; and clumsy silver hoops loosely embraced their stout necks, hanging over the breast, with a tangle of bead necklaces. Altogether, what with their awkward movements and preposterous ornaments, these heavy-featured Lashi women were not very attractive.

After halting at a hut for lunch, while the Lashis, as usual, set about combing their locks, we set out to climb the steep spur fronting us, up which twisted a narrow path overgrown with thick bush.

The steep, rocky slopes of the Ngawchang valley above the scattered paddy pockets on the river terraces are clothed with coarse grass and bracken, interspersed with pines and alder-trees; many flowers too, as white lilies, anemones (*A. vitifolia*), orchids and meadow-rue grow in this ragged wilderness. Here and there are patches of *taungya*, where meagre crops of maize and buckwheat struggle up amongst the felled trees; and dense thickets where alders, brambles (Oxyspora sp.), ferns and twining plants, all fighting ruthlessly for place, indicate abandoned *taungya*. But the streams, flowing in deep, shady gullies, are always choked with tropical forest, which thus seems to stripe the hill-side.

Presently, after a short rest on the grassy summit of a spur, I dropped behind the others, and suddenly feeling very sick, lay down and lost consciousness. It was nearly an hour later when I staggered to my feet, and pushed on up the steep path with leaden footsteps, halting every few yards. At last two of the porters, returning from the village which they had long since reached, carried me the remaining distance.

The kindly Yawyins now put at my disposal an empty hut, swept and garnished, and for the next two hours I lay on my bed in a paroxysm of fever, starting up at the blackened thatch, from which hung festoons of soot oscillating in the breeze, and at the smoked bamboo supports, gleaming as though varnished.

After a good night's sleep I awoke feeling better, and while the men were packing looked about me. There were two very pretty young girls in one hut, gipsy-like, with hazel eyes and abundant black hair; nor were they so shy as in some of the villages.

Unfortunately the Yawyins chew *pan*, which discolours the teeth; and, ageing before their time, the women at least do not long retain those bonny looks which so charm the traveller. Moreover, though cleaner than their cousins the Lashis, still an aversion to water is sufficiently marked amongst them. However, these defects are scarcely appreciated by a casual glance, and they are decidedly attractive to the eye.

This village was situated about 3000 feet above the Ngawchang hka, by a stream which tumbled over a low cliff. Now came a long pull up. Buried in scented bracken, till, having traversed two faces of a pyramid which forms the corner-stone, so to speak, where the Ngawchang turns at right angles, we reached the edge of the forest. It was a hot day, and no water was to be found, so we sat down and made a thorough reconnaissance of our position before entering the Stygian darkness of the forest, after which we should have to trust to a sense of direction scarcely checked by observation.

Ascending thus, we had gradually prised open a view, hitherto locked away out of sight, into the very depths of the Ngawchang valley, now seen as a winding ribbon of filmy blueness, chequered with gleaming rectangles of paddy-land; to the north snow shone from the clouded peaks, while looking back, across the other bend of the Ngawchang, we saw the distant Salween divide, ribbed and buttressed between its corroded grooves.

Matted forest and marbled cloud, with here and there a yellow lozenge-shaped scar where a limestone cliff interrupted the slope, or a thread of silver where some stream leapt from its bed into the air—that was the view.

How slight an impression man has made—can ever make—on these streaming mountains, whose stony heart is well hidden beneath the velvet mantle of forest! For though the life-blood throbs so near the surface, veiling the world in soft beauty, yet any attempt to disturb it brings immediate, irreparable disaster in its train. The beauty indeed is but skin-deep. Cut away a few trees on those angular slopes and the hungry water, which has been held in leash watching and waiting, instantly rips bare the hill-side, flinging everything pell-mell into the deep-flowing arteries below, and leaving behind nothing but stark staring rock, dreadful in its agony, till time and the patient lichen shall, after long ages, have raised a new film of soil where moss and ferns many perhaps bind the gaping wound.

Wherefore any attempt at cultivation is doomed. It is only in the valleys, or here and there at the mountain foot where a sufficiency of soil has accumulated, that a hill clearing can be made. Two crops cannot be raised on it in successive years—it must be abandoned to the choking undergrowth which springs up amongst the fallen tree trunks till, after six or eight years, it can be burnt, to bear again. Such is the universal method of raising scattered crops throughout the wilderness of the North-East Frontier.

Villages are tucked away out of sight in the valleys, or cling to the lower slopes and spurs, Lashi below, Yawyin above; and the proud forest tree reigns supreme in the silence beyond.

We had been on the scorched hill-side, under a hot sun, nearly five hours when at length we reached the shelter of the forest. Here we were on the crest of a ridge and there was still no water to be had, though the fever had given me a lively thirst. However, our guide came to the rescue, by cutting down some dead bamboo haulms, whose stout stems were found to contain plenty of good rain-water, though with a slightly bitter taste. This was a piece of jungle lore worth remembering.

The jungle here was very open, almost park-like, the trees small and moss-covered. Patches of balsam, iris, ferns, Selaginella and scattered orchids were the only undergrowth.

Coming presently to a tinkling stream, we halted near by, and set about making a camp. Bamboos and saplings were soon cut down, and in the clearings rough shelters, roofed with branches and bark, rigged up, while my tent was pitched on a knoll. Then the fires were lit and all made snug for the night.

It had been a warm, sunny day, with the promise of fine weather; we were camped well up on a spur of the peak to be climbed, with provisions for a week; success was in sight. The fever attack was, of course, disconcerting, but I might throw that off; anyhow, we were out to find a way to the top.

At dusk there came a mutter of thunder, and the clear sunset sky clouded over rapidly. Louder and nearer grew the thunder, and with it the wind rose.

Within five minutes of the first warning a terrific storm rushed upon us, with brilliant flashes of lightning and drenching rain. The wind tore madly at the tent, and it looked as if it might be lifted bodily up at any moment. I was grovelling inside the little bathroom annexe at the back of the tent, tightening ropes, when there came a sudden crash, followed by a rending sound; at the same moment a shower of branches rattled down, and half the tent collapsed! A forty-foot tree had fallen across it.

I crawled out from the wreckage into the main part of the tent. The centre pole, bent like a bow, still held, and one of the support poles leaned at a drunken angle—indeed the tent might collapse bodily if I did not look sharp.

Next moment Lao-niu appeared, white in the face and streaming with water, crawling through the hole in the back of the tent like a frightened dog seeking cover.

"*Ta-jen*, it is a big tree that has fallen," he said, staring wildly.

"Cut it away from the ropes," I yelled, against the noise of the storm. "The whole tent will go in a minute!" I was pulling off my clothes then.

"*Ta-jen*, it is a big tree, a very big tree!" He repeated the statement in a dazed way, as though it were some magic formula.

"Get a *dah*, call the Lashis, cut the wreckage loose at once."

"It is a very big tree, *ta-jen*," he muttered mechanically, shivering with cold and fear, but doing nothing.

By this time I was stripped, and seizing a *dah*, I dashed out into the night. Ugh! I shuddered and caught my breath as the cold rain stung my naked body.

The storm was now at its height, the trees tossing their branches madly. Then a glare of lightning lit up the scene, and I was soon warm, hacking at the tangled wreckage. A fair-sized tree had been blown down, but was luckily supported in part by the surrounding forest, one branch only having crashed through my tent. A couple of men were already at work on it and we soon had the ropes, which, owing to the limited space, were in most cases tied to trees instead of to pegs in the ground, freed.

Then we fixed up the flapping rags of canvas and I got back under shelter, all aglow with the exertion, and rubbed myself down with a rough towel till I was as red as a boiled lobster.

The wind quickly subsided, but the rain continued for a time. Then gradually

4. A Maru Matron
The head-cloth shows that she is married. She is carrying the day's water supply from the spring. The water is carried in bamboo tubes. *Photo by A.W. Porter Esq.*

silence fell over the forest, till I could hear the men talking in their shelters and the wail of bamboo flutes; through the torn-out end of the tent a ruddy glow of camp fires burning brightly once more stole cheerfully upon my solitude. This spot we christened Storm Camp.

Next morning, to my astonishment, the day was clear and sunny after the storm; evidently it was only a local disturbance, of which we experienced a much worse example later.

We broke camp early, ascending steeply, traversing, descending, but keeping as closely as possible to the crest of the ridge which I hoped to follow all the way, forest permitting. Luckily the forest was here pretty open, with small oaks, rhododendrons, Bucklandia, magnolia and clumps of bamboo, but along the traverses and in the deep cross-cuts which trenched the ridge and plunged deeply down into impenetrable jungle progress was much slower.

This bamboo forest, as one might call it after the dominant plant, in distinction to the rain forest of Hpimaw and the Feng-shui-ling, is interesting. The trees nearly all branch close to the ground, sending up a great number of twisted and bent stems which interlace above; or the trunk supports a sort of candelabra of branches. But the clean, strapping trunk shooting straight up for fifty or sixty feet as in the rain forest is rarely met with, and then it is always a conifer; also there is less undergrowth.

From tree to tree stretched spiders' webs and long threads of gossamer which, bedewed by the rain, twinkled and glittered in the breeze as the early morning sunlight sent its shafts peeping through the glades.

An hour after starting a fever attack set me shivering and vomiting again. The going too became very bad, with precipitous descents down slippery banks into gullies stuffed full of bamboo where we had to hack out steps. Now we climbed trees and, lopping off the branches, saw the Ngawchang valley behind us, far below, mottled with sunny colours, and snow on the mountains ahead, but still a long way off.

At last I could go no farther, and wrapping myself in a blanket lay down on the ground; but the men went ahead to scout for water, the presence of which controlled our camps. Happily a pool was found not far away, and I stayed where I was till the camp was fixed, when the men returned and carried me to bed.

The afternoon waned slowly, the shivering fit passed, and by evening I felt better again. We were camped on a knoll, which the men had cleared of bamboos, using them to build their shelters. On every side was the dense, dank forest, and our water was obtained from a shallow, flat-bottomed gully, treeless and open at the top, but plunging steeply and deeply down into thick jungle on either side, which cut across the ridge at right angles.

Perhaps the most depressing feature of these forests is the immense silence which pervades them; it is as if such dim, wet solitudes oppressed animal life rather than holding out promise of shelter and food, for birds are quite rare, and we saw no animals larger than voles and mice—not even a squirrel. True, at Storm Camp on the fringe of the forest we had seen a couple of snakes—these reptiles flourish to excess in the hot, wet valleys of the Hpimaw hills—and several partridges. But here the forest seemed absolutely deserted—yet once we heard the tweet-tweet of a tiny bird.

Immediately one of the Lashis concealed himself in a thicket and started to whistle a few plaintive notes in reply.

Presently curiosity got the better of that little bird's discretion, and the tweeting came nearer. Still the decoy whistle continued, was answered, and so again, till at last the poor little victim appeared, hopping cautiously from twig to twig, cocking his head perkily now on one side, now on the other, as though considering, till he was right over the thicket where the bush-rangers lay in wait; and he would assuredly have been struck dead on the spot had there been any missiles to hand. This incident may partly account for the scarcity of birds in these hills, as it does in so many of the hill jungles where the poor natives wage incessant warfare against anything that flies, creeps or crawls, for food.

I was quite unfit to travel next day, so calling the Lashis together I spoke to them as follows:—

"Go," I said, "make a path to the snow mountains and bring back all the flowers you can find."

I was not altogether certain that, blinded in the forest as we had been on the previous day, we might not have diverged from the main ridge on to some minor spur. However, from camp the ground rose above us, and by ascending as high as possible and then climbing trees the men ought to be able to get a view of the snowy mountains and of our position in relation to them.

By the plants they brought back I should be able to judge roughly what altitude they had attained, and as I expected them to reach the snow and return laden with alpines, it was with a certain suppressed excitement that I awaited their return.

The morning dragged slowly on, and my disgust can be imagined when, quite early in the afternoon, those gallant Lashis returned hours earlier than they were expected, to report that, though it was possible to get along, there was no water (hence no place to camp), and that the cliffs were still far away. As for plants, they brought me a balsam, a Corydalis which turned out to be new[2] and one or two other subdued species of the forest undergrowth!

Where were the primulas, saxifrages and Meconopsis that I sighed for? It was a great disappointment, but I consoled myself by anticipating what we would do next day.

When darkness fell I heard the fires crackling merrily as the big rhododendron logs were piled on, and the sad wail of bamboo flutes, and snatches

---

[2] *Corydalis saltatoria*, sp. nov.

of song crooned in a minor key, from where the Lashis sat huddled up in their cramped shelter huts. The weather was still fine, but the sky had clouded over and a cool breeze had rustled the trees all day, bringing down showers of leaves at dusk.

Away in the middle of the night I awoke suddenly.

Outside the trees were weeping softly under a drizzling rain and from the gloom beyond the entrance two large eyes of livid fire gazed at me unblinking. For a long time I lay looking at this apparition, as I thought in my sickness it must be; at last curiosity could stand it no longer, and rising unsteadily I found an old tree stump just outside, from the crumbling interior of which two patches of fungus-infested spunk-wood glowed with phosphorescent flame; on the ground lay scattered leaves and sticks outlined in pale fire from the same cause.

Came 27th June, after a long, long night of wakefulness, but no bustle of starting up the ridge; for another spasm of fever had prostrated me. A fierce bout of shivering and vomiting early left me in a state of collapse for the rest of that day, and on the 28th I sent a party down the mountain, telling them to seek a route straight down the flank of the spur to the Yawyin village. If this was feasible, it would save a long round, as we had ascended by an unnecessarily circuitous route.

The men were away all day, and returned at dusk, saying they had found a new route—they were willing enough to work when it came to going down! Also they improvised a chair with two bamboo poles and a board attached by ropes.

At night a gusty wind rose, sending the leaves fluttering down again, and later came rain.

The morning of the 29th dawned damp and misty, the whole jungle sobbing quietly as it seemed, and it was with a heavy heart that I gave the order to pack up and abandon Fever Camp.

We started early, myself seated in the chair wrapped in blankets and carried by two men. Almost immediately we left the ridge and plunged down a tremendously steep declivity through a dense growth of bamboo; but the men had marked a good trail, and going ahead now, cut a way for the chair, so that we went down at a great pace. Pushing through the tall bamboos, I was soon thoroughly wetted by the showers of water shaken from their slender stems; but in a surprisingly short time we emerged from the forest, finding ourselves out on the steep, bracken-covered hill-side again, and almost immediately above the village, which was reached within another two hours.

The clouds now rolled back, revealing the mountains all round, the sun shone out, and the heavy heat of the valley began to weigh on us like a hot pudding-cloth.

We rested an hour at the village and in the afternoon continued down towards the river; though shaky, I succeeded in walking most of the way.

One of the Lashis trod on a snake in the long grass—he was bare-footed, of course—and leapt clean into the air with a yell like an Apache; when he reached earth again he broke the reptile's back with his bamboo staff.

We slept in the hut of a Chinaman who told me he came from Chungking, the port on the Yang-tze at the head of the great gorges, many weeks' march distant. This is an interesting fact, as illustrating the gradual westward movement of the Chinese. I have come across Ssu-ch'uan men cultivating inhospitable-looking mountain slopes in the remotest parts of Yun-nan, which is gradually being populated from the overcrowded Chengtu plain, the richest part of the immensely fertile province of Ssu-ch'uan, with its seventy million inhabitants. And as they press peacefully westwards they eat up and imperceptibly absorb the tribesmen who lie in their way, hustling the intractable remnant farther and higher into the mountains.

This direction taken by the emigrants of Ssu-ch'uan is the natural one, the line of least resistance, southwards down the valleys into the empty spaces of Yun-nan.

North and west would only take them into the cold Tibetan mountains and grassland plateaux, a country they abhor, and where they are not wanted.

Swarms of mosquitoes kept me awake all night. My shivering fit was due next day, but the path was easy and we should reach Hpimaw in the afternoon, as I had hired four more villagers to carry my chair.

Nevertheless it was a long journey, and it took us nearly nine hours to the fort, reached by five o'clock. The evening was beautifully fine, and as we climbed the long hill from the Ngawchang valley the "pass of the winds and waters" stood out in clear relief.

Then I dosed myself with quinine and went to bed.

Thus on 30th June the first attempt on Imaw Bum came to an untimely end.

CHAPTER V

ASCENT OF A VIRGIN PEAK

Little more than a week later we set out a second time for Imaw Bum, but alas! by this time the weather had suffered a relapse.

As before, we made straight for the Ngawchang hka over hill and dale, sleeping just above that river.

Pushing through the thick growth in the stream bed hard by the Yawyin village where we had slept previously, my attention was attracted to the strange circumstance of some tall stinging nettles rocking to and fro in still air, and turning to them I found that this motion was caused by a number of large caterpillars agitating the leaves. These formidable larvæ, apprehensive at my approach, had raised their heads, snake-like, and darting them rapidly to and fro caused the leaves on which they sat to shiver and tremble in the manner described. The trembling motion became still more marked as I looked closer, and when finally I touched one, several of them ejected at me, with considerable violence, drops of dark green fluid. Such mummery is evidently designed to scare away some enemy, but whether bird, spider or insect I did not ascertain.

On the following day we crossed the Ngawchang, and ascended to the Yawyin village by the cascade, where we learnt with astonishment that since our last visit the tiny village had been scourged, three men having died and one woman even now lying grievously sick; an old man told me that they had all eaten poisoned honey.

I asked T'ung about this, thinking of the Pontine honey which poisoned the soldiers of Cyrus during the retreat of the ten thousand, as related by Xenophon.[1]

"It is true, *ta-jen*," he said. "In the fifth and sixth months the honey is poisonous, and those who eat it die; but at other times it is good."

The old man was himself ill, and saddened by the disaster which had overtaken his village; but I gave him some medicine and he eventually recovered.

Next morning we awoke in the clouds. Heavy showers continued to fall, and the steep hill-side on the direct route to Fever Camp was very slippery.

Plunging at last into the dripping forest, we reached our goal in five hours, after an exhausting climb; however, it had proved less formidable than I anticipated, and preferable to the roundabout route via Storm Camp followed on the last journey.

We found the huts at Fever Camp in good repair, and as soon as the fires were blazing we became quite merry in spite of discomforts.

---

[1] See also Hooker, *Himalayan Journals*, and J.C. Whyte, *Sikkim and Bhutan*.

Shafts of sunlight darting between the trees next morning awakened the camp at six o'clock, and we were soon on our way, the bamboos showering their burden of water on us as we brushed through.

Keeping to the ridge, and ascending gradually, we presently halted to climb trees, but though we had a glimpse into the Ngawchang valley, the mountains were everywhere hidden. Two hour's marching brought us to the end of the path previously cut by the Lashis—a sufficient tribute to their slackness—and after that progress became slower, the bamboos growing very thickly in places. Flowers were rare; a couple of dwarf raspberries, several species of balsam, a Pedicularis and an orchid being the only ones I have recorded. But there were rhododendrons and a few other small trees mixed with the bamboo growth, and now fir-trees began to appear. Birds called at intervals, but kept out of sight; and we crossed the tracks of a bear.

In the middle of the afternoon we halted by a shallow saddle where water was found, and for the next half-hour nothing was heard but the ringing of *dah* against bamboo, as rapidly a space was cleared. One by one the shelters were run up, and presently looking through the trees I saw from my tent the gleaming fires and little groups of men seated round them over their rice-pots.

Selecting a big rhododendron, I climbed to the top and settled down to wait for the curtain to go up. After an hour I was rewarded. The clouds lifted slightly, permitting a view of the Imaw Bum range away to the left, across a broad gap.

On the right lay the Ngawchang valley, but of the ridge ahead I could see nothing on account of trees; then the mist came steaming up from below again, and everything was blotted out. However, we seemed to be going in the right direction; all we had to do was to push ahead, keeping on the ridge.

I called this place Observation Camp—altitude between 8000 and 9000 feet; it was really quite a jolly spot, except for swarms of sand-flies.

On 14th July we awoke enveloped in clammy cloud as usual, and nothing could be seen from the look-out tree. After a gradual ascent, the ridge going up and down like a switchback, we went astray for a time, bearing away to the left along a lateral spur, but luckily the clouds lifted and revealed the error before we had gone very far.

Following the first early morning rush of mist out of the valley it kept comparatively fine, and in the afternoon during a burst of sunshine we had another view of the range, girded round with bold precipices; there could be no doubt that we were converging slowly on Imaw Bum itself.

Still it was an anxious day of hard work, cutting a path, or, where the ridge broadened and the bamboos grew more openly, selecting the best route. At one point we were held up by a dense growth of stiff bamboo grass six to eight feet high, which proved a formidable obstacle.

Gradually all the old familiar trees save rhododendrons died out, while fir-trees, hitherto scattered, began to increase in numbers. Still there were no flowers, though we came across a single plant of *Podophyllum Emodi*, dangling its big pear-shaped scarlet fruits, and a curious little black orchid, as fungus-like in appearance as in situation, growing in the fermenting leaf mould. There were also a few Liliaceæ in fruit, and some ferns. Everywhere our feet trod softly the same mould, beneath the tall, slender bamboos.

Camp was pitched on a knoll commanding a good view of the range—altitude about 10,000 feet—and at nine o'clock the stars were shining in a clear sky.

I awoke in a raw mist to see T'ung leaning over me.

"*Ta-jen,*" he greeted me, "there is no water; it was all finished last night, and there is no more."

Too true. The pool from which we had drawn our supply overnight had run dry. So we set out hungry.

Half-an-hour after breaking camp we found a pool in the open jungle and had breakfast while waiting for a heavy shower to pass. All around us were silver firs, big scaly-barked rhododendrons, and thick bamboo grass from six to twelve feet high; and so we marched on, up and down along the ridge, apparently as far as ever from our goal, yet in fact making real progress.

Presently we came upon some small, bushy rhododendrons—there was one with purple flowers just over, and another with bright lemon-yellow flowers. We were hot on the scent.

Up to a certain point the rhododendrons grow bigger as one ascends the mountains, the biggest tree rhododendrons occurring at intermediate altitudes, say 7000 to 9000 feet. Thence they rapidly decrease in size, till at 12,000 to 13,000 feet on the North-East Frontier, and 14,000 to 16,000 feet on the Yun-nan ranges, they grow like heather in the Scotch Highlands.

The smallest alpine species are considerably smaller than the bushes and small trees of low altitudes. But see how little effect absolute altitude has on the flora—one finds the same species of rhododendron and primula at 11,000 feet on the North-East Frontier that one finds at 15,000 feet in north-west Yun-nan!

And the matter is no doubt one of moisture and protection in winter; at 11,000 feet on Imaw Bum plants are as close to the limit of perpetual snow as they are at 15,000 feet on the dry mountains of Yun-nan east of the Mekong. Moreover, on the latter range they must ascend to that altitude in order to find sufficient moisture during the vegetative season.

Pressing on, we came suddenly to a place where the ridge contracted to a granite wall flanked by precipices, so that we must needs crawl along the top, jumping gaps, or, descending from the crest of the ridge, turn the precipices below, scrambling along under the sheer walls.

Before me lay the answer to my questions, the realisation of my hopes. For the rocks were covered with flowers—alpine flowers—rhododendrons, primula, saxifrage, Cassiope, Cremanthodium. And not only that; with flowers which, if not identical with others found on the Tibetan frontier in 1911 and 1913, were plainly microforms of them.[2] Some species were obviously identical, and of the close relationship of the flora as a whole there could be no question.

The tremendous significance of this fact was not lost upon me—but now the reader will ask: "What question was answered by this discovery, and what was its significance?" I reply:

Well, here is an alpine flora within the limits of Upper Burma identical with another alpine flora on another mountain range 200 miles to the north and many miles to the east, separated from it by the deep, impassable valley of the Salween. This latter, the western China alpine flora, has long been recognised as closely related to the Himalayan alpine flora, so that the flora we are considering must also be so related.

Now it is impossible for this flora to have reached Burma from the Himalaya, across the plains of Assam, or the lower ranges to the west of the 'Nmai hka, crossing the hot valleys of the Mali hka and Chindwin. Nor indeed is there any record of an alpine flora at all comparable to that of western China and the Himalaya on the low hill ranges of Assam or western Burma which would lead us to think that the migration could have been in this direction. On the contrary, what is known of the flora of these ranges leads to the opposite conclusion—that such flora as has travelled by this route has come to a dead stop early on.

It is equally impossible for the flora of the Mekong-Salween divide to have jumped the Salween valley and reached the Imaw Bum range that way. Either it must have passed across from one range to the other before the Salween valley was formed, which is inadmissible, or we are driven to the conclusion that it came from the north, right round the head of the Assam valley and across the extreme tip of northern Burma. This is the only route by which the flora of Imaw Bum and of the Mekong-Salween divide can have been derived, as plainly it has been, from a common source.[3]

I spent some time collecting specimens from the granite rocks, where I found, amongst others, the following:—*Cassiope myosuroides, Diapensia himalayica, Primula sciophila,*[4] rhododendron spp., Androsace sp. *Cremanthodium gracillimum*; and we then went on our way. Ten minutes later we were in the flowerless jungle again.

---

[2] The word microform is used to denote relationship, irrespective of the degree of that relationship. Thus if A is a microform of B, some botanists may call A a variety of B, another will regard them as distinct species; by denoting them microforms one acknowledges the relationship without committing oneself further.

[3] See *Transactions and Proceedings of the Botanical Society of Edinburgh*, vol. xxvii, part i, 'On the Sino-Himalayan Flora'. Also *Geographical Journal*, November, 1919, 'On the Possible Extension of the Himalayan Axis beyond the Brahmaputra.'

[4] A beautiful little gem, related to *P. bella*.

5 & 6. Yawyin Children and Imaw Bum in June.

The boy on the left is wearing the rattan cane rings below the knee, affected by all the frontier tribes.

Imaw Bum is 13,370 feet high. It was first climbed by the author following the high spur on the right, subsequently from the rear by following up the valley on the left.

Camp was pitched at an altitude of nearly 11,000 feet, not far from the last of the silver firs. In spite of a marked chilliness in the atmosphere, there were actually fire-flies in my tent. No big bamboos were found here, so the men cut slabs of red bark from the great gnarled rhododendrons with which to roof their shelters.

At dusk a flurry of cloud tumbled off the mountain-tops and sank to bed in the valley, and I perched myself in the top of a rhododendron tree and sat there looking at the main range, and the summit of our ridge, where it joined Imaw Bum, till the stars shone out almost as brilliantly as under the clear dome of the Tibetan sky. I knew that we could easily achieve the summit next day, and returned to my tent happy. But T'ung had other misgivings.

"Only three days' food left, *Ta-jen*," he said when he came with supper.

Well, we would have to make a dash for the summit next day, and as the chances of finding any water higher up were remote, it would be best to leave the camp where it was and return there.

Taking with me five Lashis, I set out early, cutting a path through the formidable barrier of bamboo which faced us the start; but the ridge soon became more open. Here scattered through the bamboo growth were the last outposts of the silver firs, stunted and ragged, their clipped branches all pointing in one direction like finger-posts of exceptional unanimity and tedious persistence. In the shade grew livid green orchids and a beautiful Nomocharis, both white-flowered and rose; here and there a break in the bamboo growth revealed open grassy glades, likewise dappled with flowers.

Soon the big rhododendrons in turn died out, and we were wading through unresisting bamboo grass little more than waist-high, clear to the screes beyond. The ascent was steady, in places steep, with none of those dips down which had caused misgivings in earlier days.

Then came a confusion of scrub rhododendron with tawny-red or flame-yellow, trumpet-shaped flowers,[5] yellow dog rose (*R. sericea*) and bushes of white-flowered spiræa, and crossing a few strips of boulder we found ourselves free, on the naked mountain flank, lashed by hard-driven rain.

Suddenly ahead of us rose several big birds, as large as geese, which flew screaming down the slope; they were dark in colour, with short fan-shaped tails barred with white, and long necks, but that was all I could distinguish through the curtain of blown rain.

In 1919 I came across this bird again on Imaw Bum, and identified it as Sclater's monal (*Lophophorus Sclateri*), one the most magnificent of all pheasants. I also obtained a specimen of the Chinese blood pheasant (*Ithagenes sinensis*) from the same peak. Both are quite common on Imaw Bum.

Clambering up some cliffs in the crevices of which crouched half-frozen

---

[5] *R. herpesticum*, sp. nov.

dwarf shrubs such as juniper, willow, rhododendron and gnarled cherry, we at last stood on the summit of the long ridge, where it joined the main range.

We had conquered our virgin peak.

The highest summit lay some distance away to the left, along the main ridge; fronting us was another deep valley at the bottom of which flowed a considerable stream, and beyond that again a jumble of ridges, spurs and valleys, but through the veil of swirling mist it was difficult to be sure of the topography. Sufficient was it for the moment that we had achieved our object.

The far side of the mountain sloped smoothly down to the stream just mentioned, and was embroidered with rhododendrons formed in the most enchanting patterns, within the web of which were included small patches of pure white quartz sand starred with the little bluish violet flowers of *Primula coryphæa*.[6]

The rhododendrons were all dwarfs, not six inches high, bearing erect trusses each of two comparatively large flowers set horizontally, with widely gaping throats. They had white flowers, purple flowers, rose flowers, lemon-yellow flowers, port-wine flowers;[7] but perhaps the most striking of all was one with pure white, waxen-looking flowers.

In this paradise we roamed for some time though shivering with cold as the raw wind beat through our drenched garments. Patches of snow still lay melting in the gullies; the mists gathered and dispersed whimsically. I would have given a lot to have seen these mountains bathed in sunshine.

Suddenly my attention was diverted by a loud snort, and looking over the ridge I saw on the opposite scree, 300 yards away, a herd of seven takin[8] standing head to wind in the driving mist, like Highland cattle. Their backs were to us, so that we had ample leisure to examine them, as the wind was coming up-valley and we were well above them. There were two big bulls, three females and two quite small calves. It was a splendid sight, and I bitterly regretted having left my rifle in camp.

After watching them through glasses for a time we halloed, and the herd started up suddenly at the sound and made off across the scree, those great lumbering brutes, almost as big as water buffaloes, leaping nimbly from rock to rock like goats. Plunging through a strip of bamboo grass, they reappeared strung out in line on the next scree and were soon swallowed up in the mist.

It was the second time I had seen this strange beast at home, for I had been a member of the expedition which discovered and shot the first *Budorcas Bedfordi* in Shensi, five year previously. Then we had hunted them knee-deep through the snow for three days, in the bitter cold of the wild Ch'in-ling mountains, the back-bone of China, and had seen a herd of over thirty.

---

[6] *P. coryphæa*, sp. nov, closely allied to *P. bella* and to *P. sciophila*.

[7] *R. nmaiense*, sp. nov.

[8] *Budorcas taxicolor.*

Very little is known of the takin's habits or distribution yet. It has been reported from Bhutan,[9] Assam, South-East Tibet and the North-East Frontier, whence it ranges into Ssu-Ch'uan and northwards to Shensi. The Indian species is known as *B. taxicolor*, the Ssu-Ch'uan as *B. tibetanua*, the Shensi as *B. Bedfordi*; but as the vast jungle-clad mountain ranges between its extreme limits are practically unknown ground, these may eventually turn out to be the same, or colour varieties of the same animal. But much remains to be discovered, especially as regards the distribution of this animal, half-goat, half-buffalo. It may yet be found to extend down both sides of the Chindwin river, for example, and south of the Zayul chu, at the head-waters of the Mali hka beyond Hkamti Long. Unless, however, it is found in Yun-nan and more generally distributed over Ssu-ch'uan, we may be certain that its distribution is discontinuous.

At the same time it is absolutely confined to the Himalayan ranges, the parallel ranges of Upper Burma and western China, and the main divide across China.

Returning now to the low cliffs and tumbled boulders up which we had finally climbed to the summit of the ridge, we prospected again for plants. Thickets of bamboo grass alternated with smooth, gravelly slopes and confused piles of boulders, amongst which grew many handsome flowers such as *Cremanthodium Wardii*, Polygonum sp., *Saxifraga purpurascens*, *Cassiope myosuroides*, and a small purple orchid; mats of silken-leafed dwarf willow spread fanwise over the ground, and mangled junipers strove to rise above the rocks; even a tortured cherry-tree, mutilated almost beyond recognition, and a Pyrus maintained the fight against cold and starvation. But the rhododendrons, even the most dwarf, never appeared disfigured. Their splendid flowers were the most beautiful of all.

There was not, however, that overwhelming profusion of flowers here that had so astonished me on the Tibetan border in 1911 and 1913.

We got back to a dismal camp, all fires out, and the rain continuing for the rest of the day, by nightfall my tent was the refuge of moths, beetles and flying creatures of all kinds.

Next morning, 17th July, we started down the ridge, reaching our third camp in two hours, and Observation Camp two hours later. Here we halted for a short meal, and starting off again, reached Fever Camp before dusk. Round Fever Camp the sodden mould was now encumbered with scarlet, yellow and purple pileate fungi spreading their poisoned gills. Several quaint orchids and lifeless-looking broomrape were in flower. Not far above a magnificent white-flowered rhododendron (*R. crassum*) was in full bloom.

---

[9] The living specimen which in recent years was to be seen at the London Zoo came from Bhutan. This animal died in 1918. There is a stuffed specimen of *B. Bedfordi* set up in the Natural History Museum, South Kensington.

Maintaining the pace down, we were out of the forest in an hour next morning, great volumes of cloud rising from the valley towards the summits we had left. We soon reached the Yawyin village, only to learn that the sick woman had died the previous day. But the old man had recovered, and with tears in his eyes thanked me for the medicine I had given him.

I went in to see the dead woman, and in the darkness of the poor hut just made out a figure wrapped in a white cloth which entirely concealed it except for the hands crossed on the breast.

An aged hag, crouched on the mud floor, was watching over it, wailing hopelessly and wringing her hands; from time to time she ceased crying and muttered incantations; then she would burst forth again in mournful wailing that had in it a note of uncontrollable despair, dreadful to hear. In the heavy darkness beyond, where the embers of a fire glowed, a white-haired old man was cooking food, and several children crawled about, playing in the dust, heedless of the ruin round them. In such gloomy surroundings, with the old witch beside it, the corpse, swathed in its coarse hempen winding-sheet, looked horribly like an Egyptian mummy, and I was glad to withdraw from that fallen house.

Outside some men were hammering a coffin together—next day the dead woman would be buried on the cold mountain-side.

Now the old man, taking me by the hand, pointed with shaking finger.

"Two have died in that hut, *ta-jen*," he said, "three in that one."

Then he broke down altogether and wept on my shoulder.

Leaving this village of the dead the same afternoon we descended to the river, the men singing as we came down the last hill-side into the semitropical warmth of the valley, glad to be home again.

Crossing the river we did not halt, but continued till nightfall, by which time we were in the Hpimaw valley.

Camping where we halted, dead tired, and starting again at daylight, by midday on 19th July we were back at the fort with our spoil.

CHAPTER VI

IN THE TEMPERATE RAIN FOREST

Standing sentinel over the green valley wherein lay the village of Hpimaw, opposite the fort, rises a high limestone peak, aloof and frowning. Towards the valley of the Ngawchang its slope, though steep, is unbroken, but facing the main range it falls away in sheer broken-off precipices. On this side too it is grooved with a deep fissure filled with forest and walled in by great slabs of bare rock. This is Laksang Bum.

In the second week of July we set out for this peak—limestone seems to attract to itself all the prettiest flowers—and descending to the village halted in a rose-scented lane for lunch, while we called for fresh porters.

Some young girls who, pressed into service above, had carried loads for us down from the fort, ministered to our wants in the meantime, bringing bamboo flagons of thick, heady liquor, and begging for beads in return.

They are not, generally speaking, pretty, these flat-faced, short-statured, corpulent Lashi girls, but in spite of their unwashed appearance—nay, it is real enough—they are, like all the hill tribes, quaintly picturesque.

A dark blue kilt-like cotton kirtle to the knees, a short jacket barely reaching the waist, grey cloth leggings and a blue turban of ample proportions—such is their dress in the main, and were their bulky figures more shapely it would be not unbecoming. Beyond this they are loaded with bric-a-brac indiscriminately, like a Christmas tree. Below the knee are the black rattan rings universally worn here, and in addition heavy cane girdles, threaded with white cowry shells, are loosely twisted round the waist. This belt plays no part in keeping the kirtle up, however, and, sagging low in front, gives a most untidy impression, as it tries to hide the breach between the short jacket and the kirtle.

But the most striking thing about them is the vast weight of blue bead necklaces—blue seems to be their favourite colour—with which they fetter themselves. How do they get them? A simple proceeding since Johnny Gurkha came to Hpimaw and made love to them like the little gentleman he is. Before that it must have been difficult, for they love not the journey to the Myitkyina bazaar. The ubiquitous Chinese pedlar no doubt aided them.

Leaving the village, we crossed the valley and ascended the slopes on the other side; the fragrance of lilies came to us from the grass, and we pitched camp on a little knoll at the foot of the peak, amidst silvery cotton grass and tangles of bryony. Here the bracken grew seven feet high, vieing with purple-flowered meadow-rue;[1] a few small trees, skerries rising from the ferny sea, grew half

---

[1] A species like *Thalictrum Delavayi*.

submerged. Here and there bosses of limestone, cropping out irregularly, were covered with the woolly white wrinkled leaves of Didissandra, which has violet lobelia-like flowers; and a dense wall of jungle, hung with an equally dense curtain of climbing plants, made the ascent of the peak by the gully, in appearance at least, almost out of the question.

The cliff which bounded the gully on one side, however, was open, and it was up this ridge, hugging the fringe of the forest—for the other side was precipitous in places and required caution, the more so as the short dry grass which clothed the ridge was slippery—that I proposed to reach the summit.

In the afternoon blood-blister flies gave us no quarter, but as usual they passed with the day, and gave the sand-flies an innings.

The evening was fine and when the moon rose over the mountains it caught the cotton grass and splashed the whole meadow with drops of glistening silver. Fire-flies twinkled amongst the trees, some coming into my tent to examine the lantern, as though jealous of its wan beams. A deer barked close by, and was answered by another, and then came a shrill scream from high up in the jungle, as of some animal in deadly fear.

Next morning, wading across the channel of deep bracken which separated us from the peak, we gained the ridge and began the ascent. No serious difficulties were encountered until nearing the summit, whereupon what had thus far been just a very steep slope was succeeded by broken precipices and rocks, necessitating hand and foot work with frequent traversing to turn awkward-looking cliffs; and the summit was reached in about three hours without incident.

We were now about 10,000 feet above sea-level, with uninterrupted views all round, but we could see very little on account of the clouds. Across the valley a white spot on the edge of the forest marked the fort, and right at our feet lay the village. But the Ngawchang hka was buried away out of sight, and the mountain ranges which enfolded us were heavily cloud-capped.

Several rhododendrons were still in flower, one a small tree with large trusses of striking crimson-scarlet flowers (*R. agapetum*), growing along the edge of the forest—this as late as 9th July! But I have seen this species in flower as late as August; in fact it appears to flower twice, spring and summer, for I have also found it in flower, and nearly over, in May.

We descended by the wooded ravine, which though steep gave secure hand and foot hold. On the damp limestone cliffs, in beds of moss, grew patches of a pretty little pink-flowered primula now in seed. Pink and white begonias and a few other flowers shone in the festering darkness of the forest, but mostly, where light filtered through from above and the awakened undergrowth sprang to meet it, ferns carpeted the warm leaf-mould.

Lower down the descent became more difficult and we came to precipices. At last we reached the bottom, we parting the thick curtain of creepers, which hung in front of the daylight, saw our camp on the knoll, not far away.

Joyfully we plunged once more through the sea of bracken, which totally submerged us, and presently reached the tents.

Back in Hpimaw after the middle of July difficulties gathered thicker. At this time I was suffering from a bad foot which kept me indoors for several days—I had injured it climbing, and the continual pressure of sodden boots had aggravated it till it festered. And now came T'ung-ch'ien weeping and asking that he might go home.

Poor T'ung! I think it was the first time I had seen him disheartened, for he was a cheerful soul, and merry. First he told me that his little daughter had died in far-away Li-kiang—but that was months ago, while we were still in Yun-nan, and could hardly be the cause of his immediate distress; for his grief was poignant.

"Don't you remember, *ta-jen*, when we were in sunny Yun-nan in the spring—we passed some Tibetan horse dealers returning from Mandalay on the road that day, and you greeted them—how I wept one evening? I knew about it at that time."

"Then it is too late, T'ung! Why do you want to go back to Li-kiang now? See, we shall only be here a few months longer; stay with me till the autumn and we will go back to Yun-nan together next year."

Then he told me that my Lashi collectors had been unkind to him on the road, so I scolded them soundly, and next morning after a night's rest—what opiate can induce an oblivion like eight hours' peaceful sleep to ease a bruised heart?—T'ung said he would stay with me till I left. And from that moment he began to recover his old spirits.

There were family troubles at the fort too, a *dooly*-bearer having unwisely mixed himself up in an *affaire* with a Lashi matron.

They are queer folk, the Lashis, impatient of restraint, restless under the closer surveillance of the *sircar*, which, since the Yun-nan Government coquetted with the villagers of Hpimaw, has been forced into a programme of direct administration which otherwise might well have been long postponed.

The commandant, missing one of his followers, heard by the merest chance one morning that he was a prisoner in the village, awaiting execution, which was fixed for noon that very day; whereupon two sepoys, rushing down, arrived just in time to save him.

Then was unfolded the usual story of love, intrigue and revenge. It appeared that the wife of a village elder, growing tired of him, had found another lover in the *dooly*-bearer, and that these two had enjoyed each other's love.

Discovery followed; the woman had been severely beaten, and the correspondent, for all that he was an Indian—perhaps the more readily on that account—summarily condemned to death. And he would certainly have been barbarously beheaded but for the prompt arrival of the relief party.

The woman's story was to the effect that her husband was an old man, and, as she bluntly told the commandant, "no good". Baring her back, she exhibited the weals and bruises inflicted on her for her conduct, and pleaded that she had but enjoyed the embraces of her lover, a function her ageing husband could no longer fulfil.

Two men who were brought up in chains, self-appointed judges and would-be executioners of the wretched *dooly*-bearer, asked, with an assumption of haughtiness, by what right the commandant interfered in the affair. It was the law in China that a man taken in adultery was executed, and they adhered to that law, since Hpimaw was under Chinese dominion!

This was a new aspect of the case, but the prisoner's ignorance, real or assumed, of the political status of Hpimaw could not condone this reckless action, and they were naturally locked up till the civil officer, who resided at Htawgaw, three marches down the valley, could inquire into the case.

The incident threw some light on the attitude of the Lashis towards ourselves and China; either they were unaware of the real significance of our presence in the valley, or by no means reconciled to it.

Towards the end of July there came one of those sudden and inexplicable breaks in the rains, characteristic of the hills. By night it poured as steadily as ever, but by day, in spite of the cloud blanket resting soddenly on the mountains, burying their summits, owing to some cross-current of air, some subtle readjustment of pressures, the rain held off for a week, while the sun even peeped out occasionally.

Then after a tempestuous sunset behind the Lawkhaung divide the clouds would close their ranks, and pressing heavily down on the valley, envelop the fort in drenching rain for the night. They were grand sometimes, those struggles at dusk between the retreating sun and the onswarming clouds. In a river of gold the setting sun, defiant to the last, would flash its fiery signals across the valley, and disappear, while the wicked-looking cloud waves quickly closed all loop-holes, and rushing up the valley, beat furiously against the mountains.

It was on just such a night, when we were sitting down to dinner, that the bugle sounded the alarm.

I heard the tramp of feet, and men came running past the bungalow. It was as thick as a London fog outside, and the finest drizzle was falling, though heavy splashes dripped from the sodden trees.

Away down the hill on the lower shoulder you heard the stamp and jingle of saddling up in the mule lines, and presently the pack-mules came trotting up the path, with the water glistening on their harness.

There was a squad kneeling at the entrance to the fort, with fixed bayonets—they shone dully through the lamp-lit mist, and a tense silence wrapped everything now as in a shroud, not altogether due to the thick mist which seemed to be slowly but surely choking the whole world to death. The Asiatic is not less brave than the European; but in the long empty spaces of the night his nerves strain and snap like parting hawsers, and he crumples up.

For he fears silence more than anything in the world.

A clicking sound from above made me look up, to see the jacketed muzzle of a machine gun thrust menacingly through a loop-hole at an angle of the fort, and a second looked sideways down the bare slope from the keep at the opposite angle. A row of dark faces dimly outlined against the slit in the diabolical gloom gave to the whole the appearance of cruel mouth grinning evilly.

Then the commandant nodded his head, and spoke to the *subadar*. The order was given to close, and the bugle rang out once more.

Of course it was all play, or let us say dress rehearsal; but the annual crop of rumours from over the frontier had been coming in and included the oft-advertised march of imaginary Chinese legions on lonely Hpimaw.

I often think that if those high-placed mandarins in Yun-nan who considered they had a grievance when we occupied Hpimaw had themselves resided there for six months, their verdict would have been: "For God's sake take the cursed place!"

The Gurkhas, it may be remarked, are very fond of flowers—they have learnt to love them in their own mountains in far-away Nepal, I expect. I often met parties of them returning laden with bunches of rhododendrons and golden marigolds, which they stuck in glasses of water to decorate the fort.

The limit of plant adolescence had now been reached, and everything was growing and spreading enormously. The turgid undergrowth stood man-high, the trees were covered with varied flowers, not their own. The thick pile of fern-like moss which covered every tree trunk and every bamboo haulm was a hive of suburban life, a world apart from the busy life of the larger forest.

Probing into its green depths, you found the most entrancing creatures in hiding, as when you lift up the fringe of seaweed lining some sapphire rock pool; and no doubt they were equally astonished at the violation of their sanctuary.

Here I brought to light a quaint green stick-insect cleverly disguised as a sprig of moss, for which, indeed, I mistook him till he showed himself capable of independent motion. Here too in the green underworld of moss were snails shaped like French horns, and slender pink, worms, leeches—but of them more anon—beetles, spiders—oh! a menagerie of creatures; the hive pulsed with silent life. Beneath an unruffled surface, what struggles took place between creature and creature, each an idea in the Divine Mind, each labouring under a blind impulse to increase its numbers without regard for others; what raids, what devilries, what tragedies!

Then came fever again, and for several days I had to depend on my Lashi collectors; nor was their enterprise great. There were wet nights when the rain pattered dismally on the roof, grey mornings, the dripping jungle only half seen, and flying cloud; but sometimes a gleam of sunshine and a few hours' fine weather in the afternoon before the watery sky suffocated the sun again.

Below the fort the ridge falls away steeply to the valleys on either side and the flank facing the village is thickly wooded with small trees and scrub—rhododendrons, oaks, willows, Hamamelis, poplar, barberry, tangled up with miscellaneous undergrowth and climbing plants. The rock where it crops out is seen to be limestone, and likely enough this ridge was once continuous with the isolated sugar-loaf peak across the valley, Laksang Bum, already alluded to, till cut through by streams flowing down from the neighbourhood of the Hpimaw pass.

The flank away from the village falls as steeply to another stream, but, facing south, is not wooded; it is clothed instead with bracken and grass, whence spring many white and yellow flowered Zingiberaceæ, besides tall white lilies one year and yellow lilies the next, at least so I was told—certainly there were only yellow ones (*L. nepalense*) while I was there; and since both are biennials there is nothing incredible in the alternation. In rocky parts, as the slope increases, scattered oaks, alders and pines struggle against gravity, flinging a network of rugged roots over the slipping rocks. It is not till you get right down to the bottom in the cool depths of the narrow glen, where the stream cascades over slaty ledges, that forest growth occurs. Here I found another patch of *Primula seclusa*.

This contrast is typical of the whole region, and not a mere accident. North slopes are forested, south slopes are grass-clad, so that looking north one sees all the south-facing slopes at once, and the mountains appear somewhat bare, but looking south, mainly north-facing slopes are exposed, and they appear well timbered.

On fine evenings the Gurkhas used to play vigorous "soccer" on the small undulating parade ground cut out of the hill-side, and I sometimes joined them in a game, till my feet got too sore from climbing. It was a pleasant change, and home-like!

While exploring the wooded slope below the fort I found as late as the last day of July the glorious crimson *Rhododendron agapetum* still in flower. This conjured up visions of possible English gardens flaming with these magnificent trees from March till midsummer. There were some ground orchids in the wood too, including *Cypripedium arietinum* and another with twin heart-shaped leaves lying flat on the rocks, variegated and glistening, as though cut from frosted glass.

Then there silently arose just in front of me a brown flapping creature which zigzagged through the trees, sawing a little up and down, before it came to rest abruptly, and—melted away. Had it been, as I at first thought, a bird, there was nothing, save perhaps its silent movements, like those of a night-jar, remarkable about it. But no bird I ever met could alight thus on a bush and immediately disappear, noiselessly. Indeed it was not a bird; its flight, its manner of settling, its power of spontaneously blending with its surroundings, all betrayed it for what it was. It was a butterfly; and with the realisation at once the incredible size of the insect struck me. But I never captured one of those skulkers, though I saw several. What I did capture in this copse was a new species of shrew.[2]

It was here too, in wet, mossy nooks amongst the limestone rocks of this slope, that, early in July, I first found a pretty little pink-flowered primula new to me, not unlike *P. malacoides*, but less tall.

And so came August. The commandant had gone on tour again and I was alone with a tiny puppy he had given me as companion. The mails arrived regularly once a week, but their news was six weeks old, and no shadow of the breaking storm had as yet darkened Hpimaw. The entry in my diary for 4th August states that it was raining day and night and we were living in the clouds. I had been in bed all day with fever, unable to take any food, but was out again on the 6th, when I discovered a dainty little meadow-rue on the open limestone slope.

At last I made up my mind to abandon my botanical work at Hpimaw and return to England in order to regain health prior to another attempt; but I would not go by the direct road to Myitkyina—I conceived a better ending to the trip. I would march northwards right along the North-East Frontier, amongst the wild mountains where rise the Laking, Mekh and Ahkyang rivers, cross to the plain of Hkamti, and thence make my way over the mountains to Assam. This plan decided on, I at once set about making preparations.

On 12th August the clouds lifted slightly, and I started on a last climb to the Hpimaw pass.

A foul, musty odour now rose from the leaf-mould in the jungle and a magic growth of meadow flowers, not unlike the meadows of the Yun-nan mountains, but less tall, covered the open hill-sides which previously had been bare save for a thin carpet of turf; but the glory of the rhododendrons was past, their place taken by these strangers on the threshold of the forest—tall meadow-rue, twining Codonopsis with yellow bell flowers, masses of Astilbe, like giant meadowsweet, chestnut-leafed Rodgersia, Polygonum, Pedicularis, geranium, Borydalis, royal fern and crimson spikes of Epilobium.

Buddleia limitanea was in flower at 10,000 feet, and the swollen infant streams were overgrown with balsams, marsh marigold and monkey-flower, jostling each other for place, with blue-flowered Cynoglossum and colonies of lanky Polygonum. There were more small birds about now, some of them very pretty little fellows, whose queer cries were pleasant to hear.

By 17th August all was ready for our departure, and on that day I dispatched an advance guard of eight porters.

---

[2] *Blarinella Wardii*, Thomas, sp. nov. This belongs to a new genus of shrews, related to the earless shrews of North America, first distinguished by Mr Oldfield Thomas, F.R.S., of the Natural History Museum; the other two known species of the genus, *B. quadraticauda* and *B. griseldi*, are both Chinese. *B. Wardii* extends the genus westwards.

All transport on the North-East Frontier and throughout the Burmese hinterland is done by porters—there are no pack-animals of any kind, and no roads either. In western China and throughout Tibet, on the other hand, though the roads are appalling, all transport is done by mules, ponies, or yak—a very different state of affairs. It is commonly said that only beggars walk in Tibet!

T'ung was sick and a little sulky, but the idea of seeing new country so cheered me that I felt better than I had done for some time. Alas! little did I realise how vastly same is all this country for many weary marches, at least all the way to Assam. However, a real break, promised for several days, had come in the rains, the sun shone from a blue sky—it was the hottest day we had had, 81.3° F in the shade at 8000 feet!—and watching the changeful sunset where invisible air currents were reshuffling the gilded clouds, I felt that we might yet achieve something from the wreck of the season.

On 18th August the main body, consisting of T'ung (Lao-niu had left me), my Maru interpreter, Lashi servant, ten porters and myself finally left Hpimaw. There was a mail due that morning and I delayed starting till it should arrive.

At last the mules appeared toiling slowly up the winding path, and I followed them up to the fort, inside which was the post office, to get my letters; but to my disappointment, receiving only a post card, I immediately turned my back on Hpimaw and followed the porters down the hill as fast as I could go.

CHAPTER VII

IN THE LAND OF THE CROSSBOW

Taking the path down the Hpimaw valley, which skirted now golden rice-fields, we crossed the spur, thrust up like a wall between the Hpimaw stream and the Ngawchang as they converge on the confluence, and dropped into the latter valley.

Here we were soon beyond the last paddy-fields, from which fat Lashi women were busy uprooting alien weeds, and thenceforward saw no more level ground, save here and there were terraces high up enfolded in the river bends, till we reached the Shan plain six weeks later.

Everywhere the steep slopes are clad with coarse grass through which bare rock thrusts itself in places, but there is a fair amount of hill cultivation for the first few miles. Scattered over the hill-sides are pine-trees, oaks, and *Alnus nepalensis*, giving to the valley a park-like appearance.

The maize crop was now ripening, and many are the devices employed to scare away the monkeys which raid the fields by night. On the very steepest slopes a small hut is built at the top, with a long diving-board jutting out, thus overlooking the entire slope below. In this forward observing-post one or two—generally two—people take up position for the night, and when the monkeys come, sally forth and drive them away by making strange noises and throwing things at them. In the slack intervals between raids they make love.

A more ingenious method is to erect bamboo poles with split tops, here and there, attaching a cord to each. When the cord is jerked the split bamboo clacks lustily, and by tying all the cords together and leading the one line to the hut the clappers can with one tug be set clacking simultaneously. Thus all the sentry has to do is to sit in the hut and give the line a sharp tug every few minutes, when alarming noises start up unexpectedly from every corner of the *taungya*. The disadvantage of this method is that as only one is required on sentry duty, the prospects for love-making are not so good.

Tins are sometimes used instead of split bamboos, and where a stream runs through the *taungya*, the line is stretched out from bank to bank with a float, in the shape of a log of wood attached to it, dangling in the water. The rush of the torrent against the float, flinging it this way and that, jerks the rope spasmodically, which in turn rattles tins or clacks bamboos all over the field; thus a more or less continuous noise is kept up, breaking out now here, now there with whimsical uncertainty.

But the most ingenious apparatus of all was worked by means of a hollow log, pivoted in the bed of a torrent. As the steam filled the reservoir with water, the log tipped up, emptied out the water and returned heavily to its original position, hitting a stretched bamboo cord a shrewd blow as it fell back. This

7. A Yawyin Lisu Family of the Burma Frontier.
The girl on the right is wearing the striped and tasselled head-cloth of the Yawyins.

in turn jerked a cord attached to all the clappers, which clacked away out on the *taungya* every few minutes as the trough filled and fell, emptied and rose.

In the evening we reached a considerable village called Gaulam—there were both Lashis and Yawyins here. It is prettily situated in the mouth of a V-shaped gully, on a shelving fan of gravel spread out by the stream, the big sixty-foot huts raised on piles sheltered by palms and walnut-trees, with tangled hedges of cucumber plants from which hang golden fruits like bananas. Below the river chatters merrily by, in a broad, shingly bed, before entering the gorge.

Clapper, clapper, clack, clack went the monkey scares, shaken by the tumbling waters of the torrent. As the full moon rose, flooding the valley in golden light, troops of monkeys came out of the black jungle above, and we heard the shrill cries of the children, and the *clap, clackety, clap* all through the night, driving them back.

The temperature fell only to 65° F, but the air was raw after a damp night.

Though the next day opened with drizzling rain, the sun quickly came through, and it was muggy in the valley.

We marched to Kang-fang in the morning, crossing several deep gullies filled with a confusion of shrubs, brambles and trees, strung together and often smothered beneath an immense tangle of climbing fern, Polygonum and

Leptosodon, whose delicate fairy bells of pale violet colour swung mutely on the breeze.

Gorgeous butterflies sported in the sunshine, and a plague of flies tormented us. Where there was any cultivation it was chiefly millet and maize, with patches of tobacco and cucumber round the villages.

There is no flat ground anywhere, not so much as to pitch a tent on, save in the river bed where the shrinking waters have laid bare a pebble bank.

Kang-fang stands on the left bank, the river being crossed by a cane suspension bridge; thenceforward we kept to the right bank of the Ngawchang. Kang-fang is also the last village up the valley where Chinese are met with, and a depôt for storing the coffin planks which are brought down from the forests to be carried into China.

This coffin plank industry is of some importance on the frontier, and considering the rapidity with which the trees are being destroyed, it is strange that the Indian Government has taken no steps to regulate the export of planks or protect the tree.

Moreover, the timber might prove of value for other purposes besides that of making coffins, and though the inaccessibility of these forests would prohibit the export of timber to Myitkyina, the tree might be introduced elsewhere.

The tree in question is a magnificent juniper, which grows upwards of 150 feet high and 20 feet in girth at the base. It is not found in the Ngawchang valley below about 6000 feet, nor much above 8000 feet, and occurs scattered or in groves probably all the way up the North-East Frontier. The finest specimens I came across were confined to the remote forests and gorges around the Wulaw Pass.

The Chinese name is *hsiang-mu-shu*—that is, "scented-wood tree"—and T'ung assured me that a conifer we had seen growing amongst arid rocks in the stark gorges of the Tibetan Mekong in 1913 is the same tree as the one which is cut here, an identification I am inclined to doubt.[1]

The juniper is cut when the wood, as judged by its scent, is ripe, it being then anything from twenty to eighty years of age; the planks are of a size corresponding to the great size of the tree, the average dimensions being—length, eight to ten feet, breadth two feet, thickness one inch, giving a weight of 100 to 140 lbs when freshly cut, though not more than 60 to 80 lbs. when dry.

Chinese carpenters come over from T'eng-yueh, a city of western Yunnan, and cut the trees themselves, hiring coolies to carry the planks back to China, as many as 150 being exported in a good season. But some years, when the rice and maize crops fail on the North-East Frontier, they do not come at all.

---

[1] Wilson mentions buried wood of *Cunninghamia lanceolata* as called *hsiang-mu-shu* in Ssu-ch'uan. Of course the name might be applied to any scented wood. (See *A Naturalist in Western China*, by E.H. Wilson.)

The price of the planks rises rapidly as you recede from their home. At the source they are sold for one *tael*[2] each. From here they are floated down the Ngawchang when the water is shallow, ten together, fifty planks requiring only five men to attend them on their twenty days' journey.

At Kang-fang they are stocked for the winter, and in early summer, when the snow has melted on the Feng-shui-ling, are carried on the backs of coolies to Yun-nan, each man carrying a single plank, taking about ten days between Kang-fang and T'eng-yueh. The minimum price of a coffin in T'eng-yueh being about Tls. 50, and the cost of four boards landed in T'eng-yueh only about Tls. 20, good profits are realised.

Why the "scented wood" is so valued in China for making coffins is explained by the passion the Chinese have for exhuming their corpses and burying them elsewhere. This is the remedy whenever the least hint, as reflected in the distress of the departed spirit, suggests that a site not in accordance with *feng-shui*, otherwise "wind-and-water", or luck, was selected for the grave.

Geomancers, though dabbling in inhuman affairs, are, after all, themselves only human, and sometimes make mistakes, though no Chinaman would think of burying a relation without first consulting a geomancer.

When it becomes plain, through the continued ill luck of the relations, that the departed spirit really is ill at ease, then the body is promptly exhumed and buried in a more favourable position.

Chinese graves are often situated amidst the most romantic surroundings, on wooded hill-sides shaded by funereal cypress, the sward strewn with dwarf irises, crimson rhododendrons afire all round. But on the great hazy plains more prosaically they pimple the landscape like mole-hills.

Tls. 50 seems a good deal to give for a coffin, but the Chinese have an exaggerated respect for the dead which reacts distressingly on the living. If there is one thing universal in China which shouts aloud for reform, it is the gross luxury in which the dead are ushered into the next world, leaving the account to be settled by those remaining behind.

T'ung inveighed bitterly against these things. He had recently lost a mother-in-law, for Tls. 150—a considerable sum for a small trader, including the provision of coffin, mourners, a feast to all his friends, new clothes, crackers to keep off devils, and a band; but perhaps it was worth it.

At Kang-fang we crossed the river by cane suspension bridge to another village, consisting of half-a-dozen scattered huts. Pursuing our way up the right bank, sometimes in the river bed, where the Lashis stopped to sharpen their *dahs* on specially selected stones, we entered a lovely gorge, forested to the water's edge; here the river was quite forty yards broad, and shallow, chattering beryl-clear over shining pebbles.

---

[2] See Chapter III.

Just below this gorge the Hpawte river enters the Ngawchang on the left bank. By following up the Hpawte hka, the Chimili (12,000 feet), the last accessible pass direct to the Salween from Burmese territory, is reached.

Climbing over a steep cliff we descended to the river, and struggling knee-deep across a boisterous torrent camped on a sand spit in the river bed. From the damp cliffs hung sprays of orange orchids, and the long, forked tongues of *Gleichenia liniaris*; bunches of striped violet Chirita peeped from amongst nests of spearhead-shaped, downy leaves, and the mottled velvet leaves of Colocasia sp. formed a beautiful mosaic; here and there were bunches of gorgeously coloured balsams, and the spikes of a Dendrobium studded with orange-yellow flowers.

At dusk a woman, followed by a little girl dragging a reluctant dog at the end of a string, waded the torrent more confidently than we had done, picking her way over the gravel bar where the water was rough, but shallower; while I went into the river for a short swim above the rapid. There is a single plank bridge over the torrent a few hundred yards up-stream, spanning a gorge, but the ford saves distance.

Then came supper under the stars, the temperature, sheltered by the trees, being 65° F.

Out of the darkness strange winged creatures fly into the wan halo of light cast by the lantern, and commit suicide in the condensed milk; slender-bodied, long-legged stick-insects follow, and hopping moths of brilliant hue.

The start was delayed on 20th August owing to the discovery that the men had not provided sufficient rice. However, we heard news of a cache in a Yawyin village above, and having climbed up to it found several bags in a hut. Two of these we commandeered, leaving a fabulous sum in payment to salve our conscience.

Then another delay occurred, the rest of the porters being discerned in the distance climbing straight up the flank of the mountain, as though to cross the Imaw Bum range and come down into the 'Nmai valley direct, instead of continuing up the Ngawchang and so into the Laking valley over the Wulaw Pass.[3] By the time we had recalled them the day was half spent; it was drizzling too, the mountains swathed in mist.

We had a fair amount of climbing up and down, often in thick forest. The undergrowth consisted mostly of ferns, flowers being rather rare in the semi-darkness. Here and there we found a small monks-hood, or species of Strobilanthes, or of orange-flowered Globba, and the huge umbrella-shaped leaf of an Amorphophallus, or the umbels of scarlet and black berries of *Panax ginseng*. Wherever there was water, rank masses of gorgeous balsams glared,

---

[3] The Wulaw Pass is not on the main Salween-Irrawaddy divide, but separates the basins of two rivers both flowing down to the Irrawaddy from that divide. It is actually a ridge, not a col.

and the tree trunks hung out orchid sprays and the slender tubes of a brilliant scarlet Aeschynanthus.

Soon we came to another suspension bridge, with an easy ford just below—indeed the river here seemed fordable in most places even now, and later in the year it would offer no obstacle at all. The bed is considerably broader than where the river enters the limestone gorge above Black Rock, though the mountains rise more steeply from the water's edge. The left bank especially, though clothed with dense forests, is very precipitous, the trees often clinging to bare rock; and as I looked at those mountains, springing tier on tier above the brawling river, I thought what a magnificent virgin field was here for the naturalist.

Fish traps are met with from time to time, both in torrents where they join the main river, and in the Ngawchang itself.

A bamboo fence is built out from the shore and a long, hollow tree trunk buried in the shingle beneath it, both ends being left open, and a conical net attached to the lower end. The water banks up against the fence, and any fish swept through the tube are caught in the net.

Unable to reach a village before dark, we camped for the night in a thicket, with tall, saw-edges grass, alders, ragged bushes and brambles all round us; a worse place for mosquitoes and sand-flies we could not have selected.

A shower passed over at nightfall, and was followed by a starry sky which lasted an hour. But had there been no drizzling rain to add, in the absence of tents or natural shelter, to our discomfort, there would have been little sleep for anyone that night, and I was thankful for daylight. The minimum temperature was 62.9° F.

Starting early, we soon reached a Yawyin village on a broad platform which sloped down to the river, the right bank being more open here, the mountains farther back. But the left bank was an uncompromising wall of forest, showing the Salween divide, separating Chinese from British territory, to be a most formidable barrier.

After leaving this village we had five hours' hard work, climbing many hundreds of feet to the summit of one spur, only to drop down on to a deep-flowing torrent on the other side and start climbing up again.

These torrents are tumultuous blasts of water leaping thunderously amongst big boulders in the cool gloom of the everlasting forest; there is a clammy feeling in the air, as of a toad's skin; no sunlight gets through the dense roof to kiss the shivering balsams that crowd at the water's edge, wetted in the flying spray, or the scarlet trumpets of Aeschynanthus that loll from the moss-coated tree trunks.

The bellow of the torrent fills the air, and every inch of ground is covered with dumbly struggling, sappy and enervated plants, which surge to the very roots of the trees and overflow the confused boulders; tall creepers hanging from aloft veil the light yet further, and one is glad to climb out of this dim oppression on to the sunny hill-side, with its rank, plebeian growths and cruel, saw-edged grass, as quickly as possible.

We passed a few men on this march, two Chinese pedlars, their goods carried in baskets on the backs of coolies, and several men stumbling slowly along with coffin planks, though, as stated, they are usually floated down to Kang-fang. From time to time a shower happened along, but it was not seriously wet.

After a tiring day throughout which the trail had grown persistently worse and the climbing more arduous, we reached at dusk two tiny hovels perched up amongst the green maize on a steep *taungya*, as remote a place as one could come across, and slept snugly.

The next day's march was very similar, but a change was stealing over the valley, the path keeping well above and some distance back from the river, which was now little more than a big torrent flowing in an inaccessible forested gorge.

From the scorching, shadeless hill-side we would plunge terrifically down into the benighted forest, by an execrable path slippery with mud, cross some ravenous torrent by a single tree trunk, and climb laboriously up out of the gulf into the hot sunlight again; and watching these white cataracts roaring out from amongst the trees and rocks higher up the glen, I always longed to start off upstream, tracing them back to their puny sources in the cloud-veiled mountains of the Imaw Bum range, where no white man had ever trod. But there was no time for any such side ventures.

At midday we reached a Yawyin village of six huts and in the evening a second one as large.

These huts are quite small, with walls of bamboo matting and plank floors, roofed with split bamboos in several layers placed alternately with convex and concave faces uppermost, thus forming a system of corrugated tiles. Being built on the spurs which slope steeply down to the river, they are always raised on piles, with rickety verandahs on two sides, along which one has to stoop to avoid the projecting eaves. The door is reached after performing complicated balancing feats on a notched log, which does duty for a ladder, and the interior is completely divided into three or four rooms.

They are nothing like as big as the Lashi, Maru and Kachin huts, and differ further in the absence of the big front porch, and in the rooms being completely divided off, without any central passage.

As for the people, we found them charming, and it is good to think that these hardy mountaineers are crowding over the frontier into the dour valleys of the Burmese hinterland. Though they are much nicer looking than most of the tribes up here—the lantern-jawed men look as proud and fierce as Red Indians—they grow cadaverous as they age, when the Mongolian relationship comes out much more clearly. They are often long-headed, with quite a fine profile, and the girls have merry, round faces, pink cheeks and large, frank eyes; they show off their figures to advantage by wrapping a long sash round the waist—a Li-kiang habit. Indeed many of them claim to have come from Li-kiang, which suggests a relationship to the Mosos, and through them to the Tibetans.

Most of them can speak a certain amount of Chinese, and there can be no doubt that they are pressing slowly up the Ngawchang valley from the south, as well as crossing direct from the Salween valley. Where the Lashi is already in occupation, they ascend the mountains and plant their villages above his, but here they have extended far beyond the limits of the Lashi, and are doggedly opening up virgin ground. Nothing could promise more brightly for this bitter country, and it may be that in time the vigorous Yawyins will over-run the indolent Lashis, and replace them in the lower valleys.

The dress of the Yawyin girls is extremely picturesque—a harlequin skirt of many colours, or more exactly three, buff, ochre-red and chocolate, arranged in broad stripes, with a short jacket; a sash tied round the waist, and an ordinary Chinese turban worn in place of the scarf affected by the more prosperous Yawyins of the T'eng-yueh district. Cloth gaiters, similar to those of the Lashis, are generally worn by the men, who otherwise have adopted Chinese dress, and all go about barefooted.

Their food consists chiefly of a sort of porridge, made from buckwheat, with coarse cakes of the same unpalatable grain, and vegetable soup, with fowls and eggs occasionally—little more than the bare necessaries of life. But they are always hospitable and even generous.

Their weapon is the crossbow, with fire-hardened bamboo arrows, poisoned with aconite; and the *dah*, a short, straight-bladed knife of soft iron.

We spent the whole of the next day, 23rd August, grinding corn for the journey over the Wulaw Pass, as this was the last village at which adequate supplies could be obtained. There was only one hand-mill, so it took a long time to fill all the skin bags with flour. I took a turn at swinging the heavy stone round and round, feeding the maize corn into a flour hole in the upper stone, and collecting the flour which was squeezed out between the two; but my shoulder, unused to the work, soon tired.

In the evening we had some sports, jumping, putting the weight—a large boulder—and a comic turn by my Maru interpreter, a most amusing fellow, who in his grotesque, but often successful, efforts to pick up sticks while tangled into knots kept the rest of us in fits of laughter.

That night, or rather in the very early morning, the temperature sank as low as $60.3°$ F, and we awoke in the clouds, which were falling about us in rain after breakfast; and so it continued all day, with the briefest intervals.

We marched four hours in the morning, and four more in the afternoon, climbing over the spurs, now grown mountain-high, across occasional *taungya*, traversing steep, forested slopes where there was scarce foothold for a goat; so that for all our marching we made scarcely five miles' progress up the valley.

At midday we struck almost the last Yawyin village, comprising three huts—the site was but two seasons old, these people having come from Yunnan the year before.

There were two remarkably pretty girls here, with whom my men promptly started an outrageous flirtation.

When these tribespeople fraternise, they break the ice by offering each other *pan* and lime from the little bamboo boxes they carry, as an Englishman would offer a cigarette; and I watched one of my Lashis, who could not speak a word of Yawyin, dumbly offer his to a pretty girl, blinking self-consciously under a glow of smiles from his companions.

The huts here had a floor of bamboo matting instead of boards, and the roof too was made of a single piece of matting bent over in the form of an arch. At dusk, in pouring rain, we reached Wulaw, a village of eight huts.

We saw many magnolia trees in the forest this day, which showed that we were steadily ascending.

Rain was falling from a perfect blanket of mist when we awoke on 25th August, and a minimum temperature of 61° F scarcely gives an indication of the chill dampness.

We soon reached the last outpost of the advancing Yawyins in the Ngawchang valley, two huts on the very edge of the forest, in a newly felled clearing not yet burnt. There was a T'eng-yueh pedlar here, selling Chinese jackets and loose trousers of dark blue cotton cloth such as the Panthay muleteers wear in Yun-nan, and purchasing coffin planks, half-a-dozen of which were leaning against a tree.

From this point we plunged into the forested wilderness, and after a stiff climb camped about five o'clock at an altitude of over 8000 feet. Those who reached the water-hole first had the pleasure of building the huts, while the sluggards came in to find camp prepared.

There were plenty of bamboos in the forest, and scarcely any undergrowth, so we had no difficulty in rigging up shelters, which were built entirely of bamboo, roofed either with branches or with split bamboo tiles, like the huts we had seen; and in spite of the rain we made ourselves snug. My own shelter was made with a central ridge pole, across which bamboos, half cut through, were bent, being tied to the cross pieces by thin strips of bamboo; and over this framework I spread my valise.

There was a very big conifer (Pseudotouga sp.) growing here, and many gnarled oaks, amongst the intricate mossy roots of which hundreds of voles[4] had their burrows. So open is this park forest that except when following some well-defined feature, such as a ridge, it is impossible to find the way, and one might vainly wander for hours through the silent glades, looking for a trail to follow.

---

[4] *Vandeluria dumeticola*, Hodgson.

CHAPTER VIII

OVER THE WULAW PASS

All night it rained, and there was a marked drop in temperature, the minimum registering 50.4° F.

It was useless waiting for the rain to stop, so we started off at nine, ascending steeply by a ridge. So slippery was it, however, that after four hours' heartbreaking work, during which little progress was made, the men refused to go on, and we halted in the forest, drenched to the skin and shivering with cold. The altitude was about 10,000 feet, judging by the fir-trees and rhododendrons which surrounded us.

Making the best of a bad business, we built our leaky little shelters and got the fires going; we even pretended to be cheerful—I believe the Yawyins really were! Anyhow, as I lay curling up on my bed, almost afraid to move lest I should upset the shelter, with streams of water dripping in, I heard them singing away by their fire as though they had not a trouble in the world.

It was a wretched night of pouring rain, minimum temperature 49.5° F, nor did it show any indication of stopping in the morning. All the fires were out, and it took so long to start them again, pack up our sodden things with numbed hands, or move at all in the confined space of our huts that it was nearly midday before we got off.

Once outside, thoroughly soaked again, it was not so bad, for movement was much to be preferred to the previous inactivity.

First came a steep climb up through fir and rhododendron forest, where there was more undergrowth than usual, to the summit of the ridge.

Here we were exposed to a raw wind from the south-west. There was nothing to protect us, and, shivering with cold, we made our way for half-a-mile or more, up and down along the open ridge through scrub rhododendron[1] and bamboo grass three feet high. The highest point of the ridge, between 11,000 and 12,000 feet, was soon reached, but ahead, dimly seen through the mist, rose a still higher peak.

Eastwards we looked over a sea of gloomy mountains, and my guide pointed out a path which he said went to the Shapa Lisu country, probably across the high range of mountains which divides this region from the Salween valley, since he said that it was eight days' march to the first village!

At last we left the open ridge and began to descend a spur on the right, soon reaching the comparative shelter of trees and bamboos again.

So far the ridge had proved rather disappointing in flowers, though I had found a solitary and bedraggled primula amongst the scrub, and presently I

---

[1] *R. oporinum*, sp. nov. flowers.

came on a fine crimson-flowered lily (*L. Thompsonianum*).

But now quite suddenly we found ourselves in a bewitching garden, the path bordered with spotted pink Nomocharis growing in the grass under shelter of the bamboos, with patches of saxifrage hard by, and grass-of-Parnassus.

Then, leaving this ridge, we plunged down the slope on our left, through fir forest, and emerged on to a grassy meadow lining a stream which splashed and gurgled amidst a perfectly dazzling display of flowers. Enclosing this enchanted spot, the forested slopes rose on every hand; but the stream meandered through them, accompanied by its strip of meadow, which floored the tiny valley with flowers.

There were purple-flowered Allium, and tall cabbage-leafed Senecio, sheets of white grass-of-Parnassus, stiff louseworts, delicate Cremanthodium, and a mammoth Rheum, standing up erect as a grenadier, six feet high. But most welcome of all, I caught sight of the twisted conical capsules, full of flat seeds, of one of that curious race of primulas (perhaps *P. Delavayi*) which now many botanists consider are not really primulas at all, but which are provisionally grouped together in a section called Omphalogramma. This was a treasure indeed, and I collected all the seed I could find, for my discovery extended the distribution of these pseudo-primulas, and might prove a link between the Himalayan and Chinese representatives.

Tramping down this steam, which swelled rapidly as other streams came gushing in right and left from the closely surrounding wooded hills, we presently came to thickets of shrubs and a wild tangle of climbing monkshood, bell-flower and starry stitchwort, with giant meadow-rue, larkspur, Umbelliferæ and many other things.

The country here was most remarkable; I have never seen anything like it elsewhere. The Feng-shui-ling was the nearest approach to it, but quite in miniature, and the mountains there were fully 2000 feet lower.

Our altitude must have been somewhere between 10,000 and 11,000 feet, and we were surrounded on all sides by a tangle of low, rounded hills, amongst which rushed hither and thither a network of frothing brooks.

The hills loomed up shadow-like and indistinct in the whirling mist, which clung like smoke to the tree-tops; wooded to their summits with rhododendrons, bamboos and fir, they peeped at us over each other's shoulders from every direction, while the streams which bubbled at their feet were lined with meadow, and the flowers grew like the magic beanstalk. Masses of violet-flowered Strobilanthes[2] flourished here. Sometimes the passage between two hills was so narrow that we had to paddle along in the stream, while giant meadow-rues and long, clinging monkshoods showered their burden of raindrops playfully on us as we brushed through; sometimes we would emerge

---

[2] Amongst them *S. oresbius*, sp. nov.

into a little grassy dell tucked away in a fold of the hills, with streams splashing down all around us.

So we went up one stream, over a low col, and down another, then across a stream to another valley, on and on, till my sense of direction was utterly mazed, and still the wooded hills, blurred in mist and rain, rose all about us, and the song of the rising torrents grew shriller.

Then quite suddenly the meadow widened out, and where the tall flowers swayed graciously all round us I came on what I sought. They were standing in a row as stiff as though on parade, just above the edge of the meadow bordering the woodland, a line of glorious poppyworts. So the missing link was found, and the flora of the Imaw Bum range definitely connected through that of the Mekong-Salween divide with that of the Himalaya.

This Meconopsis (*M. Wallichii*) grew seven feet high, and had pale purple flowers one and a half inches across, massed with a tassel of golden anthers in the centre. The flowers are small in comparison with many of its kind, but they are borne in remarkable numbers; one plant I examined, which had a seven foot stem, bore 16 buds, 27 flowers and 103 fruits—nearly 150 flowers in all, though not blooming simultaneously. It may be wondered how so many flowers of this size are crowded on a seven-foot stem, but it is quite simple. They are borne in short racemes six to nine inches long, of about seven flowers, each raceme, springing from the axil of a strap-shaped, drooping leaf, closely pressed against the main stem, which itself ends in a flower, giving a wonderful concentration of colour. The whole thus forms an immense panicle, the tall stem studded from top to bottom first with fat ovoid buds, then with flowers, and below with capsules. I collected seed of this species (familiar from the Himalaya), but it was not quite ripe and did not survive the journey to England.

But it was now growing dusk, and we were all weary, our hands and feet swollen with the continuous soaking; also we had had nothing to eat since eight o'clock breakfast, as the weather had been too bad to allow of halting for a meal, and we had been marching with scarcely a break for nearly six hours.

Consequently it was with some relief that I heard, while collecting my Meconopsis, the glad ring of *dah* against wood not far ahead; and following up the sound, discovered my men on the summit of a small knoll from which they were clearing the bamboos. Through the red-barked trees I saw the fires already gleaming.

It was dark before the shelters were finished and we snuggled into our wet nests; late before I got any dinner; but these things did not matter. What did matter was the fact that no sooner were we established on our hill-top than we were surrounded by myriads of tiny sand-flies which bit like fury. There was a perfect fog of them, and they caused us dreadful anguish, even the hardy natives hopping about; as for me, my face, neck and wrists were covered with bumps in a very short time, and I was itching all over. I lit two candles of my slender stock, and thousands rushed to their death in the flames; but their numbers were nowise diminished.

Thus with pouring rain the wicked night passed, and dawn came, lowering.

It was still pouring when we got up next morning, 28th August, after a minimum of 50.3° F, but ceased just as we turned our backs on Wulaw. In winter these mountains are covered under deep snow and it must be bitterly cold here for months. I have never seen even in Yun-nan a more wonderful place for flowers than Wulaw, nor one more difficult of access, nor more hedged round with tortures for those who would brave its terrors. It will defy the collector, and guard its treasures long, for I hardly think a white man could spend a season there and live.

Our route took us down the rocky bed of a narrow stream, the almost precipitous banks of which were smothered with flowering shrubs and small trees of cherry, birch, maple and rowan, with bamboos and rhododendron higher up. As for the giant herbs springing from either bank, they met and embraced overhead, bridging the narrow defile, so that we passed beneath arches of purple meadow-rue or brushed through tangles of yellow Corydalis and white plumes of Astilbe, which is like meadowsweet. By the water's edge were beds of orange-spotted monkey-flower, and balsam with pendent crimson bugles, saxifrages, primulas and lilies, mixed up with bushes of hydrangea, currant and hairy-leafed raspberry. It was bewildering, this rampant growth of struggling, long-limbed flowers in the dim-walled bed of the bubbling beck.

Presently a small black creature darted through the foaming water in front of me, and grabbing hastily, I caught it in my hand. It had shiny black fur like a mole's, which refused to be wetted, and the little creature proved to be none other than one of those rare insectivorous animals known as a water-shrew.[3]

But now other rills came tumbling in, laughing with joy, and the beck grew and grew, though the gorge did not broaden, only the walls rose higher, frowning down on us, with a rib and of sky visible overhead. Swifter and swifter flowed the stream down its smooth, rocky bed, till at last it leapt over a fall too high for us to negotiate, and we started traversing along the steep clay bank to a track above, which soon left the restless stream far below.

Now matters became more difficult, for we had to cross numerous torrents which had cut deeply into the soft hill-side; and the rain having turned the surface to clay, we slithered down the high banks, and experienced the greatest difficulty in climbing up the other side.

At first we were in mixed forest, but as we descended the conifers disappeared, and their place was taken by grand deciduous-leafed trees; here and there were open glades, as in a park, filled not indeed with bracken, but

---

[3] *Chimarrogale styani*, the second known example. The first was taken in Kansu, North- West China.

with masses of violet Strobilanthes and white-flowered Polygonum, growing man-high round the enormous tree trunks.

Then came gloomy, impenetrable forests of bamboo whose thick, leafy growth overhead cut out all daylight.

During a brief halt for lunch we were attacked by bees which appeared in such numbers that they eventually routed us. Continuing to descend, we at last slid down a steep clay slide and reaching the confluence of two fairly big streams, started to paddle again.

Presently crossing to the far bank, we began to climb once more, up, up, up, till we seemed to have ascended as much as we had previously descended. No words can convey how exhausting this work was.

It was unutterably dismal in these bamboo forests—no song of birds, no ray of sunlight, no wayside flowers, nothing but the patter of rain on the leaves above, and the eternal drip, drip of water.

At last, about five o'clock, the vanguard of our now straggling party, comprising three Yawyins and myself (*they* were always to the fore, splendid fellows!), stood on a low pass, looking over into what seemed in the mist and rain, to be a big valley.

Down we plunged through the cold stream, splashing along, covered with leeches, and so thoroughly soaked and saturated that the water seemed to penetrate our very skins, till at six o'clock, by which time we had come some distance and the baby stream had swollen to fair size, we came suddenly on a big shelter already set up, and halted thankfully. There was just a thatch roof, sloping up from the ground, large enough for us all; we were glad to have it.

An hour later another batch of men, mostly Yawyins, arrived, and even after dark one or two more straggled in; but several of the Lashis, including the one who carried my food, did not come in at all that night.

However, we lit a fire and spread out our bedding under the lean-to, and in spite of a coldish wind slept well after our strenuous march; for, heaven be praised, there were few sand-flies, and the bees we could cope with.

Sitting round a big fire in comfort, listening to the wet bamboos sizzling and exploding on the fire with loud pops, was pleasant enough; next day, the men said, we should reach the first Maru village.

T'ung-ch'ien was in good spirits and astonished the Yawyins by telling them of the marvels of Mandalay and Rangoon, whither he had accompanied me, and of the railway train and steamer, and how many days' march they go in a day. Or he would talk to them of Tibet, and sing Moso songs, which were always greeted with loud laughter.

Though it rained all night we kept fairly dry, and by eight o'clock it had ceased. An hour later the three remaining porters arrived, having spent an uncomfortable night in the forest higher up. So we started again.

And now for the first time we got something of a view, towering limestone cliffs looming up ahead; but whether they were across the valley we were looking into, or bounded our own valley, it was impossible to say, and seething mists soon hid them again.

We passed several bamboo rat traps set up on the bank of the stream, for the Marus catch and eat vermin; also little fenced-off places where grew the plant called by the Chinese *huang-lien* (*Coptis teeta*), a Ranunculaceous plant, the root of which is used medicinally. The Marus come up into these forests for jungle produce of this sort, also to hunt the takin, serow, bear and other animals.

Here and there gigantic trunks of the coffin-plank tree lay across our path, and as we emerged at last from the twilight of the forest we saw across the stream, high up on the opposite side of the valley, a number of these big trees; they stood out very plainly from amongst the deciduous-leafed trees which surrounded them, conspicuous by their shape, their colour and above all by their size.

Sliding and tripping we came down a tremendously steep hill-side in the open, and saw the village of Che-wen below on the left bank of a considerable stream which flowed in a deep valley.

An hour later we were splashing through the sties and mud-holes of a Maru village, its dozen huts standing amongst little fenced-off gardens, where grew beans, tobacco, opium poppies and a few peach-trees.

Pigs grunted and scuttled, an odd cow or two stood uncompromisingly in the fairway, and women seated in the porches looked up from their weaving and stared at us. However, we were well received, and soon shown into a house, whereupon the inhabitants crowded round the doorway to gaze at me.

At last I was able to take off my wet clothes, and having started a big fire in the room placed at my disposal, we set to work drying everything.

These huts, made of bamboo matting, raised on stilts with hard floors of wooden boards laid across beams, narrow verandahs and front porch, are small, like the Yawyin huts, not at all like the typical Maru huts of the 'Nmai valley. Outside the houses are small box-like granaries raised high on four stout pillars capped with circular discs of wood, which serve to defeat the rats.

Fields of maize and buckwheat slope down to the river. Beyond, the shadowy outlines of high mountains disappear into the rain mists. Up the valley and across the Salween divide, distant eight marches, lies the country of the Shapa Lisus, an evil tribe, according to Maru tradition; but this is not altogether surprising, since they wage a continuous defensive warfare against the Chinese, whose ruthless efforts to exterminate them are calculated to sharpen all their latent cunning and cruelty.

These Shapa Lisus come across the mountains selling cattle, salt, cotton clothes and iron cooking pots, all obtained from Yun-nan, buying *huang-lien* in exchange; thus they act as middlemen between the Chinese and Marus for trade purposes. Chinese traders themselves sometimes penetrate into these inhospitable mountains.

It may be remarked here that the Lisus[4] do not believe in *nats*, the elfish and capricious spirits of mountain, river and forest which watch over the lives of the great Kachin family inhabiting the Burmese hinterland; and their practice of putting the things used in this life—crossbow, pipe, wine jar and hat—on the grave, for the use of the spirit, is distinctly Chinese. These considerations point to an eastern rather than a northern original home for the Lisus.

As to the Marus, I was not altogether favourably impressed with their dirty appearance; but first impressions are notoriously deceptive, and later they displayed redeeming qualities which endeared them to me far more than their cousins, the Lashis.

Amongst their more distinctive peculiarities is the mop of unkempt hair, rarely tied in a brief pig-tail, like a Jack Tar of Nelson's day, or in a knot on top of the head. The men usually wear a brown or blue striped kilt, like a Burmese *lone-gyi*, dyed locally with jungle dyes; but occasionally Chinese fashions are followed.

It does not appear, however, that the Chinese have ever gained much of a footing over here. Barring an occasional cotton garment—for the Marus cannot sew—or a red-buttoned skull-cap, the only thing Chinese I saw was a set of scales, as used for weighing silver in China. They were being used by one of my Lashis, who was exchanging glass beads for cane rings, made of thin strips of rattan, such as all the men, and women too, wear round the leg; and a bargain was struck by weight.

As for unmarried girls, they cut their hair in a fringe all round. Their tight skirts of white hemp cloth, home woven, reach just below the knee, and they wear a low-necked blue cotton jacket with short sleeves, embroidered with cowry shells, or buttons, according to the state of the market. Other finery—bead necklaces, iron hoops with bells, and earrings, or tubes—resemble those of the Lashis.

It continued to rain, for we were still well in the mountains, but the much lower altitude we had attained was reflected in the warmer night—minimum temperature 64.8° F, nearly 15° higher than on Wulaw.

As the rain showed no signs of stopping, I felt inclined to rest on 30th August; but a break occurring in the afternoon, I changed my mind, and we started about two.

Eight of the Yawyins brought from the Ngawchang went back from here, their place being taken by Marus.

Near the village the path was frequently interrupted by stout fences, which serve to keep the cattle from straying.

In less than two hours we reached the Laking hka, of which this was tributary. The Laking is a fair-sized river, thirty yards across, flowing with a swift current; just above the confluence a cane bridge spanned the Che-wen

---

[4] Lisu is the tribal name, and includes the clan known as Yawyin.

stream, and on the far bank stood another village. But of camping grounds, save a considerable pebble bank in the bed of the Laking, there was no sign, though to the Maru and Yawyin any place where water, bamboos and firewood are obtainable is a camping ground, so there is no need for the solitary traveller to worry. Only I should not care to campaign in such a country.

Immediately below the confluence of the Che-wen stream with the Laking hka the latter enters a magnificent limestone gorge embroidered with rich forest. The track soon leaves the boulders in the river bed and climbing sharply, becomes difficult; precipices are ascended by means of notched logs, deep gullies crossed by means of tree trunks, and both were now slippery with rain and mud.

Presently we descended to the river bed again, where the water foamed over rapids, and a few minutes later were once more climbing steeply up a slippery path almost buried in vegetation.

Came yet another descent to the river bed, and comparatively easy going over the boulders. There was a quiet stretch of water here, with a rapid under the far bank, so one of the Marus, with a view to displaying his prowess, slipped off his kilt—the only garment he was wearing, by the way—and swam out to mid-river, with slow breast stroke, turning back when he met the stronger water on the other side.

Lastly we climbed by a steep, muddy path several hundred feet above the river, and emerged from the forested gorge into more open country. At dusk we reached a village situated in a bay of the mountains, a thousand feet above the river.

This village was called Magri, or Mang-yam, and I was not a little surprised to meet five Chinamen from the Mekong valley there. They were pedlars from the village of Yin-p'an-kai, and were on their way to the 'Nmai valley, selling salt, cloth and iron cooking pots. They had crossed from the Mekong to the Salween and thence by Lakhe Pass, 13,000 feet high, into the Laking valley, a fifteen days' journey.

So far it had scarcely ceased to rain, but my Maru porters were quite indifferent to the weather, for they wore circular bamboo hats almost as large as an umbrella, and long capes of palm leaves thrown over their shoulders, from which the water dripped rapidly. Also each man carried a long iron-headed spear to help him over the slippery path.

And so we entered our hut, where nailed to the central pillar of the porch, and to the beams inside, were the skulls of wild animals slain in the chase with crossbow and poisoned arrow—monkey, takin, serow and bear, besides domestic mithan, which are kept for sacrificial purposes.

CHAPTER IX

BY THE SINGING RIVER

The valley was as usual full of cloud in the early morning, but in spite of a preliminary shower it soon cleared up and we enjoyed several hours' bright sunshine, the first for some days. These continual remarks on the weather may be dull—the weather was, anyhow—but they are quite necessary for a proper appreciation of the climate on the North-East Frontier, with its consequent reaction on the scenery, vegetation and people. All of these are in the strongest contrast to those of the more familiar North-West Frontier, or (which is more to the point) to those of Yun-nan mountains farther east.

Descending to the river bed by a steep path, we pursued our way leisurely now over big bare boulders, now through the forest over some projecting cliff. Brilliant orange and purple balsams coloured the rocks, and when the sun came out gorgeous butterflies flitted along the fringing forest above the furious waters; for the river was very swift here, generally from forty to sixty yards broad. At midday we crossed a big tributary by a swinging cane bridge, and dropping into the river bed again, lay out on a sand-bank in the sunshine for lunch. Along came a man with a dead rat, which he offered us; but our supplies were not yet so depleted that we needed to accept the morsel, and eventually he ate it himself.

After a *dolce far niente*—for it was jolly here basking in the sunshine by the singing river—we went on down the valley clasped between high wooded mountains where Ficus trees, wild bananas, and plumes of bamboo, with here and there graceful tree ferns, and down by the water tall sago palms were each in turn conspicuous.

The change in the vegetation was very marked here.

Since crossing the Lawkhaung ridge in May we had seen no bananas, sago palms or fig-trees; here they abounded, with a wealth of forest trees.

Pines, alders and rhododendrons, on the other hand, were lacking. We were back in the monsoon forest, for there is probably no period of drought here, and the forest is certainly evergreen. We had passed from a preponderately Chinese flora to an Indo-Malayan flora.

Paddling through shallow water round a cliff, we presently crossed to the right bank by a fine cane bridge sixty yards in length, and toiling up the *khud* reached a village of seven huts called Tum-dang; but disdaining to quit so early, we descended to the river again, here goaded to uncontrolled fury by obstructing boulders, climbed over another cliff, and finally reached Sajor, comprising seven big huts perched on a high spur.

It was languidly peaceful up here in these forgotten villages of the warm Laking valley, the only sounds heard being the rasping *whir-r-r whir-r-r* of cicadas on the tree trunks, and the river buffeting its way through the gorge. As for birds, we rarely heard, still less saw, any.

The huts were full size now, not less than sixty yards long, with a wide open porch in front where the women pound corn or sit weaving cloth. Over the projecting front eave is sometimes set a sort of crescent, something like a pair of mithan horns, just as you see over many huts in the Naga Hills.

A thunderstorm brushed past us in the night; but though we could not see a hundred yards through the mist at half-past six, the sun was shining brightly when we started two hours later.

Sliding down a steep path of red clay, with the dew hanging in glistening drops on the ferns and grasses, and on the tall club-mosses which stood erect in the silver sand like little fir-trees crowned with cones, reminded me of an autumn morning in England; but next moment we were down by the roaring river again, amidst palms and bamboos. Clambering over boulders, along rock ledges and over cliffs, we passed several cane bridges, which must have led to villages on the opposite bank, but they were quite invisible in the forest, though occasionally we glimpsed clearings high up.

Presently we came to a fish trap out in mid-river, where stood a big boulder. A stout post had been driven into the river bed near by, and a couple of cane ropes stretched from a tree overhanging the bank to this post. Slung on the ropes were two large cane rings, about a foot in diameter, and to reach the fish trap you climbed the tree, thrust a leg through each ring, as it were a breeches-buoy, and holding on to the cables, hauled yourself along. It was hard enough work going down, with the sag of the ropes to help you, but infinitely worse getting back again. If you let go to rest your arms you fell out of the rings into the river below, or at least hung head downwards, with little prospect of regaining an upright position.

The going now, whether actually in the dry river bed or traversing through the forest on the mountain-side, became worse and worse, much labour for little progress. Path there was none, except in the forest, where there was generally a track.

Once when pulling myself up amongst the rocks I almost put my hand on a snake which was sunning itself on a flat-topped boulder; whereupon, at a warning cry from the man behind, a Maru in front whipped out his *dah* and turning cut at it so swiftly that he almost had some of my fingers off instead of the snake's head. He was only a little fellow—the snake I mean, not the Maru—about two feet long, black, with a yellow collar and coral-red speckles, probably harmless; but I always found the natives show the same instinctive distrust for reptiles that Europeans do.

The hillmen are very jealous of their *dahs*, any injury against a rock causing great distress. Whenever we halted in the river bed they would search out suitable flat stones and, squatting down, set to work sharpening their precious knives.

Farther on we came to a group of almost naked men squatting round the embers of a fire over a midday meal of boiled rice, which they were eating with their fingers from banana leaves. They looked such utter savages squatting there in the dark jungle that it was difficult to recognize in them the mild Marus.

It is rather strange that the whole Tibeto-Burman family, even the highly civilized Burmans themselves, should eat with their fingers, while their near neighbours, the Chinese, have invented the ingenious and simple chopsticks for the same purpose.

Now we crossed a tributary stream flowing in a deep gorge, by three large bamboos thrown across and lashed together, further supported by cables of twisted bamboo fastened to trees on either bank; a flimsy hand-rail was also provided, designed more with a view to give confidence than for actual support, as the bamboos were slippery.

We were down in the tropical jungles again now, though actually more than 200 miles north of the tropics. On every hand grew splendid Ficus trees, from the trunks of which dangled huge bunches of green fig-like fruit. Another species with curiously lop-sided leaves dropped from its lowest branches long whip-like shoots, which, trailing over the ground, bore luscious fruit. These we searched out and ate. Most of the vast order of figs, so typical of the oriental forests, and so diverse in habit and appearance (yet so easily recognized in all its forms, from giant tree to humble prostrate creeper), have inedible fruits, but this (*F. cunia*) was an exception.

In the river bed we found a mangosteen[1] tree and picked up some quite good fruit, which we likewise ate.

Then there were bird's-nest ferns sprouting bayonet-like from trees whose boughs were fringed with oak-leaf ferns, and roped together with corkscrew lianas; violet and yellow Chirita on the wet rocks, and in the dark dampness of the bamboos the mottled stem and solitary leaf of an Amorphophallus. But right down in the river bed, where the sun glistened fiercely on the white granite boulders, scraggy bushes of *Rhododendron indicum* recalled the cold mountains.

And yet here in the tropical jungle, where snakes and vicious-looking land crabs crawled over the rocks, and poisonous thorns grew across the path, we were far less teased by insect life at night than we had been in the wild wet mountains guarded by those terrible sand-flies.

After more climbing we came to a part of the river where the bed shelved rapidly and was choked by cyclopean blocks of white granite which reflected a blinding glare of light in the bright sunshine. Here the river, by this time swollen to a considerable size, was a wonderful sight, and from a cane bridge just below a splendid view of the water foaming down this granite stairway was obtained.

---

[1] *Garcinia* sp.

Amidst sand and boulders under the bank grew a gigantic Mucuna, hung all over with bunches of coarse, canary-yellow, fleshy flowers. They are like pea-flowers, but thick and bloated and without the wide-spreading standard. The interlacing stems grow as thick as a man's wrist, and the plant forms slovenly bushes needing support, like a wistaria. The pods are covered with short, stiff, orange-coloured bristles, which come off easily and stick into the skin, setting up irritation.

Soon after leaving the cane bridge we climbed up to another village—all the villages are perched on flat-shouldered spurs—and rested for an hour while I had some tea. There were fields of cotton here.

It seemed doubtful whether we should reach Laking, the village at the confluence of the Laking hka with the 'Nmai, that night or not; but I was determined to try, so about five o'clock we set out again.

Continuing the ascent, we were soon high above the river, which plunged down deeper and deeper into the bowels of the earth, till close upon sunset we stood on the last spur and looked clear away westward down the now open valley; and black against the western glare a high range of softly rounded mountains appeared, drawn clean across the horizon. It was the containing wall of the 'Nmai hka—the Irrawaddy itself!

Behind us grey storm clouds were piling up on the mountains we had lately crossed, but in front the sun, wrapped in mackerel sky, had turned the clouds into a broad lake of chequered silver.

Numerous deep gullies spun out the journey, and in places steep slabs of granite lay athwart the mountain-side, in crossing some of which we experienced difficulty in keeping our balance, so that one of the porters fell and cut himself painfully.

At last a deeper rent than usual yawned below us like a wound in the mountain-side, but descending the path into complete darkness far below, there was heard only a feeble trickle of water, as though the torrent, exhausted after its hard work of carving out this canyon, had slumbered.

A growl of thunder in the mountains behind now spurred us on, and climbing up from the depths, we reached the first huts of Laking at seven o'clock, just as the rain began. We had been ten hours on the road.

Men now came out with lighted torches, and we were ushered into an enormous hut quite sixty yards in length, while outside a thunderstorm swooping down from the east lit up the valley with brilliant flashes of lightning; however, it was never really very near, though the porters behind, who arrived an hour later, came in soaked.

By ten o'clock the moon was shining again, lighting up little wisps of clouds which floated far down in the valley; the night was now as tranquil as a New Year's night in the Indian Ocean.

As already stated, the Maru hut, like the Kachin, is an enormous structure, sixty or seventy yards in length, by fifteen to twenty in breadth, divided by a longitudinal partition into a passage on one side and rooms on the other.

The rooms are more or less completely divided from each other and from the passage, each room opening on to the latter by a door, and on to the outside world by a tiny window under the eave. The front room of the hut—that next to the porch—is larger, occupying the full breadth, but is not completely shut off from the passage, being divided from it by alternating walls which jut halfway across from either side, leaving a passage in between. As the whole is in complete darkness, even by day, it is by no means easy to find the way about at first, and one not unnaturally blunders into all kinds of sacred family hearths. Happily the "maidens' hearth" is not *tapu*, otherwise embarrassing mistakes might easily be made.

Each room is provided with its earthen hearth, in the middle of the floor, and the passage, being open to the public, has two or three such hearths at intervals down its length. The "maidens' hearth," reserved to the unmarried girls and their lovers,[2] is the last room in the hut, next to the back door, which is *tapu* to humans, being reserved for the *nats*, though doubtless used by sly lovers at night.[3]

In front of the hut is the huge porch, fenced round, and partly covered in by the gable roof which projects forward like the stem of a ship, being cut away at the sides. Great wooden pillars support the heavily thatched roof, that beneath the gable end being, so to speak, the corner-stone of the house.

In the porch women pound grain and weave cloth by day; cattle are tied up at night; while the pigs live beneath the hut floor, and fowls occupy baskets under the eaves.

These huts are always dark, blackened with smoke and indescribably dirty; the smell of pigs rises through the bamboo floor, and roosters awaken you at an early hour. But the people are friendly, a circumstance which goes a long way to make up for any other shortcomings.

The morning of 2nd September broke beautifully fine, and the village of Laking, with its tall sago palms, clumps of bamboo and slopes yellow with Indian corn, looked a happy spot in the mellow sunshine; it was warm down here too, the minimum falling only to 68° F.

The village is built in two parts, the upper half being several hundred feet above the lower. Far below a twisting thread of white foam indicates the Laking hka, and across the western sky, framed between bold spurs, stretches a range of forested mountains, forming the watershed between the eastern and western branches of the Irrawaddy.

---

[2] See Chapter X.
[3] In some parts the "maidens' hearth" is the *first* room in the hut next to the porch. The end room is often a store-room for grain and liquor.

The Marus of the Upper 'Nmai hka valley, being more uncouth than those of the south, are distinguished as Naingvaws;[4] but they are none the less Marus. The distinction is geographical, not racial.

Here the young girls wear girdles of cane consisting of two or three strands on which are closely strung white cowry shells, a picturesque ornament—for it does not serve the purpose of a belt to hold up the kirtle—marred only by a certain looseness and untidiness; but some of the girls wore the Kachin belt, consisting of coils of fine black rattan cane, even looser and more slovenly than the former.

Often a cloak of native manufacture is thrown over the head and hangs down behind, giving them a very *chic* appearance. It reminds one of the towel thrown over the head of a Malay girl, though the latter is probably a half-hearted attempt at concession to Mohammedan *purda* custom.

As is usual, the Marus down in the valley are better dressed, live in bigger huts and are better off in all respects than those higher up in the mountains.

---

[4] The Marus call themselves Lawng vaw. Naingvaw may be a local name, but is more likely an English corruption. The word Maru is the Kachin name (see Appendix II).

CHAPTER X

AMONG THE MARUS

First I paid off all the men who wished to return to their homes, including my Maru interpreter, who was useless, since he spoke no language known to me. Two Yawyin porters from the Ngawchang valley and five Lashis from Hpimaw went with him, leaving only five of our original party, including myself and T'ung-ch'ien.

It was late when we started with Maru porters, men, women and girls, in place of those returning; the latter crossed the river below, and started south on their long tramp, but we went on down the valley to the 'Nmai hka. They must have been back in their snug huts, away in the Hpimaw hills, long before we reached Fort Hertz.

The heat was now intense, and I was glad to halt at midday and have meal in the shade, and a shower-bath under the splash of a cascade that poured into a sandy pit surrounded by bushes. Some of the girls did the same.

The Marus, when on the march, carry their day's ration of rice ready boiled and wrapped in a banana leaf, so that they can squat down and eat it whenever they feel inclined.

For the first time I made my terrier pup, named Maru, in anticipation of his experiences in the Maru country, follow on foot instead of being carried in state in a basket as hitherto. He kept up well, and thoroughly enjoyed himself in the sunshine, finding much to whet his canine curiosity along the roadside.

Watching him as he sniffed his way along, frequently stopping to examine carefully an unknown smell, I wondered how many new ones he found, whether his knowledge was sufficient yet to enable him to classify them, and what deductions were to be drawn therefrom.

In the afternoon we had a long pull up a well-made but badly aligned path to the summit of a spur, from which we looked right down into the 'Nmai valley, though the river itself, some 2000 feet below us, was invisible.

The last part of the ascent was very steep, and the young men who reached the summit first threw down their loads; but instead of resting they chivalrously went back and relieved the girls and old men, who had lagged behind, of their burdens. I think the young Maru beaux must be very affectionate husbands, or at any rate lovers; courtship with them is a fine art.

As already remarked, the Marus are not overburdened with clothes, and during the heat of a summer's day they are reduced to a minimum.

The men wore only a short *lone-gyi* and stopped to bathe in nearly every stream we came to. The married women, who are distinguished by a sort of white turban, like a dirty pudding-cloth after a suet dumpling has been boiled

8. MARU WOMEN POUNDING MAIZE.
Note the striped hand-woven skirts. These are dyed dark blue and red
Photo by A.W. Porter, Esq.

in it, perched on top of the head, never hesitated to take off their jackets, and the girls sometimes did the same, though generally throwing it over the shoulders to conceal the breasts. The girls, however, always tucked their *lonegyi* up to their knees at least, in fact the garment is not much longer at its full extent. They wear nothing on their heads, and cut the hair in a fringe round the forehead, after the manner of a Burmese *sadouk*, the rest of it being cut short so as to form a mop.

The men also go about bareheaded in the sunshine, but if going a day's journey or more they often carry a flat, broad-brimmed hat, like a plate, with a small conical peak in the centre; the framework is of coarsely plaited bamboo, with palm leaf woven into it, but it is certainly not the equal in workmanship of the Yun-nan muleteer's finely woven bamboo hat.

Cloaks made of overlapping strips of palm leaf, arranged horizontally, or of fibrous coconut leaf sheaths, threaded on a string and tied over the shoulders, are also worn in wet weather.

Everyone goes about barefooted, and all, even the children, smoke.

From the spur on which we stood we looked northwards across to the village of Tawlang, on another lower spur, where we arrived at five-thirty. The valley was fairly open here, rather bare of trees except in the gullies, which were choked with jungle, generally clothed with high grass and shrubs.

Tawlang, where Captain Pottinger's party was attacked and forced to return to Myitkyina in 1897, is surrounded by a low stockade and looks a flourishing village.

Between the Laking hka and the Mekh, the left bank of the 'Nmai is, comparatively speaking, well populated, and there are large *taungya* of maize and mountain rice, with walnut-trees, sago palms, big clumps of bamboo, and small crops of cotton, indigo,[1] marrows, beans and buckwheat, fenced in amongst the huts.

Just after our arrival the sky darkened and a brief thunderstorm passed over the valley, travelling west, but at seven o'clock there was a beautiful moonrise. At eight the temperature was still 75° F and the moonlight brilliant, but two hours later another brief storm passed over.

It was difficult to sleep on such a bright night, nor was the continuous *whir*, *whir* of cicadas soothing. At short intervals the encircling mountains echoed to the cries of small children who, perched up in little huts on the steep *taungya*, watched the maize crops under the glow of the full moon; suddenly there would come a furious *clap, clap* as a string was pulled and bamboo rattle in a distant corner sent a frightened monkey speeding back into the jungle.

September 3rd was another fine, hot day, the minimum falling to 68.5° F and the shade temperature at eleven o'clock being just over 80° F; at ten P.M. it was still 74° F.

---

[1] *Strobilanthes flaccidifolius.*

In point of distance we were barely three miles from the next village, Ngawyaw, but the path led us up over a spur, then down into a deep gully, and so up to the summit of the next spur, high above and well away from the still invisible 'Nmai hka. The march with halts took us five hours in the hottest part of the day—for we started late, and it was a relief to bathe in the torrent we crossed, where even the mountain water felt quite warm.

In these enclosed valleys the day temperature falls very slowly with increased altitude, at least to begin with; we were over 3000 feet above sea-level at this time.

The mountains flanking the left bank of the 'Nmai hka are of granite, with occasional outcrops of limestone, as at Hpimaw; often, in the jungle especially, the granite is decomposed to a sticky red clay. A thick scrub covers the open slopes, and in the gullies are purple-flowered Melastoma, orchids, ferns, huge-leafed Alocasia and palms, with purple and sulphur-yellow Chirita on the wet rocks, giving a more tropical appearance to the vegetation. Magnificent butterflies are seen everywhere, especially at elevations of from 2000 to 4000 feet.

That night there was a beautiful sunset and the full moon rising over the black mountains and flooding the gulf below us with orange light was superb.

Heavy rain in the early morning and the valley full of cloud threatened a wet day on 4th September, but by eight o'clock it was clearing up rapidly, and after midday we had continuous sunshine. Nothing surprised me so much as the fine weather experienced on our march up the 'Nmai valley, from 31st August to 18th September, during the worst of the rains to east and west of us. A fair amount of rain fell, but it was mostly in the form of brief squalls from the eastern ranges, and generally fell either in the early morning or in the evening. It was not like a ten days' break, which may come at any time, such as one experiences in many parts of Burma during the monsoon, but seemed to be the usual thing; excluding rain after dark, we had no less than ten days without rain, a relief after our experiences on the Wulaw Pass and at Hpimaw.

Our march on 4th September was again a short one, though it took us five hours, thanks to the climbing up and down, and the partiality of the Marus for bathing; the girls, however, always stayed apart (and watched) during these ablutions—you could hear them tittering behind the bushes, and consequently I am bound to confess, with pain, that the male sex were the cleaner. I do not know why the girls were prudish about it; they were not modest about taking off their jackets, or tucking up their already abbreviated skirts, and the men did not strip themselves.

However, it was very pleasant to have girl porters, for they were always merry and bright, kept the men in good temper and were not ill-favoured to look upon.

Just outside the village of Ngawyaw were several crude images of human beings carved out of short wooden posts stuck in the ground. One of them was most obscene. A similar obscenity was noticed much later in a Kachin village far to the west, between Fort Hertz and Myitkyina, where some conical-shaped stones, probably of natural origin, and bearing some resemblance to the human penis, had been stuck in the ground at the entrance to the village. In the Maru hut too the ends of the long beams which project into the porch are finished off in a manner which might be taken to represent the penis, while on the cross-beams snakes and the head of some horned animal, whether deer, goat or fabulous monster it is difficult to say, are frequently carved. It would be interesting to know if these things have any connection with the Bon religion of Tibet, a system of phallic worship.

The most callow carving is also to be seen at the graves, which are curious. The dead are burned, and the ashes buried in a circular mound surrounded by a trench two feet deep. Over the mound is raised a conical, straw-thatched roof, and tall bamboo poles bear aloft sign-boards on which are carved human figures, birds, snakes eating each other, and heads with horns.

From the summit of the next spur we caught a glimpse of the 'Nmai hka to the north, several thousand feet below us, but this distant view gave us no idea of its size. With its endless procession of precipitous razor-backed spurs, divided by deep gullies filled with rich vegetation, it closely resembles the valleys of the Mekong and Salween in north-west Yun-nan—it would be difficult to tell from a photograph which was which, though the dryness of the Mekong valley and consequent poverty of vegetation would be sufficient to identify it.

A terrific descent brought us to a big torrent crossed by a cane suspension bridge, and then came the usual long climb up to the village.

Already three adventurous Marus, desiring to see something of the world, had attached themselves permanently to our party, thus swelling our numbers to eight. This was a great convenience, as it reduced the number of porters to be commandeered daily to six or eight, the number of loads having been reduced as our stores rapidly diminished. This balance was made up each morning from the village where we slept.

The Marus, or Naingvaws, as they are called here, are short, sturdy and deep-chested, resembling Burmans more closely than do the Kachins, though this may be in part due to their dress.

They carry their loads by means of a strap passing over the forehead and not with a shoulder-board as do the Lashis and Yawyins, a method probably learnt from the Chinese, with whom these latter came in frequent contact.

The complexion is a dark copper, the face round, nose broad and flattened, eyes almond-shaped, hair short, straight and black, usually tied in a knot on the top of the head.

They are cheerful companions, and if not very energetic, are actually capable of great physical exertion when put to the test, as we subsequently discovered.

That night the full moon rose partially eclipsed into a clear sky and by eight o'clock the eclipse was almost total; it was extraordinary to watch the glowing velvet sky, in which formerly none but the most brilliant stars had been visible, slowly turning black till stars of the second and third magnitude shone out like lamps being lit in a distant city, and the heavens sparkled with the full splendour of starlight night.

Meanwhile the villagers had become greatly excited, believing that a devil was devouring the moon. A procession formed up, and paraded with gongs, which they banged lustily, shouting as they circled round a barrel-shaped drum on which a small boy operated as it lay on the ground.

Finally the procession moved off through the village, carrying the gongs above their heads and flapping their arms to a sort of cake-walk, while a child not much bigger than the tom-tom staggered along with that instrument for another person to hammer.

After a time the efforts of these merry roysterers were rewarded, the devil grew frightened and sicked up the moon even as the whale did Jonah, and presently its silver rim reappeared, and by ten o'clock the exhausted band stood in the full flood of moonlight, their labours ended. As for me, I went to bed.

The whole performance was strongly reminiscent or scenes in a Chinese village when a big dog swallows the moon.

September 5.—Minimum 36.1° F. The day broke gloomy and threatening after heavy rain in the morning. Masses of cloud came boiling up from the gorge below, but no more rain fell, though the sky remained overcast and the atmosphere was sultry.

After crossing one spur, from which the 'Nmai was visible, we reached a village of a few huts on the summit of the next, where the porters suggested stopping the night.

However, as the Mekh rame[2] was visible just below us, and beyond that, over a low spur, the 'Nmai hka, I was anxious to push on, feeling that substantial progress would have been made once we were across that river; a dim realisation of the task we had set ourselves was beginning to dawn on me, and I foresaw a shortage of food in the near future. The four week's march for which I had prepared would be up in another four days, and we were barely half-way yet!

I had abandoned all thought of crossing the 'Nmai hka and thence proceeding through the "triangle" (the country enclosed between the Mali hka and the 'Nmai hka) to the Hkamti Long road—indeed I could get no

---

[2] *Rame* is a Kachin word for river or stream. *Hka* means a big river. *Zup* means a small stream.

certain information of a bridge over the 'Nmai, except one which was said to be destroyed.

There probably are routes westwards from the 'Nmai valley, however, for the "triangle" is said to be thickly populated; but the absence of village on the right bank of the river is curious. The mountains on that side seem to dip even more steeply into the water than they do on the left bank.

Another reason why I wished to get across the Mekh now was because there did not appear to be enough porters in this village to supply our wants, and our present lot would be sure to sneak off and leave us stranded; whereas, could I once get them across the river, we might persuade them to go on to the next village.

So we started off, and a dreadful descent of over 2000 feet down a slippery path—for the granite had decomposed to a sticky clay—brought us at last to the Mekh rame; after that the going got worse and worse.

The Mekh, up which we proceeded for half-a-mile from near its confluence with the 'Nmai hka, by a most difficult, rocky path, is a brawling river, here about fifty yards wide, crossed by a cane suspension bridge sixty yards in length and at least fifty feet above the water. Just before entering the 'Nmai it bends to the north, and has cut its way in a half-moon through the enclosing wall of the latter, so that for the last part of its course it flows in a deep gorge, precipitous cliffs rising on either side, that on the right bank forming a narrow wall between the two rivers; and having crossed the bridge—a matter of giddy difficulty, for it swayed from side to side at every step; the men as usual gallantly carrying the girls' loads across for them—it was up this rock wall we had to climb.

Along either bank of Mekh the path was difficult, as we had to clamber up and down precipices, along rock ledges and slippery logs, and over boulders, so that Maru, who so far had followed very well, had to be carried most of the way.

From the river bed we hauled ourselves up the face of the cliff by means of roots and creepers—how the porters did it with their loads I don't know to this day, but it is a fact that had they not carried them by means of a head-strap, leaving both hands free, the feat would have been impossible.

Once on the edge of the wall-like spur, matters became easier, though the path was still very steep.

It was curious to hear first one river and then the other as the path turned to this or that side of the spur between the two, first the deep boom of the 'Nmai hka like a mastiff growling, followed by the shrill rattle of the Mekh as the path crossed to the other side. From high up on the spur, which was well wooded, we looked down between the trees on to the 'Nmai hka, a cataract of foam it appeared, nearly as big as the Mekong, and then we plunged once more into the forest.

Evening now came on, and the Marus informed me that it was impossible to reach the next village that night, and that we should have to camp in the forest; but presently one of them remembered a fresh hill clearing and hut on the steep slope to the right, and down we plunged towards the Mekh again in search of it.

Stumbling and tripping over tree trunks in the darkness, we were soon aware of the clearing, and presently found the hut, a poor little shanty standing by itself in this lonely wilderness, whereupon my personal servants commandeered it for me and themselves, turning the inmates and the other porters out into the jungle for the night. Even so, there was no room to put up my camp cot, and I slept on the floor; but we had been nine hours on the march and I could have slept standing.

Next morning when we came to apportion the loads we found that what I had feared had indeed come to pass—several of the porters had decamped at dawn. We should have been in rather a fix if it had not been for a party of young men from the village above turning up unexpectedly and offering to go back with us. So regaining the path along the ridge crest, we went our way rejoicing.

Picture us, then, still toiling up the granite spur in the angle between the two rivers, the powerful 'Nmai hka and the agile Mekh rame, till never an echo of all that tumult below floated up to us.

Sometimes we were in the shade of the forest, where mosquitoes and red ants worried us, sometimes in the open, where gorgeous butterflies sported in the glaring sunshine, till at last we reached a bare shoulder of the hill-side and bore away eastwards up the Mekh valley, though that river was no longer visible.

Three hours' steady climbing up the precipitous ridge and an hour in the sunshine during the hottest part of the day had aroused in me a lively thirst, but this brown, roasting, rocky mountain-side, broken by bare granite scraps and tors to which clung a few gnarled pines and thorny bushes, looked as dry as a desert; it was therefore a great and unexpected relief when presently we came to a spring of clear, cold water gushing from the cliff 2000 feet above the river. It was, in fact, the village well, and here we slaked our thirst and rested a while before going on to the village nearly half-a-mile away.

A descent of some hundreds of feet down a villainous granite stairway, partly artificial but mostly natural, brought us to a small platform on which were perched five huts standing at various angles to each other, and here we halted for the day, though it was but two o'clock. Two hours later, almost without warning, a terrific storm, with lightning and thunder, swept across the valley, driven by a gale of wind, the leaves being whirled aloft; but in an hour it was quite still again.

I was allotted the far end of the hut, my bed, table and chair being put up in the passage by a small door which admitted light and air and opened on to a narrow platform overlooking the pig preserves and a fowl run and a rank growth of pumpkins, tobacco and buckwheat, all mixed up higgledy-piggledy.

Next to me was the "maidens' room", that convivial hearth set apart for the unmarried, where the wise virgins await the coming of the bridegroom, with stoups of liquor and flowers and pretty speeches.

And here, with no light but the red embers of the fire, and the moon rising over the black mountains, when all the household is asleep, and the noises of the village are stilled save for the restless movements of the tireless cattle and the occasional grunt of a pig under the hut, the youth whispers to the maid the same old story—only it is not always the same youth.

She does not know, and hangs her head.

Yes, she likes him, but she also likes the youth from Bum-pat, in the far valley, who sometimes comes to see her.

Last time he brought her very many *lan ka*[3] which he had made himself; and he was handsome and reputed the best crossbow shot in his village; but she fears he is also making love to Ayawng, the *duwa's*[4] beautiful daughter, and is jealous.

Besides, this new lover of hers, Wakyetwa by name, has more mithan than his rival, and he has a blood-feud against Shippawn, by whom his sister has borne a son, though he now refuses to marry her, preferring to settle in kind; he, Wakyetwa, will get more mithan for this, and a gong and a *dab*.

So Wakyetwa is encouraged to come again the next night, and before he leaves, she shyly gives him a crimson flower of coxcomb which she has plucked from her *taungya*.

It is communism. One often hears it said glibly enough, and not without astonishment implied, that the system of free love in vogue amongst unmarried Kachins—courting carried to its logical conclusion I should call it—guarantees a happy and lasting married life later; adultery, in fact, is practically unknown amongst the Kachins, it is said. Maybe this is advanced in mitigation rather than in praise of the system, but there is always a suspicion that the unexpected discovery of, after all, some good in a custom, which at first sight shocks the sensitive mind, may cause a reaction entirely in its favour; an apology, in fact, becomes a defence.

I merely point out the dander—let it not be thought for a moment that I condemn the custom, or wish to preach a moral homily; though its general application to European society would not, I fear, at this stage of evolution, achieve a similar end. On the other hand, a not dissimilar custom has long been prevalent in the back blocks of mountainous Europe.

Of course it all depends on ideals.

I dare say lots of people, asking no questions, really are satisfied with

---

[3] *Lan ka*, the rattan rings worn by the Kachin tribes round the calf.
[4] *Duwa*, a village headman.

fidelity after marriage; but on the other hand, very many stipulate for purity before, though indifferent as to what happens afterwards. Some even expect purity before marriage and fidelity after it.

However, they are not Marus.

The people of this village brought me a long-tailed harvest mouse[5] and a baby monkey for which I gave a rupee and some beads.

The monkey, a pig-tailed baboon, was the oddest little chap, his tiny face crumpled like a petal in bud, giving him an appearance of wrinkled age, though he was unweaned and his weakness, his childish clutchings, and his piteous cries for his mother, dead or wounded in the jungle, betrayed his tender age. I kept him for two days, forcibly feeding him on well-chewed sugarcane or corn, copiously emulsified with saliva, and then the newly lit flame of his little life flickered and went out in the night.

So the hot afternoon passed away, and at sunset I noticed flashes of lightning far away in the south-west, where clouds had gathered, though the wind was still from the east. The weather changes very suddenly in these mountains, however, and bright moonlight at ten o'clock was replaced by heavy rain in the early morning, the temperature falling to 67.5° F. At six A.M. the valley was filled with mist, which was rapidly dissipated by the sun two hours later.

---

[5] *Pachyura* sp.

CHAPTER XI

THE LONG TRAIL

Descending about a thousand feet to the Mekh by the usual precipitous path, now slippery with mud, we halted for a bathe, the sun being already strong. A couple of twists in the river, with big noisy rapids above and below, caused almost slack water here under the right bank, and casting off their one garment apiece, most of my men plunged into the water.

The Marus are fond of swimming, though I saw no experts, a somewhat feeble breast stroke being the only mode of propulsion. Consequently no bold spirit came forward to swim the river, here some thirty or forty yards in breadth, crossing the swift current, which, under the opposite bank, hastened faster and faster towards the rapids, to be finally sucked frothing and protesting between big boulders. Neither have they any idea of diving, my efforts in that direction, from the top of a granite boulder, causing astonishment almost to the point of attempted emulation.

For half-an-hour the air was filled with the sounds of laughter and splashing, the Marus ducking each other like schoolboys, and chasing over the hot sand, or sunning themselves on the rocks.

Our march now led us up the river bed, clambering over immense boulders or leaping from one to the other, the river a tumultuous torrent of battered, seething water, till presently we reached a cane suspension bridge. Here we met two Lisus from the hills, one of whom carried a small pig in a basket.

The Marus live in the valley of the 'Nmai hka and in the lower parts of the tributary valleys, particularly those of the Laking hka, Mekh rame and Namre rame; the Lisus occupy the hills and the upper valleys between the 'Nmai hka and the Salween valley, as well as the Salween valley itself, from where they extend into the Chinese provinces of Yun-nan and Ssu-ch'uan, though their distribution is discontinuous. They are not found west of the 'Nmai kha or north of lat. 28°.

Their villages are on an average perhaps 2000 feet above those of the Marus, and as their crops ripen a month or two later, they come down into the warmer valleys about this time for food, bringing potatoes, salt, pigs, cows and iron pots in exchange. Most of these things they themselves have obtained from the Chinese, who rarely penetrate into this part of the country. From these men I bought a few new potatoes the size of small marbles.

Presently we came upon a remarkable sight.

Some carnivorous animal had left its droppings in a rock pool amongst the boulders, and the poisoned water had tainted the atmosphere for yards around with its rank acridness. From all directions this reeking cesspool had attracted the most gorgeous butterflies imaginable, and they had come in

9. YOUNG NUNGS.
The boy on the right holds a four-foot span cross-bow. The other two have each their *dâh* or short knife. They are not blessed with abundant clothing. *Photo by P.M.R. Leonard, Esq.*

their dozens. The pool was a quivering mass of brilliant insects, and still others hovered to and fro over the unsavoury meal, awaiting their turn to alight; from time to time a butterfly, impatient of waiting, would push itself amongst the already packed multitude, causing a flutter of painted wings as the group rearranged itself like the colours in a kaleidoscope. Is it not curious that such beautiful, delicate, and outwardly dainty creatures should be attracted by such loathsomeness? It is apt to start a cynical train of thought on the corruption which underlies all material beauty and the empty vanities of life.

But it was while watching, fascinated, these heaven-born insects that for the first time I realised the full magic beauty of Mendelessohn's *Papillon*, which ran in my head even as I watched the oscillating wings at the butterfly meet.

Amongst them were many swallow-tails of the genus Dalchina, with schooner wings banded with pale green. When the insect settles the wings are folded and in profile resemble the sails of a schooner.

Butterflies, it may be noticed, when they alight do not all behave similarly; just as their flights differ, this one darting in rapid zigzags high up in the air, that one flapping sedately along on broad wings, a third swooping swiftly from flower to flower, so too some close their wings the moment they settle, while others spread them.

Amongst the former the most famous is no doubt the leaf-butterfly,[1] of which I saw one lovely specimen in the 'Nmai valley. Settled on a twig, it was impossible without close scrutiny to distinguish this insect from an asymmetrical leaf, like that of the lime-tree, which the folded wings resembled in shape, markings being readily mistaken for venation, the head tucked away, the body representing the stalk.

In spite of its strong flight and protective mimicry, this butterfly is far from common here; at least it is rarely seen.

Another butterfly[2] which at once folds up its wings on alighting is one the under side of whose wings are veined and mottled like certain kinds of rock, as, for instance, limestone with quartz veins, or schist (species of Cyrestis).

The duller butterflies of the forest, however, the sombre but none the less pretty browns and greys, generally alight with outspread wings, though some open and close them alternately, as though stretching themselves.

Most lovely of all are the swallow-tails, of which there are a considerable variety in the hot, sunny valleys. These, as they probe the flowers for honey, scarcely settle, or if they do, touch with so light a caress the damask petals that they seem poised on air; and as they hover over, or tread with fairy

---

[1] *Kallima* sp.
[2] *Cyrestis* sp.

pressure the bell-like convolvulus and trumpet flowers, their wings quiver and tremble like aspen leaves shivering in a zephyr breeze, never still for a moment. One of the most beautiful of these was a species of Leptocircus, with gauzy wings trailing out behind like fluttering ribands. How full of life they look, what restless energy in those slender bodies borne aloft on gorgeous wings! And how exquisitely the first movement of *Papillon* represents to our ears the quivering, restless vitality here seen with the eyes! This music will ever carry me back to the Burmese hinterland, where I shall see again that rancid pool with its burden of butterflies by the thundering Mekh!

On the wet rocks beneath the shadow of the high river bank pink and white begonias with mottled, velvety leaves were plentiful. Never was such a country for begonias! Indeed the shy vegetation hidden away in the forests on these damp cliffs, between 5000 and 8000 feet elevation, was remarkable for the beauty of its flowers and foliage, amongst which begonias, species of Impatiens and Chirita, maiden-hair ferns, Colocasia and Selaginella are the most noticeable.

One does not travel even over the comparatively level river beds in this country for long. We had descended 1000 feet from the last village, and we now had to climb 2000 feet to the next one. Ascents and descents, which in some places include climbing whereby one holds on to convenient rocks and tree roots, sometimes even the rattan canes insecurely fastened from one tree to another, in order to pull oneself up, are at the best by scarcely zigzag paths as steep as the pitch of a house roof. Every obstacle is surmounted by frontal attack; there are no carefully sought out alignments nor elaborately graded approaches; one cannot follow with the eye the road winding in and out round the gullies as one does the mule-roads in the hill tracts of Upper Burma.

However, as you plod wearily up, the porters toiling along behind, halting for breath at frequent intervals, you feel that at every step you are getting up—mountain ranges come rapidly into view again, faraway peaks poke up their heads beyond, the valley grows blue in the distance. One performs prodigies of accumulated climbing in a day, though you may finish at a lower altitude than that at which you started, and anyhow the net result may be only a few miles gained.

Nor is the path always safe, being indeed no broader when cut out of the cliff side or spanning a ravine than when traversing a level stretch of jungle.

Two or three logs of questionable strength, carefully concealed by earth, served as a footpath round an awkward corner in one place, and stepping confidently on the edge, it crumbled away without warning, precipitating me over the *khud*. Hence the phrase "As easy as falling off a log", no doubt first said in a country where logs are used as inconsequently as they are here. Luckily as I fell I was able to clutch the timber with both hands, and being further somewhat violently arrested in my projected course by a tree trunk below, I escaped with nothing more serous than a bruised leg and a severe shaking, being rescued from my perilous position, suspended over the precipice, and hauled up on to the path again by the porters behind.

Maru had followed us on foot ever since we left Laking, though he still had to be carried whenever we encountered a precipice or crossed a torrent. Now that he had learnt to wag his tail when pleased, hang his head when depressed by a guilty conscience, grovel on his belly when I called him to task, skip about excitedly at meal-time and give way to other expressions of canine emotion, all of which seem to have come naturally to him by degrees, since his mother was far away in the fort at Hpimaw, he was a delightful if silent companion. He made friends with the baby monkey at once, though I am not sure that the trust was reciprocated, or the affection returned.

The monkey, of course, was carried in a basket, as Maru had previously been. He was difficult to feed, because he would insist that my finger was a nipple, at which he sucked and chewed with his tiny milk-teeth all to no purpose, while my own mouth grew as dry as lava masticating and predigesting his meal of rice or sugar-cane to pulp before pushing the salivary bolus into his little red mouth. The expression on his crumpled face, which was not dissimilar to that of a new-born baby, as he looked at me with large, puzzled eyes, saying in eloquent silence, "Surely *you* are not my mother!" was sad, as though anticipating the end.

That night was spent at a village of six or eight huts hemmed in between gigantic forested spurs, and backed by the ridge above, which towered up for two or three thousand feet. When I turned in the moonlight flooding the dim Mekh valley immediately below and silvering the trees promised fine weather for the morrow.

Well protected by vegetation on every hand, the minimum fell only to $67.8°$ F, though we were quite 4000 feet above sea-level.

Next day, 8th September, we climbed steeply for three hours, pushing our way through thickets and brushing aside the long, dewy grass which concealed in path, here bordered by masses of purple-flowered Torenia.[3]

At last, passing through a belt of forest trees, we reached the open, wind-swept summit, forming the northern boundary of the Mekh basin, where there were no trees, but only dense thickets of rhododendron and other shrubs. As usual, the rock was granite.

In spite of a cloudy sky, we had a fine view of the Salween divide away to the ENE, from the crest of which this convulsion of crumpled mountains and twisted valleys stretches westwards to the 'Nmai hka, while eastwards, in amazing contrast, bold spurs dip straight down into the deep Salween which beats against their feet.

---

[3] *T. peduncularis.*

Southwards we could see far down the 'Nmai valley, but here and there the mountains were blotted out in storm, and the rumble of thunder in the north sounded ominous.

A long and steep descent through jungle brought us at length to a little cultivation, and traversing some *taungya* where millet and buckwheat struggled manfully with the weeds, we reached a village of five huts, and halted for a meal to let a storm go past. On the opposite slope, separated from us by a valley across which a bird would have winged its way in a few minutes, stood a second larger village. This we reached at five o'clock, by the more prosaic method of walking down one side and up the other.

Here the porters very naturally wished to halt, saying that we could not reach the next village before dark; but remembering how comparatively frequent villages had been between the Laking and the Mekh, and the indisposition of the Marus to exert themselves unnecessarily, I scouted the suggestion and persuaded them to go on to the next village. I felt confident we could reach it by nightfall, with an effort.

I was indeed becoming uneasy at the slow progress we were making, being already several days late on the scheduled programme worked out before starting; consequently I resolved to speed up our rate of marching at every possible opportunity.

However, I had better have been guided by those who knew something of the country and the ways of its inhabitants. The two attempts I made both failed dismally in their object, and after that I gave it up in disgust, though no doubt they sufficed to keep clearly before the minds of our party the grave fact that no unnecessary delay could be tolerated.

True, each time I cajoled the men into speeding up we covered more than the usual march the first day; but it only meant that we had less than the usual march to do the next day, and arrived exactly where we would have arrived had there been no speeding up. No amount of cajolery would make the men do three marches in two days, and in fact it was impossible, so long as we had to change porters at all; for if we arrived at a village in the middle of the day and the men dumped down their loads and refused to go on, there we had to stop till next morning.

There was no one at home in the village to take up the loads, only a few old women weaving cloth, decrepit men smoking and tiny children playing in the hearth; the rest of the inhabitants were up the mountain minding their crops, or hunting in the jungle, and would not appear till dusk. A very jolly open-air life!

There were points about the speeding-up system—for instance, it was pleasant to have a whole afternoon's rest sometimes; it gave me an opportunity to look after my plant collection and see something of Maru village life. But it never shortened by a single hour the journey to Fort Hertz.

North of the Mekh villages are few and far between. The bed of the 'Nmai hka becomes more and more confined, and though spurs are more numerous between the Mekh and the Ahkyang than they are between the Laking and the Mekh, they are also much steeper, much more rocky, and hence much more difficult to cultivate. Flat shoulders too, on which alone villages can be built, seldom break the curve of a granite spur as it sweeps down from the mountains above the river, separating one gully from the next. We toiled over an endless succession of these huge spurs; no sooner had we surmounted one, climbing from the stream 1500 or 2000 feet, in jungle, over cliffs, along ledges, through grass which buried us, than we had to begin the descent to the next torrent, and were very glad to halt and bathe when we got there.

Though the sky was still clear behind us in the south, it had clouded over from the east, so that there was no prospect of moonlight to assist us.

At dusk we stood on the brink of a deep chasm, and before the rearguard had reached the summit of the next spur, after a weary climb, it was quite dark. However, we could hear dogs barking, and occasionally through the trees see lights moving in the village ahead, which the advance guard had evidently reached, so that, as the crow, or even the careless butterfly, more typical of this country, flies, it could not be far away.

We ourselves, unfortunately, being neither crows nor careless butterflies, had to walk, and found the distance correspondingly more formidable.

As for the porters and T'ung-ch'ien, they hardly dared move for fear of falling, but an occasional fall seemed to me preferable to a night spent on the mountain-side, especially as rain threatened, so I pushed warily ahead. Though it was impossible to see the path, pale flashes of lightning revealed from time to time the contours of the land, from which the probable direction of the winding path, here buried in long grass, there concealed amongst rocks, might be gauged.

In this manner I groped my way along, carrying Maru, for half-a-mile, shouting at intervals as a light waxed and waned somewhere ahead, till suddenly, without any preliminary warning, I rolled six feet down the *khud*, losing the path altogether, and decided to stay where I was lest worse befell.

As I sat disconsolately spitting pebbles out of my mouth and combing the grit out of my hair there at last appeared round the corner a man carrying in his hand a flaring torch, which revealed the fact that I was sitting on the edge of a cliff, descended by the aid of a notched log; I could hardly have continued the abrupt descent beyond this point without breaking some arms and legs!

The new-comer, after holding his torch aloft to light me down the cliff and indicate the path ahead, now went back to where the porters had resigned, while I approached another light. Presently I reached not indeed the village, but a small mat hut on the slope above us, where the maize is stacked when ripe and people pass the night watching the crops when the monkeys come down to claim their share.

Inside the hut, which was small and draughty, I found several of the porters with my bedding, but no food. The men had lit a fire and we soon made ourselves cosy on the hard ground, roasting some maize cobs in the embers for supper, there being eleven of us altogether when the laggards arrived just as it began to rain heavily; so several must have reached the village.

During the night it rained almost continuously, and next morning the monkey was dead; perhaps this was due to cold, the temperature falling to 65.9° F; in fact it was the chill, moist air filtering through the flimsy walls which woke me before six in the dawn dusk.

Having nothing to eat, we wasted no time in packing and setting out for the village, reached it in half-an-hour, where the rest of our party met us with a suspicion of feigned surprise and fleeting smile of superiority grossly irritating.

Near the village I was surprised to find the path cleared and levelled, the grass cut, the banks trimmed, first aid rendered to the water supply, and other signs of Hodge; a Maru headman who keeps even two hundred yards of inter-village track in repair on the upper 'Nmai hka is a treasure indeed, and deserves to be encouraged by Government. In the rainy season these inter-village tracks are hardly used at all, and soon become almost obliterated by the vegetation.

We now had breakfast in the house of the headman, a tall, robust, aristocratic-looking Maru dressed like a Burman, with *in-gyi* and silk *hkoung-boung* in addition to his *lone-gyi*; in fact one might have taken him for a Burman in any other setting.

After collecting a fresh lot of porters we started off again, the weather being cool and cloudy; now we looked down on a deep valley full of mist diffusing itself raggedly heavenwards as it tried to rise into the already saturated air above.

As previously stated, we gained nothing by our forced march except an afternoon's respite from toil now; we only reached the next village half-a-day earlier, and had to stop there.

The Marus, unlike the Yawyins, do not care to travel far from their homes, and generally object to going beyond the next village.

Asked for information about the road three or four marches ahead, they can tell you nothing except in the vaguest terms, so that when the villages are close together progress is necessarily slow, porters being changed at every village and, for the reasons given above, a change being impossible except in the early morning.

Yet every morning you may see the young men of the village saunter out with *dah*, crossbow and arrow-bag of black bear skin to hunt in the jungle and pass the day smoking, chewing *pan* and talking idly; while the women and children do the work in the fields and in the house, making food and clothes for all.

I was very lucky to have got ten porters, including five Marus, to go with me the whole way to Fort Hertz, otherwise I should never have got there without jettisoning half my loads, since these villages north of Mekh could not have furnished the requisite number of porters.

The prejudice against travelling far from their home seems to be characteristic of people whose lives are spent in the jungle, whose vision is circumscribed by impenetrable vegetation in the midst of which lurk all those evil spirits, here called *nats*, bread of an imagination unfettered by knowledge.

The mountain peoples, the men who reach the passes and meadows above the forest, in contrast to these others, travel far and wide, fearing nothing. They are the people who emigrate, and emigrating, come into contact with new civilisations; they are the people who eventually shoulder their way into the fair places of the earth.

Such are the Yawyins. Such too are the peoples of the wide, windy plateaux of Tibet, great travellers all, nomads some. Their horizon is bounded only by the limits of human vision, and a vast curiosity assails them as they stand beneath the blue dome of heaven and look across the mountains; nothing stands between them and far lands but these same mountains that they know so well—why then should they not go to those dim distances, strange and full of unknown things, but not mysterious, not exciting unbridled imagination!

So even when they desert the wide, windy pastures and take to agriculture in the warm valleys, they lose not their love of nomadic life, but become great traders, venturing far afield in search of what they need in their newly settled homes.

And such, too, are the children of the desert, on whom the stars twinkle at night with an unearthly brilliance, and the rising and setting sun slants its rays over vast, bare spaces.

A steep ascent now brought us out on to a narrow granite ridge bare of trees, from which we had a fine view down the 'Nmai valley, the river itself being visible far below.

The ridge fell away to the next stream in a precipitous spur running parallel to the 'Nmai hka, and we found ourselves walking along a knife-edge, the summit of which was formed by a jumble of granite tors; so we turned back into the mountains to avoid it, immediately descending the east flank of the spur by a steep, zigzag path, sticky with red clay and very slippery.

No sooner were we on the inner face of the spur, behind the main river, than we plunged into thick jungle again, the high, precipitous banks loaded with the usual maiden-hair ferns, yellow and blue flowered Chirita, Selaginella and brilliant Impatiens.

Just before crossing the spur I noticed a tumultuous movement of the clouds, a fantastically fringed black plume sailing over from the west and, as soon as it reached the river, sending forth vivid tongues of lightning.

This evil-looking cloud banner now performed some extraordinary gyrations with the lower clouds which already brooded over the valley, a sort of cloud-spout or water-spout, anyhow a funnel-shaped object being formed in mid-air by the rubbing of opposing air currents; and next minute to the roar of thunder and a blast of air out of the sky as it seemed a deluge of rain fell, the storm lasting two hours.

Consequently our descent down the clay path was more hasty than dignified, and by the time we had crossed the torrent and climbed the opposite slope to a village perched a few hundred feet above we were all drenched to the skin and caked with mud.

However, in the afternoon every vestige of cloud disappeared, the sun shone out, and the temperature went up with a bound, reaching 83.1° F in the shade.

I spent the afternoon skinning the dead monkey and looking over my accumulating collection of plants, not sorry for a rest.

I also bought another pig-tailed baboon from the villagers, in exchange for some beads. He was older than the last one, and only took to me very gradually—indeed it was several days before he could bear to look at me without facially expressing his displeasure, though he was soon smiling at the natives.

This village was like many others—half-a-dozen rather poor huts scattered on the hill-side amongst patches of cultivation and little fenced-in gardens of Capsicum, pumpkins, yams, and tobacco.

CHAPTER XII

AMONG THE LISUS

September 10th.—Minimum temperature 65.2° F after a good deal of rain in the small hours.

The start was delayed owing to the fact that the path had been washed away and it was necessary for men with *dahs* to precede us and effect what repairs they could; vegetation had to be cleared, saplings cut, bridges thrown across gullies and brackets built round cliffs before we could get out of the cul-de-sac we had entered the previous day.

It was one of the most difficult marches we had yet experienced. Numerous notched logs and rickety bamboo ladders had to be negotiated, leeches worried us, and, as the day was hot, I was thankful when at four o'clock we reached a small village high above the river, amongst patches of cotton and *taungya* of ripening maize. Here we halted for the night.

This place commanded a good view of the 'Nmai hka to the north, which was the more welcome as, in spite of our continuous proximity to it, we rarely caught even a glimpse of this elusive river. At no time during our march north did we descend to its bank till we finally crossed it on 13th September, though in crossing both the Mekh and the Ahkyang we were only a little way above the junction of those rivers with it.

At nightfall a white mist softly filled the valley and wrapped everything below in slumber; only our heads were amongst the brilliant stars.

September 11th.—Minimum 63.8° F. The valley was still full of cloud at six o'clock, but there was blue sky overhead. Heavy dew gave an autumnal bite to the air, but as soon as the sun was up the mists disappeared and another fine day followed, the sweat bubbling out of us as we climbed up and down, rarely finding shelter from the sun's rays.

At the start we had a very deep gully to cross, the opposite ascent being exceptionally difficult. Then followed the long descent to the Namre rame, which valley may be considered, for this part of the world, thickly populated.

After crossing the stream by a cane suspension bridge we again ascended steeply, and passed through two small villages before halting at a larger one near the summit of the spur. Just across the valley, which was open, with cultivated slopes, on the left bank of the stream, two more villages were visible, and there were others higher up the valley out of view.

Five villages in view at once, say forty or fifty huts with perhaps four or five hundred people! We had seen nothing like it since leaving the Mekh!

When we arrived at the Namre rame we found between thirty and forty villagers, men, women and children, engaged in a fish drive. This operation consists in damming and diverting the torrent and securing any fish unlucky

10. "Black" Lisus.
A "black" Lisu of the Ahkyang. Note the cotton "gown", all in one piece and the *dâh* under the left arm. *Photo by A.W. Porter, Esq.*

enough to be left behind in the pools and channels below, which are gradually half drained.

Here, just above its junction with the 'Nmai hka, the Namre rame is a boisterous torrent, tearing amongst huge blocks of granite. At one point, where the water poured over a boulder into a deep pool, a dam had been built across the stream and the water confined to a single lateral channel, the crevices through which it might find its way beneath and between the boulders having been plugged with banana stems and a pulp made from the sheaths of sago palm leaves.

Thus for fifty yards or so down-stream there were only a few trickles and quiet pools of water lost amongst a wilderness of enormous boulders, glistening white in the sunshine.

It was difficult work scrambling about here in the torrent bed where the tumbling water had worn deep chasms and polished the sheer-sided boulders.

11. "Black" Lisus.
A "black" Lisu girl of the Ahkyang. She is wearing a Chinese jacket over her gown and a head-dress of beads. *Photo by A.W. Porter, Esq.*

Sitting or lying full length on these slabs, or lowering each other down into the pools, the Marus swept the hushed waters with conical bamboo sieves on poles, or turned over stones and grabbed, putting any fish they caught in baskets. I saw several taken, but the biggest was not more than seven or eight inches long, though every capture was hailed with a universal shout of applause.

The higher we travelled up the 'Nmai hka the uglier became the Marus.

The small children go about naked, and are always filthy. They have the usual pot-bellies and thin flanks of Eastern children, making them look as though they were in a perpetual state of unstable equilibrium, and trying to correct it by running faster than they were meant to.

September 12th.—Minimum 64.4° F. The sky at day break was perfectly clear and we got off soon after nine, climbing steeply to the summit of the spur which divides the Namre rame from the 'Nmai hka, and following its broken crest some distance up the valley; below us, on the Namre rame side, were scattered villages and cultivated slopes, but luckily (for as usual it was very hot in the sun) the crest of the ridge was more or less covered with forest.

On beginning to descend again we presently found ourselves, to my surprise, on quite a good path—not well graded, of course, for in several places it descended by abrupt steps down which one lightly leapt, but fairly broad, and cleared of undergrowth; evidently it had only recently been repaired.

This path took us down quite 2000 feet through forests in which I noticed two species of tree fern, and a species of oak with enormous acorns in squat cups, to a torrent where we halted for our usual daily bathe. In diving into a shallow pool here I had the misfortune to hit the bottom rather hard, cutting my head and chest on the sharp rocks.

A short climb up the opposite spur soon brought us to a village insecurely perched in an exposed position on the hill-side, where some slabs of slaty rock stood on edge like low walls; one hut was built close to the brink of a small scarp formed by one of these outcrops. To the west the mountains, in the form of a small horseshoe-shaped bay, stood up very steep and menacing, as it seemed.

Since four-thirty P.M. I had noticed an occasional growl of thunder, and when I looked out of our hut at six-thirty the wind was rising; before eight it was raining, a strong wind was blowing and frequent flashes of lightning illuminated the dark sky; evidently it was working up for a storm.

Quite suddenly it burst upon us with awful fury, the wind blowing with hurricane force. Now the lightning blazed incessantly, flash following flash with such rapidity that we could see everything—bending trees, whirling leaves, and the dark outline of brooding mountains; and to the continuous roll of thunder, like heavy artillery, was added the shriller rattle of drenching rain as it beat viciously on the stiff palm leaves.

The storm simply crashed down on to the village from the mountains, as though someone was tipping barrels full of water and compressed air on top of us.

Water poured through the thatch roof of our hut, bringing with it dirt and leaves which it splashed everywhere, quenching the fires and soaking our belongings; the hut rocked and shook on its piles like a liner in a gale; people screamed, dogs barked; every moment I thought the hut must collapse. Now the voice of the wind in the stiff-leafed sago palms and amongst the tall clumps of bamboo rose to an angry scream, and above all this tumult could be heard the deepening roar of the torrent below.

There came an ominous crash, and a shower of sodden leaves, dirt and debris from the roof littered the room where I sat, the earth floor of which was already a puddle; but in the furious gusts which came raging down the mountain-side I could not tell what had happened.

Then the people of our hut, snatching up torches, rushed out into the darkness, scared and weeping, and in the dim light cast by the quivering flames I saw the hut just above ours lying on the ground, a mass of broken beams, torn thatch, and split posts; the wind had simply crumpled it up like brown paper. Around it stood a group of wailing villagers, who seemed more concerned in rescuing a little food and a few stoups of liquor than in looking to see if anyone lay beneath the wreckage, though that may have been because they knew all had escaped. However, one of my men said there were people in the hut when it was blown down, so taking my lamp I climbed up the shattered roof and dropping through a hole found myself in the midst of a dreadful tangle through which it was very difficult to crawl; in this way, partly on my belly, partly on my hands and knees, I explored such of the interior as was not absolutely razed to the ground. However, there were no victims. The villagers were somewhat concerned for my safety, as they feared a further settling down of the huge mass, for their huts are enormously long, and it had been simply doubled up. As a matter of fact, little of it could have been laid much flatter than it was already.

Luckily for us this hut stood near us and to windward, otherwise *ours* would have gone! As it was, fragments had beaten against our roof, sending showers of debris into the rooms.

Close by a second hut, in which less than an hour before a dozen people had been seated round their family hearths, lay a shapeless mass on the ground, but from this too the inhabitants had escaped just in time, so that our further explorations led to no sad discoveries. Had anyone remained in the wrecked hut he must have been crushed by the falling beams, or suffocated beneath the weight of sodden thatch.

After paddling about in the mud outside and delving amongst the wreckage till I was festooned with soot and leaves from the thatch roofs (for chimneys there are none, and the interior of the hut is black with the smoke of generations of fires), while people shouted to me as I crawled here and there to hand out bite and sup which they specially prized, I returned to my quarters, thankful they were safe. The fire had been lit again and T'ung was preparing my dinner, though even here, so much water and rubbish were scattered about, it looked as though there had been a small earthquake.

It was nine o'clock and the storm was fast disappearing in the south-west—you could still hear it, growing fainter and fainter as it died away down the valley. By nine-thirty it was all over, the wind hushed, even the thunder too faint to be heard. A great stillness seemed to come upon the wrecked village as suddenly as the storm itself had fallen on it.

Such was the result of the last ten days of sultry weather, this furious rush of air and electricity from the eastern mountains.

September 13th.—Minimum 61.8° F. The storm had perceptibly cooled the atmosphere, but at six-thirty we could see nothing either above or below, or a hundred yards away in any direction, for we were in a bath of mist. However, it soon rolled back on to the mountains, and the day was as fine as ever, though less sultry.

The misfortunes of the previous night prevented us engaging porters at this village, all hands being required to repair the damage but we prevailed on those who had accompanied us from the last village to go on with us another stage.

Ascending the ridge above the village in the track of the storm, we found the path blocked in places by broken branches and uprooted trees, mostly young alders, the mountain-side here being, as usual, open, covered with high grass, shrubs, bushes and small trees forming thick copses. Here I found that curious parasite *Aeginetia indica*.

Later we met some travellers, small parties of Lisus and Marus, a sufficiently rare occurrence to comment upon.

After marching through the forest clothing the crest of the ridge we began the descent to the Ahkyang valley, following a very good path recently cleared of undergrowth and made with some ideas on the subject of grading. Presently we reached a fair-sized village, which, however, appeared to be quite deserted.

We could see some distance up the Ahkyang valley, which was broad and open, quite different to anything we had yet seen in this country, following with the eye paths on either side leading to more villages; but the river itself, some distance below, was still invisible.

The porters wanted to halt here, protesting that we could not reach a village across the river that night; they even unearthed a man who readily perjured himself to say that there was no way of crossing the river till the morrow.

However, having, after a prolonged halt at the deserted village, unearthed a few men, we descended by a narrow path so buried in grass from eight to twelve feet high that we could not see our way, and so steep that we could hardly feel it, to the Ahkyang.

Meanwhile three of the girl porters who had already come two marches with us struck work and ran away to the village above, determined not to cross the river.

This extreme dislike of travelling far from their own village evinced by most of the Marus may be a relic of a time when every village was against every other village, and to enter rival territory risked being captured and held as a slave. Kachin villages of different clans to this day raid each other and capture slaves of their own race.

A quarter of a mile up the left bank of the river we found a bamboo raft and set about crossing to the other bank, a long business, as the raft would only take two men and two loads at a time, besides a crew of one who squatted in the bows paddling and steering.

The river here was smooth and deep, about fifty yards wide, with a gentle current; just above was a big rapid, and the water became turbulent again fifty yards lower down. Both banks were rocky, fringed with a great variety of forest trees, and the view down-stream where the river swept in a broad arc between high cliffs to join the 'Nmai hka not far below was most striking.

It was a beautiful sunny afternoon, and while the raft was plying backwards and forwards I went in for a swim.

We camped for the night on the far bank under the rocks and trees, one of the latter being a tremendous fellow, two huge plank buttress roots of which facing me looked like the widespread legs of some giant. Between these my bed was set up.

We were poorly sheltered from rain, but the evening was fine, and at eight o'clock the stars were shining. I had supper to a chorus of insects buzzing and whirring in the jungle, accompanied by attacks from mosquitoes and sand-flies which lasted all night. Before we turned in the Marus from the village above, who had rafted us across and replaced the runaway girls, returned to the left bank, promising to come back again early next morning, a promise which, rather to my surprise, they kept.

September 14th.—Minimum 65.6° F—much warmer down here. Heavy rain in the early morning so that we all got wet in our natural shelters which were not sufficiently large to protect us. The river water had changed colour from green to brown telling of rain in the mountains; its temperature was 65° F. I saw a big grey kingfisher here, and the Ahkyang looked an ideal river for mahseer.

We started about nine on a most appalling climb straight up the cliff. Once out of the fringe of jungle the narrow path was completely hidden by the tall, saw-edged grass, twining Leguminosæ, birch and alder saplings, and shrubs, but mostly tussocks of twelve-foot grass, so that we were buried in it. Through this unyielding tangle we had to push our way, sometimes crawling on hands and knees, so tightly was the vegetation laced together above, cutting our faces on the sharp edges of the grass. The sun was blazing hot, there was no shade and the flies gave us no peace. On the whole, I thought, the jungles of the Wulaw Pass were preferable to those open hill-sides in the 'Nmai valley.

It took us two hours to reach the crest of a spur, after which the going was better to the top of the ridge.

Keeping along the ridge for a bit, we presently found ourselves on another good path like the one which had attracted our attention the previous day, and descending a little, reached a small village.

It was barely one o'clock, but here we had to halt, having gained nothing but moral satisfaction from crossing the Ahkyang the night before; it was the last attempt I made at speeding up. We heard that a British official and some soldiers had just gone up the Ahkyang valley, having slept in the hut we now occupied; however, he was expected back in a day or two, whereat I rejoiced. Still, we could not wait, as we had so little to eat, and besides he might be short of supplies himself on his return march. But I hoped he might overtake us before we reached Hkamti Long.

12 & 13. Nung Maidens and Iron Smelter.

Dressed in cloak and skirt of home manufacture; those on the right have girdles of cowry shells, threaded on bamboo; those on the left wear girdles of black rattan cane.

The smelter is holding the skin bellows by which the draught is maintained. The furnace is made of mud. *Photos by P.M.R. Leonard, Esq.*

As it turned out eventually, it was not a British officer at all, but a native Government employee.

We spent a beautiful sunny afternoon drying our things. It was quite pleasant here at an altitude of 5000 or 6000 feet, with a cool breeze, the shade temperature at three P.M. being 79.1° F. At dusk a wind sprang up and rain threatened, but at seven o'clock the stars were shining. However, when we turned in at nine-thirty it was raining steadily, and it was a fact that you could not depend on the weather for an hour in this valley.

September 15th.—Minimum temperature 64.3° F. For several days past we had been inquiring how many marches it was to Hkamti Long, but no one knew; they did not seem to have ever heard of the place. However, I reckoned from the map it could not be many marches now; but the worst was yet to come.

As usual, the valley was full of cloud when we got up, but presently patches of blue sky began to show through the breaking mists overhead. After nine we had continuous sunshine and blue sky over the valley, with clouds only on the mountain-tops.

It was, too, distinctly cooler again, and there being very much less climbing than usual, I was able to take more interest in my surroundings, in spite of a long eight hours' march. There were certainly plenty of things to interest one on every hand—plants, trees, butterflies, birds, to say nothing of the few people we met on the road, and those in the villages.

In the very next village we came to we met a party of Lisus from farther north, quite different from any we had yet come across. Each carried a very long, straight, pointed *dah*, similar to the Burmese weapon, in a proper sheath, not like the short, broad-headed *dah* of the Kachin tribes, with its open scabbard. This *dah* was about four feet long and had a scarlet handle.

They also had bags made from the fur of a silver-grey monkey, whose paws were crossed pathetically over the lid of the bag.

The first half of the march we were in the jungle nearly all the time, the path quite good, with easy ups and downs. Mosquitoes, flies and bees were rather a pest here.

Amongst the trees I noted two species of oak, a Castanopsis, a Ficus, two tree ferns and several big lianas. Many of the trees had conspicuous plank buttress roots, and a climbing Aroid was common, besides bananas, begonias, Impatiens and other jungle flowers; but I saw no palms or screw pines. The most interesting plant met with was a species of Piper, the leaves and fruits of which were eagerly plucked by my porters to chew; they said it improved their stamina.

In the southern parts of Burma *Piper betle* is cultivated, and the leaves chewed with lime and the betel palm nut (Areca sp.) by the natives.

On the open hill-sides grew two species of Rubus, *Alnus nepalensis*, Ailanthus sp., shrubby Polygonum, a poplar, a birch, Melastoma sp., tall, yellow-flowered Hibiscus, *Urena lobata* covered with pink flowers, and any amount of saw-edged grass.

On a plant of Polygonum I saw a caterpillar of the Geometræ class, which at first I took for a dead leaf. There were several shrivelled brown leaves on the stem, and this cunning caterpillar, by standing on the stem at the same angle as a dead leaf, being of the same colour and shape, readily passed for one.

Another caterpillar might easily have been mistaken for a muff, so densely was he clothed with hairs; he must have found it very hot in this climate, I thought!

Several birds whose voices are familiar in Burma were heard calling, and on the banks brown, smooth-skinned, shiny lizards disported themselves; we also saw a couple of green snakes, neither of large size.

After emerging from the jungle on the summit of the ridge, and descending a little, we came to some Lisu huts, and here the men got a few yellow-skinned cucumbers, two of which constituted my lunch; they were very juicy, and splendid thirst-quenchers.

The path here was pretty good, winding round a few small gullies which did not give us much climbing up and down. We passed through two more small Lisu villages, and then a climb to the summit of a spur, with a view of the river to the north, and a longish descent, brought us to Wakawatu, the first Lisu village of any size. We did not arrive here till after six, when it was already dark, having done about twenty miles.

At nine P.M. the sky was cloudy, the temperature 69° F.

We had great fun with the baboon this march. He generally rode on top of one of the loads, or on a man's shoulder, or even on his head, where he spent the time looking for lice, an occupation which amused him greatly and was certainly attended by a fair measure of success. Now that he had come to recognize in some manner my claims on him, I could pick him up and perch him on my shoulder, from which vantage point he would pull my hair vigorously—I couldn't offer him the same amusement as the natives did. However, he was not quite reconciled to me yet. When I picked him up, he would look up into my face with a surprised, questioning expression, as though asking me what I meant by taking such a liberty with him, blink his eyes very deliberately once or twice, keep still for a moment, and then give a sudden wriggle, at the same moment biting my fingers. The suddenness of the attack often ensured its success, and then he would drop to the ground and make off at full speed, in a series of leaps which took him along at a great pace.

Then perhaps Maru, seeing him and thinking it was rather a good game, would rush after him, and it was laughable to see them together, the one fleeing and dodging as though for his life, the other in hot pursuit. Eventually the pup would catch him up, and roll him over, and the monkey would lie low by the roadside for a minute, covering his face with his hands.

Presently Maru would begin to lick him and give him little playful nips, and the monkey would shut his eyes and tilt up his chin and smooth a few of the creases out of his face with a pained, resigned sort of expression which said us plainly as words: "I suppose I had best submit to the ill-timed levity of this plebeian beast."

Maru was always very gentle, but the monkey never became quite reconciled to him, escaping as soon as he could and swarming up the nearest man's leg, from which safe retreat he would chatter with rage at the indignity of it all, and grin horribly at the puzzled little dog, who did not understand.

He expressed his emotions volubly. When his attempts to escape from my clutches met with no success, he would give a shrill, querulous call, as though he were lost and required immediate assistance. It was a plaintive cry for help to one of the natives. When annoyed, as he was when I smacked him for biting, he always gave an angry little scream; at meal-time he mewed like a kitten, which was his way of asking for food, and again he would change to a coughing purr, which seemed to indicate contentment.[1]

September 16th.—Minimum temperature 65.5° F. In contrast to the Maru huts, the Lisu huts, though of a more substantial build, are quite small and have scarcely any projecting porch in front; nor is there any passage down the length of the hut—instead the interior is completely partitioned into three rooms, as in the Yawyin huts already described. Like the Maru huts, they are raised on piles, with walls and floor of bamboo matting, and thatched roof. In the middle of each room is the usual earthen hearth.

Besides being much smaller, the Lisu huts are more scattered, and the villages are situated in the bays between the spurs, instead of being perched up on the spurs themselves. The Lisus we met all spoke Maru, though none of the Marus could speak Lisu.

We continued our march northwards in drizzling weather, though it improved in the middle of the day. The path was fairly easy, though we had to cross one big gully. Just here the 'Nmai valley was more open, the slopes more gentle, the spurs falling less abruptly to the river, so that when, in the afternoon, we got up to a fair height, looking back we had quite a striking view of the river, hitherto so rarely visible.

---

[1] *Macaca assamensis.* "Anger is generally silent, or at most expressed by a low, hoarse monotone, *heu,* not so gular or guttural as a growl. Ennui and a desire for company by a whining *hom.* Invitation, deprecation, entreaty by a smacking of the lips, and a display of the incisors into a regular broad grin, accompanied with a subdued grunting chuckle, highly expressive, but not to be rendered on paper. Fear and alarm by a loud, harsh shriek, *kra,* or *kronk,* which serves also as a warning to the others who may be heedless of danger. Unlike the Presbytes (Semnopitheci) and Gibbons, they have no voice if calling to one another" (Tickell, in *Fauna of British India,* by W.T. Blanford, F.R.S.).

About one-thirty we halted at a Lisu village for rest and refreshment, having been going for nearly five hours.

These Lisus must not be confused with the Yawyins (*hua* Lisus) of the Burma–Yun-nan frontier hills farther south. True, they speak practically the same language, and are probably different clans of the same tribe. But they differ considerably from the Yawyins in dress, and to some extent in appearance, being taller but less sturdy. They are, in fact, identical with the redoubtable "black" (*hê*) Lisus of the Salween valley, from which region they have emigrated into British territory via the Ahkyang valley, probably within recent years, as a result of the recent Chinese occupation of the Salween valley, just as the Yawyins are doing farther south. I saw evidence of Chinese influence in their clothes, cooking pots and household goods.

I found them rather shy and suspicious; they asked prohibitive prices for eggs, and beyond that we could buy hardly anything from them, though my cook commandeered a fowl about the size of a dove, for which I paid a rupee.

It would seem that the *hê* Lisus are a degenerate clan of the great Lisu tribe, who have been adversely affected by living in the enervating Salween valley, which, from latitude 28° southwards, is low-lying, rain-drenched and pestilential.

The *hua* Lisus, on the other hand, many of whom, as we have seen, are now migrating into British territory from across the China frontier, owing to the pressure of the Chinese, are a typical mountain people, hardy, resourceful and pleasant to deal with.

The dress of the *hê* Lisus women is characteristic, and quite distinct from the harlequin skirt of the Yawyin, which latter peculiarity is said to be due to local influence.

She wears a thin, pleated skirt down to her knees, rather full at the waist, made of white hemp cloth with thin blue stripes, and a loose jacket to match. Feet and legs are bare, but below the knee a garter of black cane rings is worn. There is little display of jewellery such as the Tibetan woman wear, this being confined to large earrings and silver bracelets, while hoops of bamboo or iron are worn round the neck. The ears are not bored like those of Burmans, Shans and Kachin tribes, nor are masses of beads, such as the Lashis, Marus and others delight in, worn—probably because they are not obtainable. The hair is done in two hanging pig-tails, and round the brow is bound a fillet of white shirt buttons, or, in rare cases, of cowry shells, from which dangles a fringe of tiny beads ending with dummy brass bells. Cowry belts like those of the Maru girls were not seen.

The men wear a long cloak like a dressing-gown, of the same thin, white, striped cloth, which is slit up the sides to the middle and tied round the waist. Often short, baggy trousers of blue cotton cloth, obtained from China, are worn underneath, and not a few of the men wear Chinese trousers and jacket only. The hair is done in a single pig-tail which is not bound on top of the head. Large *dahs*, crossbows and bags of monkey-skin, in which tobacco and food are carried, are in everyday use.

So much for the *hê* Lisus of the Burmese hinterland. They do not differ materially from their relatives in the Salween valley immediately to the east, though some of the latter are even more uncouth.

In the afternoon we continued our march, reaching another village after dark, by which time we had covered over twenty miles.

CHAPTER XIII

A DESPERATE MARCH

September 17th.—Minimum temperature 63.7° F, the valley below us full of cloud in the early morning as usual.

We were told we could reach Hkamti in six days, but that as there were no villages *en route* we should have to engage porters for the whole journey. That meant a delay anyhow, to prepare food. Unfortunately all the men of the village had gone as porters with a Government party which had been up the Ahkyang valley a fortnight previously and were not back yet.

I therefore decided to push on with our permanent men—namely, four Marus and three Lashis—leaving T'ung to follow in charge of the remaining loads as soon as possible; meanwhile we sent a Lashi and a Maru back to the last village to engage porters there.

Starting late, we crossed several deep gullies filled with dense jungle, the path becoming worse and worse, and presently reached a few miserable Lisu huts, where we halted for an hour. Continuing, we crossed more gullies, and at length obtained a good view of the river, to which we descended gradually.

Now for the first time we found ourselves by the great river we had followed so persistently for over a fortnight, with rarely even a glimpse of it, though so close. It was a fine, swift river seventy or eighty yards broad, broken here and there by rapids. The temperature of the water, which was deep green in colour, was 63° F, two degrees colder than the Ahkyang.

The thick jungle came down almost to the water's edge on both sides, but there were sand-banks and coves, and stretches of boulders covered with azalea (*Rhododendron indicum*), Pyrus and other shrubs like those we had seen previously. The river was not in full spate, for the winter snows had long since melted on the northern mountains, and probably the worst of the rain were over.

We halted before dusk in a sandy bay where stood a few old bamboo shelters, roofed with banana leaves, which the men proceeded to renovate. Close beside us was a glorious tree, like a weeping hornbeam, from which suspended hundreds of long yellow ropes of winged fruits. This was a species of Englehardtia.

The view just before dark, with wreaths of thin mist forming over the river which twisted away into the twilight of the forested mountains, was extraordinarily solemn; the cicadas were making such a noise we could barely hear the splash of the water below our sand-bank, or the occasional hoot of an owl. But the low-hanging clouds were not reassuring, and the sand-flies and mosquitoes were a nightmare.

September 18th.—Minimum 65.7° F. When we woke up at daylight banks of mist lay over the river, which was scarcely visible except immediately below, but there was blue sky overhead.

Following up the left bank, we reached the crossing in an hour, and here happily met the returning Lisus of the last village, otherwise we should probably never have got across at all. In winter at least rafts can cross near where we camped, and probably they could have made the trip safely now, only there were none. Here the river was narrower, and flowed swiftly between high, rocky walls of vertically tilted slates and schists.

From bank to bank were loosely slung two ropes of plaited bamboo, their ends tied to trees; and by one of other of these ropes, it did not matter which, we had to cross.

Such rope bridges are common in Tibet, across bigger rivers than this, but how different!

In the first place, each rope is attached high up on the bank from which you start, and low down on the bank at which you arrive, and is kept taut; thus you cross the river by your own momentum, and the object of having two ropes is to enable you to cross in either direction.

In the second place, the Tibetan ropes are of finely plaited bamboo, and are well greased (with butter) before starting, to reduce the friction. But this rope was made up of three coarsely woven strands, so splintered as to look very unsafe, and there was no grease. The wooden sliders too were broad and ill-balanced, adding to the friction. Finally, instead of stout leather thongs such as the Tibetans use for slinging men and loads from the slider, the Lisus used their waist-cloths and turbans, both of which were yards in length. It was evident the Lisus were not accustomed to this method of crossing a river, and the whole outfit was very second-rate in consequence.

Every man had to pull himself across more than half-way. As for the loads, they would not budge down the rope of their own accord, and each one had to be laboriously hauled along by a man in front, who clasped his legs round it and then slowly pulled himself and the load up the rope. No wonder the crossing took four hours! The Tibetans would have had us across one of *their* rope bridges in an hour.

Meanwhile, waiting on the steep river bank, we were tortured by mosquitoes, bees and biting flies of many descriptions.

The men crossed one by one, clutching the rope with their toes and pushing, as well as pulling with their arms.

My turn to cross came last. Accustomed to being whisked across the great Tibetan rivers in one grand rush, I did not at all relish the prospect of hauling myself up this sagging rope.

Just before I startled the monkey, seeing none of his friends round him, jumped from my shoulder on to the rope and began running across, crying out as he went. In the middle he stopped, as though frightened by the rush of water beneath him; once or twice he slipped, and I thought he must go over, but he performed the hazardous feat of turning round without mishap.

I then started and slid less than half-way over. It was a most horrid sensation lying on one's back beneath the rope, perched in a cloth noose suspended from a slider which threatened to slip off the rope, leaving the cloth to be cut through by the sharp bamboo, arms stretched out at full length over one's head, clutching the rope.

Tremendous exertion was needed to pull oneself up the steep rope in such a position, against the friction of the slider, and when I was over the very worst bit of water, a broken rapid, running like a mill race, I felt thoroughly exhausted, and had to hang on there for a rest. Thus, looking down at the raging river forty feet below, from which I was preserved by a cloth band and the strength of my own arms, I could not suppress a shudder.

I had now caught up the monkey, seeing which he sat grinning at me for a moment, and then jumped on my shoulder. Slowly I pulled myself up the remaining distance, and as I at last neared the bank, the waiting men threw a rope and hauled me up the last few yards like a sack. It was good to stand on solid earth again.

One of the Lisus returning from Kawnglu, the outlying British post our informants had referred to when saying we were six marches from Hkamti, brought me a note from Mr J.T.O. Bernard, the frontier officer there, enclosing a telegram from Mr Hertz, Deputy Commissioner at Hkamti Long.

I was glad they were expecting me; it seemed to bring the place nearer. No mention was made of the war and we were still in complete ignorance of that astounding news.

We now climbed up the steep river bank in thick jungle by an execrable path till we joined the main path a few hundred feet above the river. Except for ankle-deep mud, which had been a feature of the path ever since leaving the Lisu village, the going was not bad.

Crossing a large torrent, we ascended gradually, approaching a considerable lateral valley, and halted at five o'clock by an old camping ground. Here we settled down for the night in a perfect haze of sand-flies, did up the old tumble-down shelters, and cut bamboos for new ones, roofing them as usual with leaves of wild banana.

Breakfast had consisted of tea, two biscuits and a plate of boiled rice and pumpkin, followed by a boiled egg.

This last was sprung on me as a surprise, having been commandeered by my Chinese cook, who, ignoring the protests of the Lisus that they had none, had gone the round of the baskets hung beneath the eaves of the hut and resurrected six. At two o'clock I had a small piece of chocolate for lunch, and when we reached camp, at five, I had a cup of tea with two biscuits and a maize cob. For supper, a plate of boiled rice and pumpkin, apple rings and some maize liquor obtained from the natives. The biscuit, egg and tea ration were carefully apportioned to each day, in the hope of making them last out, but with the rice, pumpkin and maize cobs I could afford to be fairly reckless. There was nothing else.

September 19th.—Minimum 66° F. The weather was very unsettled all day, with showers at intervals.

Shortly after starting we came to the big torrent up which our route lay westward to the pass, and turning our backs on the 'Nmai hka began the ascent. We were now over our ankles in mud the whole time, which made it very tiring—loose sand is the only thing to compare with it. Presently the stream branched into two, and the ascent became steeper. Nearby we saw a mule skeleton and broken pack-saddle, grim reminders of the previous year's expedition to the Ahkyang!

Some Lisus on their way down passed us, and at three o'clock we halted by the torrent, which here tumbled noisily down a steep granite stairway, camping beneath a huge boulder which afforded ample shelter for all; and a very cosy place it was, though chilly chiefly on account of the torrent. A large torrent always causes a cold draught.

On the rocks grew several species of Impatiens, including the one with bright magenta flowers, and an orange one with a long spur; another pretty one had large rose-pink flowers. In the jungle I noticed walnut-trees, but the nuts are like stones and contain no edible kernel.

The monkey was quite friendly with me by this time, and rode on my shoulder most of the way, eating chocolate. He was very fond of maize liquor too, and would fill his cheek pouches with food to be chewed at leisure later on. He had a curious way of sleeping on his belly, all bunched up into a ball, and his little cry of pleasure, his querulous scream and his shrill scream of anger were frequently heard.

In the forest I saw an enormous butterfly, similar to one noticed at Hpimaw. It flapped its great wings slowly and sedately, and settled with them outspread, the hind wings being purple and brown, fading to white on the front wings. It haunts shady forests at moderate elevations.

At eight-thirty the thermometer stood at 60.5° F.

September 20th.—Minimum 50.8° F. For nearly three hours we climbed steeply up the mountain-side in the deep mud, while it rained steadily throughout. In some of the steepest places attempts had been made by the Chinese muleteers who had accompanied the expedition in the previous year to improve the track by laying down bamboos; but as these were laid lengthwise we could not stand on them, whatever the mules could do, and slipped so badly at every step—for wet bamboo on a slope is like ice—that we were content to plod through the thick, sticky mud instead.

At last we reached the pass known as the Shing-rup-kyet, 8000 feet, and stood on the water parting between the 'Nmai hka and the Mali hka, the two great branches of the Irrawaddy which unite above Myitkyina, nearly 1000

14 & 15. A Maru Grave and a Nung Rope Bridge.
 The grave has a sugar-loaf thatched roof. It is crowned by a painted design. Inside is the coffin, containing ashes, not bones. *Photo by A.W. Porter, Esq.*
 The man's body is thrust through a large cane ring, threaded on the rope; he hauls himself along, pushing with his feet. *Photo by P.M.R. Leonard, Esq.*

miles from the sea and 200 miles from where we stood. Through the thick rain mist we could see a loop of the 'Nmai hka to the north-east, which was within a short day's march. Had we been able to see westwards we should have seen nothing but range after range of forested mountains, stretching to the horizon, all of which had to be crossed before we reached the Mali hka and the broad, open plains of Hkamti. However, we were spared that sight—perhaps it was as well not to know what was in store for us—and looked down into a cauldron of obliterating mist instead.

Following the stream down between high banks covered with variously coloured begonias and balsam, we presently came on an open meadow in the jungle, where a species of Impatiens grew four feet high, and scattered in its midst were bananas, oaks and Ficus trees, covered with climbing Aroids.

Then down, down, a long way, till it seemed we must be coming down to the plains almost, so big had the stream grown.

But no sooner had this thought come to me than we began to climb again, ascending a steep spur. Up and up we went, while the rain poured down, making the track hopelessly slippery, till we had re-ascended as many thousand feet as we had previously descended.

At last we came to some shelters, built by previous travellers, and the men wanted to halt—it was then about three-thirty. But camp was so dismal and we were so short of food that I was determined to march while there was daylight, so on we went, now up, now down, with occasional peeps through the trees and broken mist of endless mountain ranges in the west.

Finally we started definitely on another long descent, and did not halt till nearly six, when we came to a miserable shelter. The men soon ran up some new ones and built smoky fires to keep down the sand-flies which swarmed. Leeches too had begun to worry us, particularly little Maru, who ran along with his nose on the ground and got them up his nostrils, under his eyelids, and in his ears. Big blood-sucking horse-flies were another pest, and at supper nasty-looking stick-insects got bogged in the butter, and drunken cicadas dropped into the food from the trees, protesting stridently. But the most remarkable change on this side of the divide was the sudden appearance of screw pines (Pandanus sp.) in large numbers, growing fifteen or twenty feet high, propped up on their stilt roots.

In the afternoon the monkey ran away into the jungle out of pique because I smacked him. I thought he was lost, but presently I heard him screeching away, and caught sight of him crawling along the branch of a tree farther down the slope. I called and called, but he ceased crying, and I had almost given him up when he reappeared sitting on the path below. When he saw me coming he grinned, ran down the path a little way, I after him, and then sat up again, waiting; when I came to him he climbed up my leg and seemed pleased to be back. I don't think that he liked that five minutes at home, for it was raining hard at the time and he hated rain. Whether it was a momentary twinge of home-sickness or a joke he was unable to tell me, but he never ran away again. We passed many more discarded pack-saddles on this march.

September 21st.—Minimum 62.7° F. It rained steadily all night and continued most of the day, the longest and most trying march we had yet done, ten hours in the sodden jungle.

First we continued the descent of the previous evening, crossed a big torrent, and traversed for some distance, winding our way round gully after gully. The whole region was a perfect maze of mountains, cut up by hundreds of streams flowing deep in their jungle-hidden ravines, and the road was marked by the skeletons of mules and broken pack-saddles. All the time we were squelching ankle-deep in mud, tortured by leeches which dropped on us from the trees.

My feet and ankles were now covered with dreadful sores brought on my being always wet, and the bites of leeches which easily got through my wornout boots. Every night the continuous irritation would awaken me, or even prevent me getting any sleep at all sometimes.

A long climb brought us to the top of a ridge, and this we followed up and down for mile on mile. A gleam of sunshine at one o'clock was a false alarm, but another gleam about four proved less fleeting. At five, when I was tramping along mechanically, noticing little, I saw something better than sunshine, for the white mist between the trees suddenly gave place to a deep blueness, and I knew what that meant—it was the blueness of distant mountains. The plains at last! I thought. At the same moment we began to descend into a deep valley, and presently the fretted mountains on either side of the ridge showed up momentarily through the changeful mists; far below we distinctly heard above the patter of raindrops the unmistakable chatter of a river.

It was now getting late and we raced down the almost precipitous path as fast as we could go. Down, down, several thousand feet, till the whir of cicadas filled the air again, and it grew perceptibly warmer. At last we could see the valley below us, and at six-thirty we reached a considerable river, the Shang wang, a tributary of the Nam Tisang, which flows into the Mali.

Crossing by a bamboo trestle bridge, we reached a small hut at dark, built by the expedition in the previous year. Never had I been so tired as I was that night. Next day I anticipated an easy walk down the river valley to the plains.

September 22nd.—Minimum 67.2° F. It was very close down here and I slept badly in consequence of the sudden change and on account of the sand-flies.

We started late, and immediately faced a mountain once more. There was no easy march down the valley after all!

Showers fell throughout the day, the clouds moving up and down rhythmically. First the clouds would be lying down in the valleys, where it was raining, though we, high up, could see blue sky overhead; then they would start climbing up, and we would get glimpses into the valley below.

Presently, having concentrated their forces against the mountain-tops, they would drip rain for an hour, and having exhausted themselves, sink back wearily into the valleys again, leaving the wan sun to warm us. And this performance would be repeated again and again.

The long climb up the steep spur was wearying, and I was nearly exhausted before we reached the summit. Happily I found hidden away in my box a packet of crystalline jelly, such as cooks use for mixing with boiling water to make ordinary jelly, which I ate greedily.

At three we began to descend, and just afterwards the leading men stopped on the edge of a cliff, where the trees had fallen away, and pointed dramatically.

A thousand feet below, seen through a mist of rain, were the roofs of a frontier fort!

Joyfully we stumbled down the path in the jungle, passed through the barbed wire and found ourselves inside the British post of Kawnglu.

Here were Gurkha sepoys, Babu clerks and—yes, a white face again!

How they stared at us to be sure; and well they might, coming unexpectedly out of the jungle like that, from God knew where!

And what sights!—I with a six weeks' growth of beard, dirty and haggard, my clothes worn out, my boots flapping, my hair long, the men soaked to the skin and covered with mud!

Captain Clive greeted me heartily and sent me down to the bungalow, where I saw Captain (now Major) Conry; I had met him only eighteen months previously, but he did not know me!

Neither officer could do too much for me. They gave me a hot bath and a shave, clean clothes, and then sat me down to a tea I shall remember as long as I remember my travels. How I gulped down cup after cup of tea, and made inroads on the ham, poached eggs, and bread and butter! It was weeks since I had a proper meal.

And then came the bombshell!

I was not particularly interested. At home one rushes for the morning paper at breakfast, but it is more habit; deprived of daily news, one soon ceases to worry. It is like giving up drink or smoking, or going without little luxuries when travelling—after the first week you find they *were* only luxuries, and don't miss them, indeed forget all about them. And I have always found when going for months without news of the outside world that it went on just the same, my not knowing did not seem to affect it much; anyway it never stopped. But now—

"You know about the war, I suppose?" said Captain Conry.

"The war? Not China? Or do you mean civil war in Ireland at last?"

"No," he said, staring; "England, France and Russia against Germany and Austria!"

CHAPTER XIV

INFINITE TORMENT OF LEECHES

In the evening we sat out on the verandah and talked. My hosts brought out all the papers they had, which were not many, for mails took three weeks to come by mule from Myitkyina, and during the rains often did not come at all, so bad was the track; but for a long time my head was in a whirl, and I could not adjust my ideas to this novel perspective—war!

The *canard* of the North Sea fight in which most of the German navy had been sunk reached even to this remote outpost, only to be contradicted. Already the Russians, according to our newspapers, had captured the entire Austrian army, and the decisive battle was even now taking place in France. I wondered vaguely if I could get home before it was all over, and mentally kicked myself for coming such a long way round when I might have gone straight down to Rangoon!

Kawnglu fort is, like Hpimaw fort, situated on the shoulder of a steep spur. It was impossible on account of the clouds in which we lived at this altitude (about 6000 feet—that is, 2000 feet lower than at Hpimaw) to obtain a comprehensive view of the surrounding country; but immediately behind us rose the mountains, densely clothed with thick forest, which we had just crossed, and below the country fell away rapidly to the bottom valleys and foot-hills bordering the plain, which, as the crow flies, was not far distant. There were no more mountains between us and Fort Hertz, six marches away.

Towards sunset a magnificent sight, marred by rather too much cloud, burst upon us, for we looked right across the Hkamti plain, which lay invisible in white wrappings, to the mountains of Assam, standing up clear against the western light; and northwards to the towering snow-clad peaks of the Lohit divide, mysterious Tibet! In the growing dusk the long waves of ghostly vapour, from amongst which shot up into the blue haze above, lit by a crescent moon, the flanking ranges of the Himalaya and Tibet, was a sight worth marching all those miles to see!

Early next morning too the mountains were visible above an ocean of cloud, which lay heavily over the plain, but the clouds soon rose and masked everything.

So we sat talking till the young moon set, and then I walked down the hill to the civil officer's bungalow, where I was to sleep, he being away. I should probably meet him on the third march to Fort Hertz, they told me.

I could not envy those two officers in their lonely fort, much as I had appreciated what seemed the luxuries they had placed at my disposal after the discomforts of a long march.

16 & 17. A Duleng Village and Shan Girls, Hkamti Long.
Long, low, grass thatched huts, raised on piles; the typical hut of the Kachin tribe. The sacrificial stake can be seen on the left. *Photo by T. Hare, Esq.*
Note the dainty dress of these civilized folk. *Photo by P.M.R. Leonard, Esq.*

They lived for nine months of the year buried in cloud, surrounded by jungles in which nothing was heard but the dismal drip of the rain. What a relief it must have been to go off to the Ahkyang for a month on escort duty, as they did occasionally, or down to Fort Hertz, where at least there were four more white men!

But they stood it, though they confessed it was dull.

It is no use for the student to say: "But what an opportunity to study languages, or literature, or other academic pursuit!" The men who find themselves in such places are just the men who cannot readily do these things—energetic, active, high-spirited, and adventurous. What have they to do with scholarship? Nor is the necessary attitude of mind to be achieved at short notice. Most men do, however, readjust themselves somewhat to the altered circumstances—sufficiently so to pass an examination in at least one of the local dialects, sooner or later.

This by the way. The lot of these men on the extreme fringe of the Empire is often cheerless enough, and at this time it seemed doubly hard to be chained to such a spot. But as Captain Conry said: "If I cannot go myself, I'll take care that my Gurkhas, who have volunteered almost to a man, know something of their job!" So he worked them night and day, sparing neither himself nor them, night operations being a feature of their training.

September 23rd.—I was awakened by the calling of gibbons in the jungle, and having packed, sent the porters on ahead while I had breakfast in the fort. So loath was I to tear myself away from the hospitality extended to me that it was nearly midday before I started.

Descending to the valley below by a steep path, I caught up the porters, who had not hurried themselves, and we went on leisurely through the jungle, by a path which except for the mud was easy compared with some we had seen. Passing through two Duleng villages, we halted at a third close to the Nam Tisang, a tributary of which, it will be remembered, we had crossed two days previously.

The Dulengs are a Kachin tribe, and are the great iron-workers of this country, making the *dahs* and spears used by the Shans, Chingpaws and others. The iron comes from mines in the Kachin country to the south, between the Mali and 'Nmai rivers.

Their huts are similar to those of the Marus, built on piles and thatched with leaves of the fan palm; but the front porch, instead of being fenced round, is open. The great central pillar in the porch of the Kachin hut, whether Maru, Duleng or Chingpaw, is as it were the corner-stone of the building, a fowl or pig being killed when it is erected. On it are hung the skulls of sacrificed animals, mithan or buffalo.

The Dulengs, both men and women, tie the hair in a knot on top of the head, and wear a coloured handkerchief over it. The only garment worn is a *lone-gyi*, or skirt, usually dark blue striped with dull red, and fastened rather above the waist. In place of a jacket the women wear coils of black rattan wire round the breasts, drawing attention to rather than modestly concealing them. Indeed they have rather fine figures these Duleng women, being bigger than the Marus, and well made; but their looks are nothing to boast of. Very few beads or cowries are worn—a great contrast to the Marus—and practically no other ornaments; a roll of paper or a bamboo tube is thrust through the large hole bored in the lower lobe of the ear, a few rattan rings passed round the calf below the knee, and that is all.

It was hot and muggy in the valley, for after heavy rain about ten it cleared up, the sun shining out and the storm passing up into the mountains, though we were treated to showers again in the afternoon.

The vegetation now took on a more tropical appearance. There were many palms, including sago, rattans or climbing palm, a species of Nipa by the river and a tall, fan-leafed Borassus or cabbage palm, Selanginella, including a tall, erect species, and hundreds of bird's-nest ferns; one tree supporting a whole series from base to summit, so that the rosettes of foliage seemed to belong rather to the tree itself.

Later, in the more open country, we found the villages sheltered beneath fine clumps of bamboo growing sixty feet high. There were sacred *nat* trees too, generally figs, with matted, snaky roots, the far-spreading branches supported by thin pillars taut as steel rods, beneath which stood little bamboo tables with food offerings to the *nats*. But of flowers there were none, save here and there a white convolvulus and the usual, or often unusual (for every district seems to harbour new species), gaudy balsams. Strange, therefore, that there should be so many butterflies; but indeed they seemed to live on filth rather than on nectar.

September 24th.—Minimum 69.2° F. The Maru porters turned back from here as they did not wish to go to Fort Hertz. This caused a delay, as new ones had to be found to replace them, and we did not start till ten, crossing the Nam Tisang, a broad, swift stream, in dug-outs. The water was several feet below its highest flood-level, as indicated by the bedraggled vegetation, covered with flotsam, which grew thinly on the sand-banks. In many places these sand-banks were deeply trenched by rain channels where the water had poured down from the steep slopes above. On the far side the sand had been cut up by the rain into a curious appearance of bas-relief, due to rubbish protecting it from being washed away, leaving imprints of leaves, often perfect, standing up as much as two inches above the general level of the sand. The granite of the mountains had given place to laterite, which had been pounded into a sticky clay, retarding us considerably; but it was a relief having no mountains to climb, the path crossing small spurs only.

The land leeches, however, were dreadful.

These little fiends are about an inch long and, at a full stretch, no thicker than a knitting needle. They progress similarly to a looper caterpillar, though they are not, of course, provided with legs. Fixing one end, which is expanded into a bell-shaped sucker, the leech curves itself over into a complete arch, fixes the other extremity in the same way, and releasing the rear end, advances it till a close loop is formed. The process is then repeated, the creature advancing with uncanny swiftness in a series of loops. From time to time it rears itself up on end and sways about, swinging slowly round in larger and larger circles as it seeks blindly, but with a keen sense of smell, its prey; then suddenly doubling itself up in a loop, it continues the advance with unerring instinct. There is nothing more horribly fascinating than to see the leaves of the jungle undergrowth, during the rains, literally shaking under the motions of these slender, bloodthirsty, finger-like creatures, as they sway and swing, then start looping inevitably towards you. They have a trick, too, of dropping on to the traveller from above into his hair and ears, or down his neck. Cooper[1] says there are three kinds of leeches in Assam, including the red or hill leech, and the hair leech. I do not recollect coming across either of these last two on the North-East Frontier, but I have no doubt that if they are found in Assam they are also found in the Burmese hinterland.

Poor little Maru suffered most of all. I halted continuously to relieve him, on one occasion pulling six off his gums, two from each nostril, several from inside his eyelids, and others from his belly, neck, flanks, and from between his toes. Sometimes his white coat was red with blood, or rather with a mixture of blood and mud.

As for me, leeches entered literally every orifice except my mouth, and I became so accustomed to the little cutting bite, like the caress of a razor, that I scarcely noticed it at the time. On two occasions leeches obtained such strategic positions that I only noticed them just in time to prevent very serious, if not fatal, consequences. I also ran them down in my hair, under my armpits, inside my ears—in fact everywhere. My feet and ankles were by this time covered with the most dreadful sores, the scars of which I carry to this day.

At the village where we halted I bought a few eggs, a pumpkin and some cucumbers, and the *duwa* gave me a fowl, for which I paid him eight annas. The afternoon and evening were quite fine, but I was too tired to do any work, and lay down, though jungle fowl were calling from the thickets. At dusk I heard the low, plaintive cry of nightjar.

September 25th.—Minimum 69.1° F. An easy up-and-down march, the country much more open than hitherto, covered with tall grass twelve feet high and thickets of scrub. There was little jungle, and in consequence fewer leeches, though the path was as muddy and slippery as usual. Weather showery and close, the rain driving the sand-flies into the huts at night and making life miserable.

---

[1] *The Mishmee Hills,* by T.T. Cooper.

In the afternoon we crossed a fair-sized stream, the Ta hka, another tributary of the Nam Tisang, by canoe, to the village of Kumlao. Just here the scenery was very pretty, several villages half hidden amongst palms and clumps of bamboo being scattered along the gently sloping grassy banks of the river, where homely buffaloes grazed. I had expected to meet Mr Barnard,[2] the Civil Officer of Kawnglu, here, but to my disappointment there was no sign of him.

As soon as I got in I helped myself to a packet of fermenting rice tied up in a banana leaf—there was a tub full of them in the hut—and ate it. The curious, sticky mass with its musty alcoholic flavour restored me, but at the end of my diary for the day I find this entry: "It will be a struggle to get through, but I am at least sleeping fairly well."

September 26th.—Minimum 70.8° F. The entry in my diary at seven-thirty A.M. is:

"Pouring rain in the night and still continues. This will make the path terrible for our last march before the plain is reached; I scarcely feel as though I could do it."

It rained all day, and not caring to halt in such weather, we marched steadily from nine-fifteen A.M. till four-fifteen P.M.

Just above the village we came upon a magnificent clump of bamboos, about sixty feet high, the largest of them eighteen inches in girth at a height of two feet from the ground. There were nearly a hundred stems in the clump, springing up close together and gradually spreading out above till they finally drooped over in graceful Prince of Wales' feathers.

This was our last hilly march; we even crossed a watershed, but the ascent was so gradual that we scarcely noticed it, though the descent was steeper and more continuous. Down, down, down to the plains, crossing torrent after torrent of chocolate-red frothing water, now knee-deep, now waist-deep, till once I was nearly swept off my feet.

The climax in leeches was reached this day. From all directions they seemed to be looping inevitably towards us. Every leaf of every tree seemed to harbour one of those blind mouths, standing on end and at full stretch *feeling* for its victim; they lurked in streams, on the trees overhead and amongst the undergrowth, and took their toll in blood.

The easiest way to get rid of a leech is to drop salt on it; the pressure set up through its porous skin soon sucks it inside out practically.

But one does not as a rule carry a salt-cellar in one's pocket.

The natives, bare from the soles of their feet to half-way up their thighs, and from the crowns of their heads to their waists, were better off than I was. For they could get at their tormentors immediately, and perceive them before they did much harm. You would see one stop, draw his *dah* and *shave* the blood-sucker off his leg as with a razor; or seat himself and deliberately spit

---

[2] Mr J.T.O. Barnard, C.I.E., now Deputy Commissioner, Fort Hertz.

betel he had been chewing on to it, which was almost as effective as salt in making him relax his hold.

But for poor little Maru there was no cure, save that of stopping to pick them off from time to time. Even the baboon, who had lain rather *pianissimo* the last few days, was troubled, though he took care never to walk.

Presently we emerged from the jungle on to another grassy knoll, where stood some huts, and there before us fluttering in the breeze was a small Union Jack! How I blessed that flag!

While I was changing my sodden clothes Mr J.T.O. Barnard, whose name and fame are written across the North-East Frontier from the Hukong valley to the Ahkyang, came over from the hut where he was inquiring into village cases, and invited me over to a substantial tea, to which I did full justice.

Mr Barnard was on his way to Fort Hertz, and luckily had halted here for a day, enabling me to overtake him; otherwise I sometimes wonder whether, without the food he gave me, I should have been able to struggle over the last two marches.

September 27th.—Minimum 70.8° F. I got up while it was dark as the sand-flies were giving me a bad time and went across to Barnard's hut for breakfast.

Maru had not turned up the previous night, and though I had sent a man back to look for him, no trace of the poor little pup could be found. As he had not arrived when we started at eight o'clock, I asked Barnard to tell the village headman to look out for him. He turned up all right, and Barnard found him in the village on his way back to Kawnglu, and took him along with him. He was quite well apparently, but died suddenly on the march a few days later.

Thus passed away my brave little pup, who had never uttered a sound of complaint all through the long march, in spite of manifold discomforts. I was sorry he had come to near Fort Hertz only to be lost at the last moment.

We were still in the jungle, but it was thinning out. We passed numbers of magnificent Ficus trees, and ferrying across the Ti hka, a considerable stream flowing direct to the Mali hka, reached the last Duleng village, situated on a broad, grassy mound. Outside their long, low huts women sat on the ground weaving cloth, the warp stretched over the toes and kept taut by a band passing round the waist. Others were winnowing rice with large fans made of palm leaf, or stamping paddy in wooden mortars.

We sat down on the knoll for a rest; and there just below us spread the broad, flat valley of the Mali hka, the plains at last, covered with palm-trees as it seemed in the mist. Here and there a low mound stuck up out of the grey-green sea, otherwise the valley spread away level to the horizon.

Then we plunged knee-deep into a stream, and following it up for a mile, tramped through mud to the last low pass.

18. A Duleng Girl Ginning Cotton.
The seeds are pressed between wooden rollers, which take off the cotton hair and leave the seeds. *Photo by T. Hare, Esq.*

A gibbon leaped lightly across the path, but I scarcely noticed him; a gay Kaleage pheasant ran into a thicket, but I would not be beguiled. We slipped and slithered down the slope, past a few paddy-fields, and quite suddenly emerged on to the bank of a big river.

It was the Mali hka!

The western branch of the Irrawaddy is here, 150 miles above the confluence, a fine river in full flood, about 200 yards in breadth, running swiftly but smoothly in mid-stream. The water was a dull greyish-brown in colour, carrying much mud, temperature 69.8° F, or 6.6° warmer than the 'Nmai hka!

Ferrying across in canoes, we reached the Shan village of Nong-hkai on the edge of the plain, about 1200 feet above sea-level, and found everything suddenly changed—vegetation, crops, people.

September 28th.—Minimum 71.3° F. A fine drizzle was falling when we got up in the dark at four-thirty for the last march, hoping to arrive for ten o'clock breakfast.

Starting at six in dismal weather, we splashed through mud, waded streams, lost our way in the paddy-fields, and presently found ourselves in the large village of Langtao. Yellow-robed priests were just starting out in procession with begging bowls to collect the day's food from the pious Buddhist villagers, and the sweet-toned notes of a Burmese spinning gong, carried by a small acolyte, vibrated through the air. Close by stood a row of Shan women. Their dress—a long, close-fitting blue *lone-gyi* and jacket trimmed with red, with glossy black hair piled up on top of the head—was most picturesque. As the silent procession passed, with downcast eyes, they emptied their offerings of boiled rice from the leaves they carried into the bowls.

It almost gave one a shock to see that some of the black piles of hair were fastened on heads covered with *white* hair! Well, there was no deception; they were quite frank about it.

And now the long tramp of twelve miles across the plain which was something like Wicken Fen without the flowers, and is evidently an ancient lake bed.

Several very prominent river terraces, one of which is about eighty feet high, traverse the plain in various directions. Away to the east, eight miles distant, flows the Mali hka, but the whole horizon was wrapped in cloud, and nothing but the pale outline of mountains was visible.

It was a cold, cheerless tramp. We were soaked to the skin, and I lagged behind dreadfully. But about half-way we met two natives leading a pony for Barnard and a mule for me, sent out for us with a note of welcome from the Deputy Commissioner, and now we got along faster.

Floundering across streams, up to the girths in mud and water, we at length saw the ridge on which Fort Hertz is built. Now we reached a village, and had to wade across a considerably swollen stream, beyond which we caught sight of the Union Jack flying outside the Deputy Commissioner's bungalow. Climbing the steep side of the terrace overlooking the paddy-land, we dismounted at Fort Hertz.

We were welcomed by Mr W.A. Hertz, C.S.I., the Deputy Commissioner, whose guest I became from that moment for two months, and after a clean up and change I sat down to a sumptuous breakfast, followed about an hour later, for we arrived late, by an equally sumptuous tea.

In the evening Hertz gave a station dinner, and we foregathered five strong—Hertz, Barnard, Captain Burd the Battalion Commandant, Dr Brooks, the Civil Surgeon, and myself.

We heard little war news, for the telegraph line had been destroyed—not by the Germans, but by the weather. We learnt, however, that the great blockade had begun, and that a censorship of unprecedented discretion was being maintained.

And yet I suppose we five Britons, on that wet September night in the remotest post on the Burma frontier, knew as much of what was going on as the fighting men in France. The difficulty was to visualise the great change that had come, and was to come, over the world we knew.

September 29th.—Minimum 69.9° F, Maximum 83.2° F. There is one entry in my diary under this date. "Fever to-day. Temperature in middle of day 103.2°. After tea I went to bed under the doctor's orders."

Except for a few desultory pages, written at odd moments during convalescence, there is no further entry in my diary till 22nd November.

I was ill for six weeks, during which time the Deputy Commissioner and the doctor did everything possible for me, and thanks to them I was able to start for Myitkyina, in the doctor's company on 30th November.

CHAPTER XV

THE PLAINS

The romantic history of Hkamti Long may yet be outshone by its future, but for the moment we are concerned rather with the past.

Briefly, Hkamti Long[1] is a mountain-girt plain, 1200 miles up the Irrawaddy, yet only 1200 feet above sea-level. It lies on the west bank of the Mali hka (or western branch of the Irrawaddy), and covers an area of nearly 300 square miles—35 miles from north to south by 10 from east to west, at its longest and broadest. The greater part of the plain is covered with tall grass and scrub, or with jungle, only the northern end being cultivated.

At the extreme end of a tongue-shaped terrace which juts out northwards into the plain from the western foot-hills, and drops steeply to a small river flowing sixty feet below, stands the British post of Fort Hertz. The Shan village of Putao (from which the post formerly took its name) is two miles away to the north, on the flat paddy-land by the Nam Palak.

This terrace, or natural embankment, is about 600 yards wide, and across the tongue tip, where stand the military police lines, is a deep dyke and rampart, long since overgrown with thick jungle. To the south beyond the court-house, where the terrace is smothered beneath high grass and jungle, are many grave mounds.

Mark then this dyke, at the end of the terrace, and these graves in ominous array; for it may be that the terrace, deserted when the British first came to Putao, had its defenders in the great days of the Shan invasion.

The northern end of the plain, beyond the post, is cultivated, and there is much grassland where herds of cattle and buffalo graze between swift-flowing streams. Hedges of orange-flowered Lantana, prickly Euphorbia and golden sunflowers envelop the villages, which are full of trees such as sacred peepuls, sago palms, cabbage palms, lemon-trees and pumelos, with clumps of bamboo and patches of banana, from amongst which peep grass-thatched huts.

To the south stretches a broad plateau some fifty or sixty feet above the level of the paddy-land, covered with high grass and scattered shrubs, flanked by jungle.

Standing aloof down the paddy-fields like derelicts are clusters of ancient bell-shaped pagodas, made of sun-dried brick. Now they are overgrown with flowers and bushes, and are fast falling to ruin.

There is perhaps no more lovely experience on earth than to awaken slowly to life after a long illness, much of which was a dark blank, with vague shadows

---

[1] Hkamti Long, the Shan name for the plain, means literally Great Gold Land.

projected on it from time to time; to see again the blue sky overhead, the golden paddy-fields, green forests and distant snow-clad mountains; to wake in the radiant dawn at the cry of gibbons shrilly calling from the jungle, when the mist hangs over the river and the first rays of the rising sun are sparkling across the blue mountain-tops; to hear the birds whistling and trilling and the silver-throated gong vibrating in the monastery. A vast peace seems to have enfolded the whole world in its embrace. You tread on air with winged feet, and sing, nay shout, for the very joy of living. Every leaf and flower, every bird and beast, every cloud in the sky, is revealed as an object of beauty, welling life and love. Happy the man to whom such revelation is permitted.

Therefore shall I ever remember with gratitude those convalescent days at the end of November in Fort Hertz, when, having emerged from the Valley of Death, I walked a little farther, and grew a little stronger each day.

From the apex of the tongue, beyond the military police lines, where, as stated, the ridge falls steeply to the plain, you look northwards across a fertile country dotted with clumps of slender palms spreading out their great fan-shaped leaves, and of graceful bamboos, clasped by a semicircle of mountains. Immediately to east and west rise high parallel ranges, ridge beyond ridge, all cut up and smoothed off by flowing water, and covered with green jungle, looking in the distance like velvet; at their feet nestle low rolling hills merging into the plain. But straight ahead, beyond the sparkling Nam Palak, which winds at our feet, beyond the thatched spire of the village monastery, beyond the betel palms and sacred fig-trees, and the grey-green middle distance, there lifts itself up proudly above the early morning mists the sentinel range of Tibet, all white with snow. That graceful, rounded peak visible in the north-east, called Noi Matoi, is over 15,000 feet.

At sunset jungle and grassland are straightway drenched with dew. The tops of the eastern ranges turn crimson, changing to violet in the shadow below, but the snows of the Tibet frontier still gleam in the gathering darkness.

Out of the dusk a bat flits into the luminous western sky like an evil spirit, and a moment later is swallowed up in the gloom. An owl follows, flapping noiselessly across the compound, and is lost amongst the trees. A fire-fly glimmers for a minute and is gone; then one by one the stars peer down on us from the darkening sky.

So creatures dimly seen pass and repass before us as we watch, presently to go out of our lives into the mysterious beyond whence they started. Night has come.

At dawn long silver threads and wisps of cloud press closely against the blue mountain-tops, which appear floating on an ocean of milk-white mist. Presently the sun, rushing up, begins to break through, and the drenched grass sparkles with diamond dewdrops. Now gibbons begin to hoot in the hills, and

19 & 20. A Hammock Bridge and the Cane Bridge Over the Ngawchang River. The bridge is made entirely of climbing palm (rattan cane), and is slung between trees on either bank.

their glad voice is taken up by all the birds of the forest, warbling their praise at the coming of another day.

It is impossible to walk over the green fields by the Nam Palak without thinking of home. Here in the ditches are familiar catmint and buttercups, in the hedges white convolvulus and fragrant oleaster; there are golden cornfields beyond—only it is paddy, and the grazing herd whence arises the ding-dong of bells happen to be buffaloes.

Nevertheless, if the vision of England is dispelled by the sweet-scented lemon-trees laden with flowers and fruit at the same time, and by the palms and clumps of bamboo outlined against the evening sky, yet we might well believe ourselves back in Burma—that is to say, Burma proper—200 miles south of where we stand.

Here in the midst of the wilderness—for similar country to that which we have just crossed lies to north, west and south, and must be traversed ere we shall see sunny Burma again—here are the same people, the same crops, the same trees and flowers that we meet with on the banks of the Irrawaddy below the confluence.

Isolated, surrounded by trackless mountains and by wild tribes—Hkanungs, Hkakus, Dulengs—this outlier of the once mighty Tai race which had spread from Tibet to the China Sea and founded powerful kingdoms in Yun-nan, Burma, Assam and Siam, the last of which, shorn of power, alone survives today, lies dying at the sources of the western Irrawaddy!

What a pitiful tragedy—to have journeyed back to die near the old home their ancestors left when they went forth to conquer southern Asia, unknown centuries ago!

For the Hkamtis are slowly disappearing. The strongest long ago emigrated to Assam, and the degraded remnant, rotted with opium, ruined by slave dealing, preyed upon by the virile Kachins, are dying out.

How is it that they have not long ago been blotted off the plain by the Kachins? Because they are, in the language of the hill-men, "the fire that keeps the Kachins warm". In other words, the raiders batten on them. Every year when the crops are ripe the poor Kachins come down from their hills and billet themselves on the indolent Shans for a month or two, and eat their fill; and when the time comes for them to depart they take with them a few baskets of rice or a few pigs, or poultry or cattle, even a girl or two—anything, in fact, for which they have a fancy.

Between host and parasite the utmost friendliness prevails, and the transactions are marked by profound peace, for though the Shans loathe the Kachins, their loathing is tempered by a wholesome fear.

In return—for the transaction is not entirely one-sided, and, to borrow a term from biology, might be cited as an example of commensalism, a living together for mutual benefit—in return the Kachins assist the Shans in their eternal intertribal feuds.

Thus one tribe of Kachins will be parasitic in one Shan state, or in one village, another tribe in another; and if those states or villages are at enmity, as is often the case, the parasitic Kachins espouse the cause of their respective hosts, and fight their battles for them; which is as bad for the Kachins as it is for the Shans. But perhaps the Kachins do not really fight each other—more likely each party in turn wreaks vengeance on the village indicated by its hosts, so that everybody is paid full value, and all live happily ever after—except the Shans.

They are a house divided against itself, and in this wise cannot stand.

Since the British came to Hkamti Long this amiable relationship has ceased, and the Kachin is no longer permitted to act in a fiduciary capacity for the trusty Shans. Slavery has also been gradually abolished, and the isolation of the Hkamtis brought to an end by the opening of a mule-road between the railhead in Upper Burma and Hkamti Long, 200 miles distant. Thus the poorest man may safely travel through the Kachin country to the bazaars of Myitkyina, without fear of being captured and sold into slavery.

It is notable fact that when the British came to Putao in 1913-1914 one Chinese and five Indian slaves were found, and the Chinese muleteers with the party at once clubbed together and bought out their fellow-countryman!

There is more glory and tragedy in the age-long history of the Tai race than of that in any other people of south-east Asia. The tale of their migrations and dissensions, their struggles and successes, and the rise and eclipse, one by one, or the great kingdoms they founded—Nan-chao in Yun-nan (the modern Ta-li-fu), conquered by Kublai Khan in the thirteenth century, Pông bled by the Burmans, finally conquered and sacked by the Kachins as recently as the nineteenth century, and the great Ahom power in Assam, which after six centuries of rule, waging victorious war against the Moguls and others, was ruined by civil war and finally overthrown by the Burmese, in whose train followed such chaos that they were speedily replaced by the neighbouring British power in India—all this seems incredible to anyone who knows only their descendants to-day. For the peaceful, kind-hearted Shans of Upper Burma and western Yun-nan, the indolent Siamese and the lazy, opium-sodden Hkamtis are all that remain of the once merciless and mighty Tai!

The Shans came to Hkamti via the Hukong valley—that is, the Upper Chindwin—from the kingdom of Pông, which is the Mogoung of Upper Burma. They found the fertile plain occupied by Tibetan tribes,[2] and after their struggles in the jungle they were sad. Then their leader prayed that if they were destined to occupy the fertile plain they had found, might they be given a sign; might it snow heavily on the mountains, and block all the passes, so that no help could reach the trapped inhabitants of the plain. And it snowed heavily, and blocked the passes, and the Tibetans were driven back

---

[2] There are still a few Tibetan villages in British territory at the sources of the Irrawaddy.

and slaughtered by the Shans, as the numerous grave mounds testify.[3] (But there are some who say that these mounds date from a dreadful pestilence and famine which visited the plain.)

This, however, is legendary, for no written records of Hkamti Long have been discovered. If there is any truth in the story, these things must have happened many centuries ago, for later the Kachins (of whom no mention is made in the legend) grew sufficiently powerful to advance in turn down the Hukong valley and threaten the kingdom of Pông. But the latter, growing stronger again, drove the Kachins back eastwards towards the Mali river, though not far enough to re-establish communication with their brethren on the Hkamti plain; and it was not till much later that the Kachins completed the ruin of exhausted Pông. The Kachins who were driven east gave origin to the Lashis and Marus of the 'Nmai valley.

Thus it comes about that we find this outlier of Shans at Hkamti encysted amongst the Kachin tribes, dwindling in numbers as the latter increase. Isolated they truly were, for no man dared leave the plain—did he do so, he was soon captured and sold into slavery by the Kachins.

Even after their isolation the best of the Shans migrated, for it seems certain that the people who came to Assam over the Patkoi range at the end of the eighteenth century, though simply referred to as Hkamtis, were Shans, and not Tibetan tribes.

In 1794 these people took Sadiya, assisting the effete Ahom dynasty to its downfall; and in 1835 there was a fresh immigration of Hkamtis into Assam. A few years later, being dissatisfied with the British, who had released their slaves, they rose and attacked Sadiya again, but after the inevitable humiliation which eventually overtook them for this brief triumph, they were scattered, and were scarcely prominent in Assam again.

Cooper,[4] however, writing about 1870, speaks very highly of their descendants who, living in the neighbourhood of Sadiya, formed a screen between British territory and the warlike Mishmis.

Those who were left behind, the weakest, the less enterprising, the most contented, are to-day the sorry remnant of a people who fought their way up the Hukong valley to the open plains beyond.

Such in brief is the history of the Hkamtis—what is known of them.

The days when they were great hunters and fighters are gone, never to return. About the year 1860, in an evil moment, a Buddhist priest came from Burma and converted the Shans of the Hukong valley to Buddhism, and they forsook hunting and fighting, being forbidden to take life; and the Hkamti Shans did likewise.

---

[3] Mr J.T.O. Barnard, however, informs me that the snow tradition is of much more ancient origin.
[4] *The Mishmee Hills*, by T.T. Cooper.

Therefore we find many pagodas, all overgrown with trees, at Putao, some on the outskirts of the villages, others standing aloof in the paddy-fields.

It is wonderful, after weeks of marching in the dark, dismal jungles, hearing nothing but the roar of torrents and the everlasting drip, drip of the rain, to emerge suddenly on to the broad plain and hear again the silver-toned gong of the yellow-robed priests.

As yet, however, the Hkamtis are not very thoroughly converted. True, they conform outwardly to the doctrines of Buddhism—they do the things which those who believe do, and leave undone some of the things which those who believe do not do; but deep down in their hearts they know that the *nats*—the invisible spirits of the mountain and forest—attend them capriciously, as they attended their grandfathers before them. They practise Buddhism; but they do not understand. There are pagodas and *chaungs*—priests' houses—in the peaceful palm groves, where the old priests still teach the village boys—not how to succeed in the difficult battle of life, but the doctrine from the Pali script. It is a beautiful story; but it is difficult, and the Shans, who are timid children of the forest, know that the *nats* still live in the old grove where the shaky-rooted Ficus tree stands, and in the singing stream hard by, and on the distant mountain.

So they worship the Great Sawbwa mountain and sacrifice a buffalo to it every year, and even when dedicating a pagoda the ceremony is witnessed by such *nats* as Wé-Sôn-Vari, the *nat* of the earth, and by Ma-Da-Ri, the *nat* of literature, as inscriptions in the pagodas themselves testify.

But the blighting influence of the peaceful Buddhist religion has done its work. No longer able to hunt and fight, the men have found time hang heavily on their hands, and sitting at home in their huts watching the guns and *dahs* with which long ago their ancestors performed wondrous feats of arms, rusting on the walls, they have found refuge in opium.

The dress of the Hkamti Shans differs considerably from that of the southern Shans inhabiting the country round Bhamo and Myitkyina, as well as the Shan States proper; the latter have been influenced by the Burmans.

In the early morning, to the throb of the spinning gong, a procession of yellow-robed monks and boys, with downcast eyes and slow step leaves the wee wooden monastery, and starts on its begging tour through the village.

Then from each hut emerge the pious women storing up merit with their offerings of rice, which they tip silently into big bowls borne by small boys. We can see them well now—they are very dainty, in tight skirt of dark blue cloth relieved with a few stripes of red or brown, reaching to the bare ankles, and close-fitting, short-sleeved jacket. Perhaps they are proud of their neat figures, these charming little Shan girls, for their clothes are always tight-fitting, and the trick of edging the trim sleeves of their dark coloured jacket with brighter red, and wearing a low turban of white or scarlet, draws attention to just those points they would have you look at. Often a white wrap with coloured stripes at each end in flung loosely across the breast, over the left shoulder.

Like the Tibeto-Burman tribes, the ears are pierced to hold metal tubes, but the rattan cane rings with which the rude jungly people adorn their persons are not worn; for the Shans have emerged from the wood age into the metal age, and naturally (but silently) despise their uncouth though powerful neighbours.

Their large huts, built entirely of bamboo matting thatched with grass, are raised three or four feet from the ground on a perfect forest of piles, and entered by a ladder, or, in some cases, by an elaborate stairway with carved posts. The front of the hut is closed in, but from the back room you step straight out beneath the typical Shan half-dome-shaped eave on to an open balcony. Here the women of the household sit together gossiping, smoking and weaving cloth. Except in its large size, the Hkamti hut does not differ materially from the Shan huts seen in Upper Burma.

In winter the village, with its palm-trees and pagodas, its pumelo-trees laden with golden fruit nearly as big as a man's head, its gardens hedged in with sunflowers and Lantana, its slaves thatching huts anew and weaving fences, is picturesque enough; but during the rains it is a morass through which squelch grunting pigs and fawning cattle, with a sprinkling of clucking hens. So deep is the mud that a narrow gangway of planks, raised six inches off the ground, is laid down the streets, and by using this fairway it is possible to avoid some of the quagmires, unless a lurching buffalo, with bovine humour, pushes you into it.

As for the forests and mountains which enfold this smiling plain, it is difficult for me to convey any adequate idea of their immensity and utter desolation.

To the north lie the sources of the Mali hka, flowing in half-a-dozen big rivers down from the snowy Lohit divide, on the other side of which is the Lohit river, with the Mishmi Hills and Tibet beyond.

To the west lie ranges of mountains, tier on tier, inhabited by Singphos (who are none other than Kachins), beyond which the waters flow down to the Brahmaputra and the Chindwin.

To the south lies the unexplored country between the two branches of the Irrawaddy, known as the "triangle".

To the east lie the mountains we had crossed with so much difficulty, and beyond them the wonderful mountains of Yun-nan.

All this country is scarcely known—the few travellers who have crossed it here and there have done so as quickly as possible, often starving. Much of it is known to a few frontier officers only. Yet there are wonders hidden behind the black wall of forest, such as the dwarf Nungs of the Taron, to the north-east, whose huts are built in the tree-tops; the black Marus, spearing their fish from canoes; the unscaled peaks of Noi Matoi, Daphla Bum and many other snow-capped giants; unexplored rivers, and the passes into

21. A Religious Festival on the Hkamti Plain.
Note the silk umbrellas held over the Shan *sawbwas* or chiefs. Cymbals and drums comprise the band. *Photo by P.M.R. Leonard, Esq.*

Tibet—oh! wonders for the explorer and naturalist.

Big game is said to abound in the mountains, though I had found the sodden jungles apparently devoid of life. Tiger, rhino, sambur, elephant, bison, *burhal*, pig are all spoken of—Prince Henry met with tiger, two horned rhinoceros, and antelope on the Assam ranges to the west, and British officers have told me of many tracks on the path between Fort Hertz and Myitkyina. Musk deer and takin are common, so it is said, on the mountain ranges to the north, and barking deer came right into Fort Hertz.

But the reader must not imagine that Hkamti Long is a sportsman's paradise—he certainly will not if he has followed me closely.

The jungle is all but impassable, the climate very bad. There is no food, transport is often unobtainable, and there are all the discomforts of a hot, wet country to contend with—leeches, ticks, sand-flies and many more.

However, there is a certain amount of snipe and duck shooting on the open plain, imperial pigeon in the forest, and jungle fowl and pheasants in the long grass round the fringe of the jungle; while in the Mali hka is to be had some of the best mahseer fishing in India, fish up to eighty pounds in weight having been taken in its waters.[5]

---

[5] The record for mahseer taken at Fort Hertz, an eighty-six-pound fish, belongs to Mr Langley of the P.W.D. But the most successful fisherman is probably Mr P.M.R. Leonard, of the Frontier Service, who has captured many big fish from fifty to seventy pounds in weight.

One evening I walked out to see some pagodas near Putao village—they stood alone in the paddy-fields, shaded by palm-trees, green islands in a golden sea.

Entering the biggest through a narrow tunnel, the sides of which were decorated with small mural paintings, I found myself in a circular brick vault tapering up to a pointed dome crowned by a lotus bud. Most of the space was taken up by a life-size recumbent figure of Buddha in alabaster, which had once been covered with gold leaf. A spiral of writing in Shan characters[6] encircled the narrowing dome, and just below was a frieze composed of fifty-five niches, each containing a tiny gilt image of Buddha only an inch high.

In another pagoda was a seated figure of Buddha, round the pedestal of which were small paintings on plaster, covered with glass, of Bodhisattwas in grey monk's garb with legs crossed in the orthodox attitude of meditation, each with a palm-leaf fan; their faces were curiously Chinese in expression.

From the ordered pagodas and trim gravel paths bordered with beds of Michaelmas daisies and shrubs I wandered out into the wildness of the paddy-fields, along the ditches of which grew a tall grass whose hard grey 'seeds'[7] are much prized by some of the jungle natives, as beads for trimming their bags.

The pagodas of the farther cluster were smaller, and contained, in some cases, dozens of small Buddhas, arranged round a cone-shaped pillar, on which one might gaze through small openings in the outer wall facing north, south, east and west.

By the end of November I was fit to start again. The doctor was going down to Myitkyina on leave, so I accompanied him, abandoning all idea of lengthening the journey by crossing into Assam.

The Deputy Commissioner lent me a mule to ride. For transport we had Nung porters, and two elephants, hired from one of the Shan *sawbwas*, or chiefs, who keep a certain number of these beasts.

On 28th November the doctor started, and two days later I followed. As usual, a heavy white pall of mist lay over the plain in the early morning, but up on the ridge we were almost clear of it—we could see blue sky overhead through the thin veil—till it gave a heave as the sun rose.

Then it was slowly rent aside and rolled up into puffs which clung to the mountains, and disappeared mysteriously, and the whole plain was flashing and smiling in the glorious sunshine.

So I bade farewell to Mr Hertz, and to Hkamti Long, where I had been so long, and turned my face southwards.

---

[6] There are several totally different Shan scripts.

[7] *Coix Lachryma* (Job's tears), cultivated for food in many parts of south-east Asia, more particularly in Assam. At the base of each inflorescence is a hard, polished, grey, pear-shaped body, resembling a seed. This is really the bract of the inflorescence, and belongs to several spikelets, not to a single flower.

CHAPTER XVI

THROUGH THE KACHIN HILLS

Fording the Nam Palak, now quite a shallow stream, we passed between gardens where pink roses and scarlet Canna were jumbled up with climbing marrows, pumelo-trees and papaws, crossed a strip of low-lying sand freckled with scrub jungle, and emerged on to the open plain.

How different it looked to the swamp we had floundered through, beneath dripping grey skies, two months back! Now the grass, brown and shrivelled, was burning in many places close to the path; the smoke and crackling bushes frightened my mule, but the elephants took no notice of them.

Dropping down the steep slope to the lower terrace, we crossed a belt of jungle, where I noticed several screw pines. These have great bayonet-shaped leaves arranged in close spirals at the summit of a palm-like stem, giving a most curious effect, as though a giant hand had tried to wring the plant's head off!

And so we came to the village of Langtao, where I found the doctor keeping vigil by the broad Nam Lang, waiting for the homing duck to fly over. It was a beautiful evening, the clean-cut mountains a deep purple against an orange sky; and presently a wedge of duck winging across, one fell to the doctor's gun.

Next day we crossed the Nam Lang, a clear, swift stream ninety yards broad, by a trestle bridge, and turning our faces to the south, plunged into the jungle, where many streams, now mere trickles, but in summer yelling torrents, flow down to the Nam Lang. Up the Nam Lang lies one of the three known routes from Hkamti to Assam.

At midday we left the last Shan village behind and entered the Kachin hills. Immediately the country became more undulating, and by evening we had reached the first Kachin village, built on a high bluff overlooking a flat valley, across which, a mile or two distant, was a long line of cliffs several hundred feet high. At the foot of these cliffs we could hear a river rumbling along, but it was not the Mali hka; many days were to pass before we would actually see the Mali, though we were never very far away from it.

The Kachins are animists, pure and simple, and buy off the evil *nats* who, together with good *nats*, inhabit the jungle, by setting up little bamboo tables outside their villages on which food is placed for the hungry spirits to help themselves. At the entrance to every village are also *nat* trees, inhabited by spirits; they are nearly always fine old Ficus trees, often covering a great area by means of their prop roots, and, like the village bamboo clumps, are carefully preserved.

In the middle of the village are two big wooden beams about a dozen feet long, stuck in the ground and crossed so as to make a framework something like a multiplication sign. To this frame sacrificial buffaloes are lashed before being beheaded; and to the great central supporting pillar which stands out so prominently in the front of the huge hut are nailed the skulls of buffaloes and pigs slain at every *natgalore*.

These huts are quite like the Maru huts, but even bigger. I generally slept inside the porch of one, having no tent; and the poultry roosting in baskets hung beneath the low-pitched eaves, or the pigs grunting and scratching themselves against the piles (happily fenced in all round), did not suffer me to oversleep myself.

Drinking our early morning tea at five A.M. on 2nd December, while it was still quite dark, we listened to the heavy dew dripping like rain from the trees and shivered, for the temperature at this hour was but 50.5° F.

Immediately we descended into the valley, and fording the river already noticed—the Nam Yak, here fifty yards wide—followed up the stony bed of a watercourse, presently to enter what has been picturesquely called the conglomerate *nalla*.

High cliffs of sand and boulder gravel hidden beneath a mosaic of velvety leaves rose precipitously on either hand as the *nalla* narrowed. The stream dashed this way and that, swinging round bend after bend, and ahead one could see the big trees which crowned the cliff almost touching each other.

At this hour a faint mist still hung over the gorge, but presently shafts of sunlight came slinking between the trees and glanced on the leaves of some strange tropic plant far above. We were now completely hemmed in by these fantastic cliffs of gravel and red-stained sand, crushed so tightly together as to have become almost solid rock. Here and there a silver thread of water leapt from above and frayed out into tassels. It seemed almost absurd to believe that so small a stream could have carved out this profound gorge, but it was now the dry season, and from the way the cliffs had been undercut, one could plainly see that during the rains a powerful torrent must fill the bed of the *nalla*.

Most wonderful of all was the rich mosaic of foliage, interspersed with bunches of violet and lemon-yellow Gesnerads, pale begonias with elephant's-ear leaves, and delicate maiden-hair fern, which paved the walls; it was a paradise for the shade-loving plants, and they revelled in the damp gloom.

At last we left the *nalla* and climbing up, up through the forest till we were more than a 1000 feet above the stream, presently looked down on the valley of the Mali hka and across to the blue mountains beyond.

From this ridge we descended again to the Nam Yak, flowing through the forest, which, bordered by strips of blazing white sand, came down to the water's edge; and crossing it several times camped finally on the right bank. Strapping Dipterocarp trees with glistening white trunks bearing heavy crowns of foliage striped the dark green forest; many were draped with ample

22. A KACHIN VILLAGE ON THE BURMA FRONTIER.
Women weaving. Sacrificial buffaloes are lashed to the cross-posts by the fence on the occasion of *nat* festivals.

folds of creepers, and the showy pale violet trumpet flowers of *Thunbergia grandiflora* were often seen.

We camped on a sandbank just above the river, putting up bamboo shelters roofed with tarpaulins, or banana leaves and grass; but the Nung porters scraped hollows in the sand, animal fashion, and slept by their fires in the open, merely sticking up a few fan-shaped palm leaves to keep off the wind. Long-haired, dirty and unclad—they possess only a hempen towel and jacket apiece, with a blanket for night use—these poor wild jungle folk are hardy and cheerful.

December 3rd.—Minimum temperature 51° F. A thick cloak of mist swaddled the river, and the air was raw at six o'clock; but the sun coming through, the thermometer stood at 70° F in the shade by the middle of the afternoon.

The day's march was a short one, about eight miles to a P.W.D. bungalow situated on the bank of a river, the Wot hka, in the midst of the forest.

We passed through two Kachin villages, where stood trees laden with huge limes, besides orange trees, whose good-looking fruits were, however, a delusion, the skins being very thick and full of oil; the flavour was sweet, and there were no seeds—but neither was there any pulp; it was all skin.

We saw a number of duck on the Wot hka, but though the doctor spent an evening with them, he had to be content with nothing better than a merganser.

In the afternoon I found several of our porters searching beneath the shingle of the river bed for a species of bug, which when captured was decapitated between the finger-nails and dropped into a bamboo tube. These bugs are fried in oil and eaten as a delicacy, despite their horrible odour!

The Kachins here were dressed very similarly to the Marus of the 'Nmai valley, the *lone-gyi* being usually dark navy blue striped with dull red—very jungly colours. Kachin women have no excuse for keeping their husbands waiting; they have no hat to be set at an accurate angle in front of the glass, and their raven hair is simply tied in a knot on top of the head. English girls, when sea bathing, do likewise, but have evolved something more elaborate for everyday use. But small children shave their heads—wisely, seeing the collection of vermin harboured by adults—leaving only a small wisp in front, perhaps a handle for angry mothers to catch hold of.

They were not particularly affable, these Kachins, but they tolerated us in their villages without welcoming us inside their huts; though, as already recorded, I usually set up my bed under the frowning eave of the porch where the womenfolk pound rice of an evening and weave the family clothes.

Inside, the Kachin hut closely resembles the Maru, the "maidens' hearth", which is the only room completely walled in on all sides, being in front.

The fact is, the Kachins realise they will have to give up their thievish, domineering ways, and abandon slavery, for even their jungles can no long hide them from the prying eyes of the *sircar*.

As you watch the unaccustomed white men passing through your deep forests with their elephants and ponies and their thousands of mules, and hear the tramp of armed men following on, Kachins, you must understand that the time has at last come for you to submit to the dominant race.

But your religion, your customs, your huts, and crops, and women, and property will be left to you, untouched; only in return, and for the privilege of admission to the great brotherhood, you must pay a trifle towards the maintaining of security, and supply porters to travellers. These things you will come to do gladly in time, and prosperity will be your lot. So speaks the *sircar*.

We passed some Kachin graves this day—they are similar to the Maru graves already described. The coffin, a hollowed tree trunk with a carved lid, sometimes wrapped in a cloth, stands on a circular mound surrounded by a trench. Sometimes there are two coffins, side by side. Over them is raised a conical thatched roof, surmounted by a tall pole. Coffin lid and pole are rudely carved and crudely painted—there is usually a bird perched on the summit of the pole (for birds figure in all primitive Oriental religions previous to Buddhism), with a couple of snakes below, while the coffin lid terminates in a beaked dragon or bird's head.

If the man dies in debt the trench round the grave is left incomplete, an insult to the family. As soon as the debt is paid the trench is completed. In some places we came on Maru graves extinguished under a tall sugar loaf of thatch, fifteen feet high, with no opening save such as made by the weather.

It must not be imagined that the coffins thus laid out contain corpses; they contain only calcined bones, or ashes, for the dead are burnt, with little ceremony, and the ashes subsequently buried in season (or when the family has accumulated the necessary funds)—it may be several months later, at a public funeral wake. It is the burial, not the cremation, which counts.

This is a great orgy, at which buffaloes are sacrificed and unlimited feasting and drinking indulged in. The ashes are then interred in the mound under the thatch umbrella.

During the rains, or while the paddy is being cut, no burials take place.

Many of the huts flew what looked like a publican's sign at the fore—a long bamboo tube ending in a flat palm-leaf plate surrounded by a ring of similar tubes; which was in reality a device not to attract good drinkers, but to repel bad spirits.

As the wind caught the plate it swung to and fro, and all the bamboo tubes did likewise, clapping and rattling together in a way to scare any *nat* with an evil conscience.

The Kachins in some parts seem to have been tainted with a breath of Buddhism, for outside a few villages were banners hung from tall poles and small mud pagodas crowned by a bamboo spire and imitation *hti*, or umbrella, as seen in Burmese pagodas.

In one village was a magnificent fig-tree, its branches, supported by prop roots which had dropped to the soil from above and held fast, spreading twenty-five to thirty feet from the central trunk, so that the area covered was over 300 square feet.

The villages are always perched up on the hill-tops, with a steep descent in every direction, so that from them we had good views of the high ranges to the west, separating the Mali and Chindwin basins, and of the parallel ranges in the trans-Mali country to the east; but the country in between these main north and south trending ranges was so cut up that spurs seemed to run out in every direction. Travelling south, parallel to the Mali hka, we were crossing rivers running down to it between high ridges; but often we would go for miles along the crest of some ridge trending at right angles—that is, north and south parallel to the main divides.

It was noticeable that the Mali receives big tributaries from both sides, whereas the 'Nmai receives none worth speaking of from the west. On the other hand, no tributary of the Mali which we saw could be compared with the big rivers which roar down to the 'Nmai hka from the China frontier.

All round us as far as the eye could reach was dense forest or high grass and scrub. The big elephant, an enormous beast from Assam, found it difficult to get through in places, and the *mahout* was sometimes threatened with decapitation by the branches of trees. However, seated on Jumbo's neck with a foot behind each ear, he guided the wise old beast skilfully, and the pair of them provided us with plenty of amusement, especially the small Hkamti animal, who always insisted our rising while he was being loaded.

Bat! Bat!! Bat !!![1] screamed the *mahout*, as the kneeling elephant, with half his load on his back, leisurely proceeded to stand up; then he would slowly sink down again and allow the men to put some more on him. In the hilly country, however, the elephants proved only a nuisance, moving with extreme slowness; indeed the big animal became almost useless, so thoroughly exhausted was he, and at one time we quite thought he was going to die by the wayside.

The jungle on this side seemed far less dismal, more pulsing with life, than did the forests across the 'Nmai; but this may have only been due to the season; no doubt the fine dry weather made all the difference, but we must also remember that the Mali valley is far more thickly populated than is the valley of the 'Nmai.

Every day we heard parrots and monkeys screaming, and often the sweet song of a thrush. Sometimes a golden oriole or a gay woodpecker was seen, or a gorgeous kingfisher would flame by, and at night we heard the sharp bark of the muntjac. There were plenty of sambur about too, and the Kachins shot them by night, while watching their *taungya*, so that we were able to buy excellent venison. There is a little white-polled red and black water-wren commonly met with throughout this country as well as over a large part of China, and a big grey kingfisher, also Chinese. We saw striped squirrels too, and occasionally a gibbon travelling at enormous speed. I watched one clear the track at a leap, judging his distance with consummate accuracy.

When, as sometimes happens, we met big mule convoys going north with rations, great delay ensued, for the elephants stalked along as kings of the road, and the opposition mules did not like the look of them. However, there is no room to stampede in these jungles, and any attempt to do so makes for terrible confusion. Some of the convoys we met contained over five hundred mules, mostly from Yun-nan, but a few big Government animals with their ridiculously heavy and clumsy trappings. Even the war does not seem to have stimulated the Indian Government into abandoning these obsolete contrivances.

Mountain rice, raised on hill clearings, is the chief Kachin crop, besides a little maize for brewing liquor. In the villages are grown cotton, beans, cucumbers, pumpkins, sweet potatoes, oranges, limes and tobacco. Unlike the Shans, the Kachins do not indulge in opium, but they all smoke. The Shans grow two kinds of tobacco, one for smoking and another for chewing.

At sunrise on 7th December the eastern mountains were ink lined against a rosy sky; below us mist filled the valley and shone like silver under the waning moon. We marched twelve miles through very hilly country, with fine views of a high, rocky range to the east, probably the 'Nmai divide.

---

[1] *Baitho* = sit down (Hindustani). *Bat* (pronounced *but*) is obviously a corruption.

The mountains here are composed of loose sediments—a friable yellow earth containing scattered pebbles of granite, silver-grey, buff and reddish sandstones, grey clays with dark leaf beds, and nodules of iron pyrites, all derived from the disintegration of granite and other crystalline rocks, and have clearly been laid down in a lake or shallow sea or perhaps in an estuary. To the north the material was always coarser—conglomerates, gravel, and sands instead of these argillaceous rocks, from which it may be inferred that the water deepened southwards, and was shallower in the north. The Hkamti plain and much of the country to the south may have been a lake, into which rivers flowed from the north, and the iron mines scattered throughout these mountains probably derive their existence from vegetable deposits. The sediments laid down have been subsequently heaved up into a series of wave-like parallel ridges from 3000 to 5000 feet above sea-level, and cut across by streams flowing down from east and west.

Still farther south mica schists make up the bulk of the ranges, these rocks dipping SE or ESE at angles varying from 30° to nearly 90°; and in the bed of the Mali itself are dark grey slates with quartz veins, dipping east at about 90°. The Mali hka seems to be merely the overflow of the Hkamti lake, long since drained either by the river keeping open a passage while the country was being buckled up, or by cutting back at the head.

All the villages are fairly open, the huts more or less scattered, so that, being enclosed by forest, they are nearly invisible till one is right into them; for they reserve to themselves the highest hill-tops in the neighbourhood. Thus they deny a view down on to them from above, though occasionally looking across a valley one may pick out patches of *taungya* chequering the hill-side, and glimpse the grey thatch of huts.

As to the forest, which has been described as over-running the whole country, it is a glorious sight on a sunny day, especially in the wide river valleys where the laughing water is walled in with many-hued evergreen vegetation, against which white tree trunks stand like temple pillars supporting the turquoise dome of heaven.

There are oaks and fig-trees in great variety, sago palms, Palmyra and climbing palms, tree ferns and a wealth of bamboos, many with prickly stems; Pterospermum with huge shield-shaped leaves, Bauhinia, screw pines, walnut, tree-of-heaven, Cassia, Dalbergia, Acacia and many more Leguminosæ; Sterculia, Dipterocarpaceæ, tamarind; and in the valleys open areas filled with patches of banana and elephant grass. A dense tangle of climbers—in the sunlight, rosy convolvulus, *Thunbergia grandiflora*, Lygoduim, Smilax; in the jungle, lianas, some flattened to ribands, others like whipcord, some smooth, others warty, or covered with knobs, or prickles, or spurs, or roughened like the bark of an oak, some black, some green, some yellow or brown, tie everything together. Then there are the epiphytic orchids, Dendrobium, Vanda and others, not yet in flower; bird's-nest fern, oak-leaf polypody and moss-like ferns carpeting the tree trunks; Aroids such as Pothos, and a few epiphytic trees as *Ficus benjamina*. On damp, shady cliffs or in the forest undergrowth are many Zingiberaceæ, such as Globba, Hedychium and Cautleya; striped Gesnerads, more Aroids, and begonias with their curious lop-sided leaves resembling an elephant's ear, by which name the plant is known.

It is the flora, not of China, but of the Indo-Malayan region; not of the Sino-Himalayan ranges to the north and east, such as we had found beyond the 'Nmai hka, but of the Assam valley, and Lower Burma, of Siam and the Straits. And the farther south we travelled the greater the number of leafless trees which showed up, skeletons bleaching in the sunshine.

For on the Hkamti plain there is no long dry season, and the forest is evergreen in spite of chill winter nights; but as we go south, we get more and more into the region of the regular monsoons, where wet and hot dry seasons alternate. During the dry season, about March or April, just before the rains break, many trees shed their leaves for a brief period and burst into flower.

Although these miles and miles of jungle appear monotonous, yet looked closely into, the monsoon forest is exquisite, as though peering beneath the surface, one grew conscious of the real spirit of the forest behind its plain exterior. The temperate forest, changeful as a petulant child, may be admired as a whole; it is the detail of the monsoon or tropical forest, in its limitless diversity, that attracts.

Thus its foliage, differing so in colour, but more in its arrangement; how on one tree the leaves are held out boldly at arm's-length, vertically, as shields, owing to the bending of the petiole where it meets the blade (Petrospermum); how leaf chains of great length and delicacy are fashioned by one creeper which, with a cunning kink of the petiole, brings all the circular leaves into line, overlapping each other like mail armour (Aristolochia); while another spreads its long, thin blades alternately right and left of the stem, desperately seeking light; how this leaf is hinged in two halves which close at night like the pages of a book (Bauhinia); that one drawn out into a long point that the rain may drip rapidly from its downward-pointing apex (*Ficus religiosa*).

There are shiny, leathery leaves, and delicate velvet leaves, red leaves, yellow leaves, leaves of a hundred greens, fitting into each other, overlapping each other, embracing each other, all pushing and hustling for light and air. It is a fairyland wherein to roam, while every bush and tree astonishes you with some dainty device you had not noticed before.

On 8th December we did a short march to Laza, perched on an isolated sugar-loaf peak, with a clear view across the Mali valley to the distant 'Nmai divide, and a peep through the trees to the snow-clad Zayul range, 100 miles north.

We rested a day at Laza, where we met two officers from Myitkyina on their way up to Fort Hertz. There were rumours of a Kachin rising, and it was not certain whether we should get through before the whole country-side was up.

The shade temperature rose as high as 67° F that afternoon, but it was 15° colder when we rose at six next morning, 10th December. The Mali valley was at that hour a great lake of foaming cloud splashing up against the dark line of mountains just visible against a lemon-yellow sky; overhead the stars were paling, with Venus rising like a diamond.

From Laza, in the crystal atmosphere above the miasmas of the river valley, we plunged down some 2000 feet to a torrent, and then up, up again till on the crest of the next ridge another invisible torrent suddenly burst into clamour, and we descended to *that*! So it continued all day.

Presently from beneath a tree an emaciated, raw-backed pony whinnied to us as we passed. Poor beast! He would never carry his burden again—his very hours were numbered and he had been marooned in the jungle!

The villages hereabouts were poor, the huts small and dilapidated, the graves with their conical thatch roofs falling away, their trenches filled with undergrowth so that it were easy to step into one unawares.

CHAPTER XVII

BACK TO CIVILISATION

Long ago the Shan *sawbwas* of Hkamti Long paid tribute to the kings of Burma, thereby acknowledging them as overlords.

No doubt they were actually independent, but would, if necessary, ask the suzerain power for assistance against their enemies. A century ago the king of Burma could, and would, have marched an army from Ava to Hkamti Long if required and thought nothing of it.

In those days Burmese armies marched far south to Siam, westwards over the mountains to Assam, and eastwards into China; but with the wars between Burma and Great Britain, and the rise of the Kachins, who swept southwards, the Hkamti Shans became isolated, and emigrating, as previously described, to Assam, were no longer of account. There was no one to whom they could appeal for help, and so they pined away.

The British were far too occupied with their own affairs in Burma proper to think of going so far afield as Hkamti Long; yet after the annexation of Upper Burma from time to time deputations of chiefs travelled to Bhamo, there to acknowledge British overlordship and claim British protection. No change in the government of Burma altered the status of these tributary Shans, and while for thirty years the suzerain power had been unable to help them against the growing oppression of the Kachins, here surely was a power which might!

Another twenty years were, however, to pass, during which British power was firmly consolidated in Burma proper, before Government would move in the matter; and then it was not Kachin oppression, but Chinese activity, which settled the issue.

The Chinese having as the direct result of affairs in Tibet established a comparatively powerful military autocracy in western China, naturally looked beyond their immediate frontier, and seeing Hkamti unoccupied, stepped in with a view to annexation.

Here was just what they wanted—a big open plain where paddy could be cultivated, lying on the flank of their main line of advance into Tibet.

Their design was, however, not entirely unknown to the Indian Government, and three separate British expeditions were sent to Hkamti to counteract Chinese influence before the final occupation in 1914. The first of these expeditions took place during the cold weather of 1910-1911.[1]

The Kachins were not pleased at what they regarded as an intrusion into their fastness, and with their usual truculence asked the British the reason for

---

[1] Under the leadership of Mr J.T.O. Barnard, C.I.E.

this. The chiefs, however, brought presents, receiving others in exchange for allowing the expedition to pass.

One chief, indeed, sent to demand how it was that the British were passing through his territory without first obtaining his permission. He was curtly requested to come and see the British officer, to which he replied that to do so he required an escort of fifty sepoys and five hundred rupees travelling expenses!

This was refused, the official bluntly pointing out that since he was travelling in his own country he required no escort. Three hundred rupees travelling allowance was, however, sent, and eventually this haughty chief came in, bringing as presents a lump of iron ore and an elephant's tusk. In the symbolical language of these unlettered tribesmen the former signified that he, the chief, was the owner of all the iron mines in his territory, and would brook no interference.

On the arrival of the expedition at a certain village the British official saw, stuck in the ground outside his tent, a fine spear, transfixing a pumpkin, together with a *panji*—that is, a sharp bamboo stake. Not very valuable gifts, perhaps, but then the Kachins are poor.

Puzzled, but taking these things for presents from the village headman, the Englishman was about to accept them when the Kachin interpreter prevented him, saying that an insult was intended, the interpretation being as follows.

The *panji* meant war. The pumpkin meant that the English thought the Kachins a worthless people, a sentiment they bitterly resented; and the spear that they were united against the common enemy.

Hearing this, the official asked for an explanation, at the same time ordering the chief to remove the offending articles. But he came in person, refusing to remove them, and offering quite a different interpretation.

The pumpkin, he said, meant that the Kachins were a poor, simple-minded jungle folk, living on jungle roots; the spear that the British were a powerful, upright people; and the *panji* that the poor Kachins, children in the art of war, and untutored, fought with bows and arrows.

In the end the chief was prevailed upon to remove the offending articles, whereupon he waxed wroth.

"You may," he said, addressing himself to the British official, "pass through my country if you wish to go to Hkamti Long. You may come back again next year, and go backwards and forwards—my people will not molest you. But we will never pay tribute to the British, nor be ruled by them."

The Kachins have at various times given a good deal of trouble, especially during the years immediately succeeding the annexation of Upper Burma.

It is estimated that there are at least a million Kachins in the mountains between Assam, Upper Burma and the China frontier, but luckily they are far from being united, and in spite of difficulties owing to the bitter nature of the country, Government has never yet failed to exact summary retribution for any hostile act of these freebooters.

However, there are still large tracts of country—notably the "triangle", between the 'Nmai hka and Mali hka—where the Kachins are quite independent. Nor is any Englishman permitted to wander into these preserves, lest, should any untoward fate befall him, Government should be forced to take action.

At sunrise on 10th December we saw the eastern ranges boldly outlined against a rosy sky; we were above the mist, on which the waning moon shone brightly, filling the valley below with a faint silvery light.

Twelve miles were covered in very hilly country, with good views of a high, rocky range, devoid of forest, to the east. This might be the 'Nmai divide, which is sixty miles distant as the crow flies.

The path we followed next day was better than usual, though soft, the animals raising thick clouds of dust; but a little rain would have turned it into a stiff clay. This powdery earth, derived from laterite, took on a beautiful rich brownish gold or ochre tint in the sunshine.

There were some fine sago palms near the villages, and castor-oil plants up to fifteen feet high, growing semi-wild.

There is a regular colony of Marus here—they seem to be much worse off than the Kachins, and I bought a fowl for a handful of beads, where the Kachins had mulcted us to the tune of eight or twelve annas.

A prowling tiger roared defiantly close at hand during the night, and one of the elephants distinguished himself by gobbling up a whole basketful of yams, for which we had to pay compensation. It is unwise to leave anything edible or inedible in the neighbourhood of an elephant, though ours always went out into the jungle first and devoured whole clumps of bamboo.

Yams of various kinds were eagerly sought for and dug up by our Nung coolies while on the march—so perhaps it was they, and not the elephants, who were the real culprits.

The elephants were very slow now—the endless hills seemed to break their hearts. It was amusing to watch them fill their trunks with saliva and spray it over their huge bodies, or with sand, and give themselves a dry shampoo, to drive away the flies which irritated them so.

When we met mule caravans coming north, as we sometimes did, there would be a stampede, the mules sidling up towards the giants, with their ears at the alert, and then passing them with a rush.

On the 12th the rocks began to change their character, mica schists replacing the usual sandstones and clays. These schists were much crumpled, and stood nearly vertical; but they gave origin to the same reddish earth and stiff clay as the others had done.

Now the country began to open out more, the mountains to spread apart and grow flatter; looking south from a high ridge we saw the hills beginning to fade away into plains.

Each day our order of march was the same. We got up at five, while it was still quite dark, with wet mists lying in the valley and brilliant starlight

23. KACHIN RAFT ON THE MALI HKA.
The raft will be broken up and the bamboos sold down the Irrawaddy. *Photo by P.M.R. Leonard, Esq.*

overhead; had breakfast at six, and started at half-past seven. After four hours on the road we would halt by a village or at some wayside stream for lunch; then, pursuing our way till about three in the afternoon, reach another village, thus completing the day's allotted stage.

On the 13th, passing through Bumpat and other Maru villages, we camped in an abandoned *taungya*, which was lying fallow, where wastrel plants of cotton and Capsicum, with gaudy yellow and magenta coxcombs, had sprung up amongst a wilderness of weeds.

The Marus in these parts were better off, and possessed that hallmark of aristocratic Maru society—cowry belts. In the good old days, they said, they had visited the jade mines.

There were tiny tea gardens in these villages. As cultivated here, it is a slender-branched tree, fifteen to eighteen feet high.

The method of making tea is as follows:—

The leaves are rammed into a bamboo tube, which is roasted over the fire till on again ramming down the leaves juice can be squeezed out. More leaves are added, and the process repeated, till finally the tube is filled with a compact mass of leaves like plug tobacco; and it is cut up in the same way, to be used as required.

Such tubes of compressed tea sell for six to twelve annas, though one would imagine that by this process all virtue had been expressed from the leaves.

We were able to get good-flavoured bananas here, though they were rather full of hard black seeds. Walnut-trees are found in the jungle, but the nuts are useless for eating, the thick shell being as hard as stone. The bark is said to be used for poisoning fish, which rise to the surface when it is thrown into the stream. At Hpimaw, however, edible walnuts are found. This is evidently another variety altogether, probably introduced from Yun-nan.

The mulberry is cultivated for rearing silkworms, from which the Kachins weave their head-cloths and beautifully worked bags, decorated with silk tassels.

Wild rubber (*Ficus elastica*) is still fairly common, and is planted near the villages. We saw many trees criss-crossed all over with V-shaped incisions made to tap the latex, some so exhausted that they were already dead. But the natives, finding rubber valuable, are now more careful of their trees.

On 14th December we crossed the Daru hka. It was a lovely day, the shade temperature rising to 74° F in the afternoon, which contrasted with an early morning temperature of 50° F seems very hot.

The Daru hka, like the other rivers crossed between Hkamti Long and Myitkyina, flows down from the Kumon range, separating the Chindwin basin from the Mali valley.

The early mornings continued dewy and misty, but the days were radiant, with enough snap about the nights to brace us.

The 15th was a great day. The road was fairly good, descending in abrupt sweeps, and then suddenly, at out feet, broad and strong, crystal-clear, the Mali at last, rolling between banks of glistening sand.

A steep descent and we lay by the river in the smiting Burmese sunlight, watching the water slip swiftly by and listening to the murmur of a small rapid lower down.

After lazing thus for an hour, drinking in the peace and beauty of the scene, we continued our march, soon leaving the rocky river bed for the jungle again.

Presently we passed several groups of Kachins returning from Myitkyina driving cattle before them, sure sign the new leaven was working. Formerly a man who went to Myitkyina to buy anything got back with a very small portion of it, having paid the greater part away in taxes to be allowed to pass. But with the picketing of the road by military police every fifty miles an impetus has been given to trade.

No wonder the short-sighted *duwas* are sad, now that they have to go down to Myitkyina to buy their own salt and cattle, instead of stealing from weaker brethren or from the Shans! They do not yet perceive how immeasurably to their ultimate interest is the opening of the road. Nor, perhaps, do they greatly care about their ultimate interest!

On 16th December the temperature fell as low as 49° F—the lowest I recorded on the road. Dew was streaming from the trees, and through the opaque mist our camp fires gleamed thickly.

We had only ten miles to do, starting with a long climb up from the valley till we stood over 3000 feet above the river.

A few miles more and then from the ridge just above the 'Nsop stream we had a clear view southwards of the Mali hka, blue as the cold weather sky, twisting through the forested mountains; the bare, white-barked trees striping the green wall of jungle made a very pretty scene, bathed in the golden afternoon sunshine.

A precipitous descent brought us down to the 'Nsop zup, splashing over its bed of jagged slate rocks, and crossing by a bamboo trestle bridge we reached the military police post above.

That night we sat down six to dinner—two P.W.D. men, an officer of the 32nd Pioneers at work on the new mule-road, a military police officer, the doctor and myself. The talk naturally ran on exploration at the sources of the Irrawaddy, of dead and dying mules, of trackless forests and strange beasts, of rations and ammunition abandoned and buried in the jungle for lack of transport, of wild savages and wilder mountains, remote valleys and unknown rivers. It was a picturesque gathering on a far frontier of the Empire, while Britain was fighting for her life in Flanders.

Country boats were expected to arrive from Myitkyina any day, and I awaited their arrival, while the doctor, who was going on leave, hired carts for the remaining forty-six miles, preferring to start at once by road rather than await the mythical boats. As it turned out, none came for a week.

Meanwhile the porters and elephants had started back; for the Nungs were fearful of being bewildered in the mighty bustle of Myitkyina! We had two chill days of rain now, but they soon passed, and it was beautiful to see the sun climb into the valley and roll up the quivering mist like a curtain.

Each day I wandered in the jungle, never far from the bungalow, lest the boats should come during my absence. At night the familiar bark of the muntjac and the tiger's appalling roar sounded very close in the stillness.

'Nsop fort crowns a small knoll overlooking the river at the limit of boat navigation, nearly 1000 miles from the sea.

See now 'Nsop post during the 'open' season, when it is the rationing base for Hkamti, 160 miles distant by road.

A mule convoy is picketed in the hollow, and a dozen bullock carts are straggling through the gate in the barbed wire, loaded up with rations.

Thus the small *maidan* below the fort is crowded with Chinese muleteers, Indian *drabis*, Burmese, Kachins, Shans and Gurkhas, all shouting at once; to the Englishman's eye they are apparently mixed up in helpless confusion, actually they are evolving some sort of order out of the chaos, in the peculiar Oriental way.

The carts are being unloaded, and the loads transferred to mules. Now the Pathays leave their fires, the squatting circles dissolve, and presently the convoy of 150 mules, with one man to every five, starts on its long march northwards.

No sooner has the last mule been swallowed up in the forest than from beyond the rocky promontory which juts out into the river bed is heard the jangle of mule bells again, and the head of an incoming convoy appears. Here they come, strung out across the hot white sand, the weary little mules, though empty, hanging their heads; for they have marched twenty-five miles this day.

As soon as they are within the barbed wire, pack-saddles are removed, picket lines set out, and in half-an-hour they are contentedly crunching their ration of beans; while the muleteers, their fires blazing again, are squatting round the big iron pot bubbling in the centre, each with his rice bowl and chopsticks. So they chatter away as only a happy-go-lucky Panthay muleteer can.

Before he started back, the big elephant was taken down to 'Nsop stream and scraped clean with a *dah*.

It was as good as a play. First he knelt down gently, so as not to upset the *mahout*, who was performing hazardous antics on his back. Then he rolled over on to his side, raising a tremendous wave, and completely submerged himself save for his hind quarters, which appeared like a great grey glistening hill of leather. Next, his trunk appeared out of the water momentarily, and sank again, followed by a sizzle of bubbles.

Meanwhile the *mahout* was dancing with agility on his back, scrambling to a flank as the lusty brute rolled over, and hitting him unmercifully across the head with a *dah* blade, till once the elephant fairly roared with pain. After coming up, he rose heavily to his feet, ploughed tempestuously through the water, the *mahout* still balanced on his back, knelt down, rolled over and sank again. At last he was clean, scraped all over, and emerged shaking himself.

Orchids were by no means so common or various here as they were in the wet Hpimaw hills between 3000 and 6000 feet; they do not get so equable a supply of water here, in the regular monsoon climate, with its long period of drought.

At last, on 22nd December, the long-expected country boats arrived, and were quickly unloaded. These boats, laden with stores, are towed up from Myitkyina, and drift back with the current.

After breakfast T'ung and I went on board, preferring to start late rather than kick our heels at 'Nsop for another day. It was pleasant to be lolling in a boat on the last lap of our journey.

We had three boatmen, one in the stern with the steering sweep and two in the bows hoiking away with short strokes, while we seated ourselves amidships on the luggage. However, our crew did little rowing once we were adrift, enticed from work by the lure of opium; but the breeze being dead astern we pinned two blankets together and raised a sail. So with the help of the breeze we scudded along steadily, and soon shot into a race which took us along well for half-a-mile, the little boat jogging merrily over the choppy waves which slapped against the gunwale.

Long jagged peninsulas of grey slate jutted out from the shore, or showed up in mid-stream, and we floated between well-timbered hills whose lower slopes were covered with plantations of mulberry. Three hours after starting we danced suddenly between a maze of rocks, and there before us, flashing in the sunshine, smiled the broad Irrawaddy, the great river of Burma, placid as a lake.

We had reached the confluence.

The 'Nmai hka here joins the Mali hka at an angle of about 90°, flowing from nearing due east, boisterous and wilful as ever. Behind us lay the wicked mountains of the Burmese hinterland; in front lay the fair land of Burma.

Progress now became slow, for the current was feeble. As the sun sank to rest we passed Watungy post and immediately after came one quick hair-raising rush through the big rapid, where the channel is choked with sabre teeth, leaving a single narrow passage. Into this maw the water hurls itself with an angry roar.

The boat seemed to leap into the jaws of a monstrous shark with triple rows of cruel teeth which had bitten off and cast aside great tree trunks, now stranded thirty feet above water-level. The passage is barely a score of yards in breadth and the water boils and foams in its rage to get through.

My heart was in my mouth as we swung round towards a wicked-looking rock which just showed above water. We were right on it, I thought. Then the vigilant pilot gave a warning yell which sent the opium smokers to the bows in double quick time, from where they fended us off with a pole not a moment too soon to save our boat from going to the bottom of the Irrawaddy.

Now the journey became a tranquil dream; the sun set, and the primrose sky faded out as dusk came on. So broad and still was the great river, so remote the low, tree-clad banks, that we seemed to be motionless under the stars; but a glance at the bobbing buoys which here and there marked the deep water channel showed that there was a good stream running.

A strange throbbing noise grew on us, and after a time resolved itself into the rattle of machinery, rising louder, then falling again. A black shape, glowing with lights, loomed up ahead, and the noise grew to a full-throated roar as we floated past the dredgers sucking up gold from the mud of the river. Then they too fell astern and their voices sank to a whisper.

A heavy dew settled down on everything, and the stars glittered more brilliantly than ever. Feeling cold, I took a turn at the oars; then fell to dozing.

Suddenly a bugle close at hand rang out "Last Post" and I sprang up with a start. The high bank of the Myitkyina shore rose above us, and a moment later we were alongside.

Without waiting for anything I leapt ashore to stretch myself, stiff with cold and cramp—we had been thirteen hours in the boat.

Here were the grass lawns, the roads and shaded bungalows just as of old; everything seemed to be wrapped in slumber; but I must wander through the familiar scene like a restless spirit revisiting its beloved haunts, drinking in the scent of roses.

The crisp challenge of a sepoy sentry startled me for a moment, and then came the muttered "Pass, friend. All well." So I wandered about, caring not whither my footsteps strayed; and, returning to the boat after midnight, slept under the stars.

Next morning I missed the train, but that afternoon, watching the polo, I met several old friends, and dined with a party of officers.

Christmas Day.—The sun rose over the mountains into a cloudless sky, splashing its golden light into every nook and corner, and sparkling on the dewdrenched grass.

Soon the mountains bordering the China frontier and away up north took on that warm blue tone that you see in nothing else except the smoke of a wood fire, and as I looked eastwards for the last time before turning away to the railway station I felt a dreadful home-sickness stealing over me.

In that moment everything—rain, fever, hunger, unending weariness of body and spirit, even infinite torment of flies—was forgotten, except that I loved the mountains.

T'ung-ch'ien was to accompany me as far as Naba, where he changed trains *en route* for Bhamo and Yun-nan. Brave soul! He had been with me, away from his home in Li-kiang, for nearly a year, ever a staunch companion, and cheerful through all our trials. Would I ever see him again, I wondered.

Our boatmen and some of the Kachin porters who had come by road were there on the platform, waving us a last farewell; and as the train steamed out of Myitkyina and I turned my back on those dim mountains rising tier on tier in the pearly haze I could have stretched out my arms to them and cried.

CHAPTER XVIII

THE NORTH-EAST FRONTIER

I have given in the previous chapters an account of our march along the North-East Frontier and through the Burmese hinterland, pointing out the interest of this country as regards its flora and people, and showing how it is all part of the one region of parallel rivers which stretches from the Brahmaputra in Assam to beyond the Yang-tze in China. But the work would be incomplete without some reference to the future of the North-East Frontier, though in this case it is necessary to be brief.

It is only within the last six years[1] that the North-East Frontier problem has become prominent, though it has been maturing ever since the Tibet mission of 1904. Even now its scope and significance seem to be frequently obscured by side issues.

As late as 1906 there was no defined frontier at all. Administered territory stopped short a little north of Myitkyina, the present railhead on the Irrawaddy, twenty miles below the confluence.[2] North of that lay the vast unadministered territory of the Burmese hinterland about which very little indeed was known.

True, the central plain of Hkamti Long had become familiar from the journeys of British officers who reached it early in the nineteenth century from Assam, and much later, in 1895, it was visited by Prince Henry of Orleans on his famous journey from Tonkin to India. But the greater part of the territory, especially towards the Salween divide, was entirely unexplored, though in 1899 Captain Pottinger had gone up the 'Nmai valley as far as the Laking hka, where, coming into conflict with the 'black' Marus (Naingvaws), he was compelled to retreat over the Wulaw Pass to Hpimaw, and so back to Burma by Htawgaw and Lawkhaung. There was no mule-road between Myitkyina and Hpimaw in those days.

In 1906 Hkamti Long again came into the official limelight. In that year a Chinese mandarin named Hsia-hu, whom I met in A-tun-tzu in 1911, visited the plain from A-tun-tzu, and made proposals for its annexation to Yun-nan.

But whatever justification there may be in the Chinese claim to a part of the Irrawaddy basin, there can be no question but that they had no shadow of a right to Hkamti Long. While, therefore, the Indian Government was willing to waive a long-standing interest in the extreme north-east of the hinterland,

---

[1] Written in 1914.
[2] That is, the confluence of the eastern and western branches of the Irrawaddy, the 'Nmai hka and the Mali hka, in Burma called always 'the confluence'. The former is now recognised as the main stream.

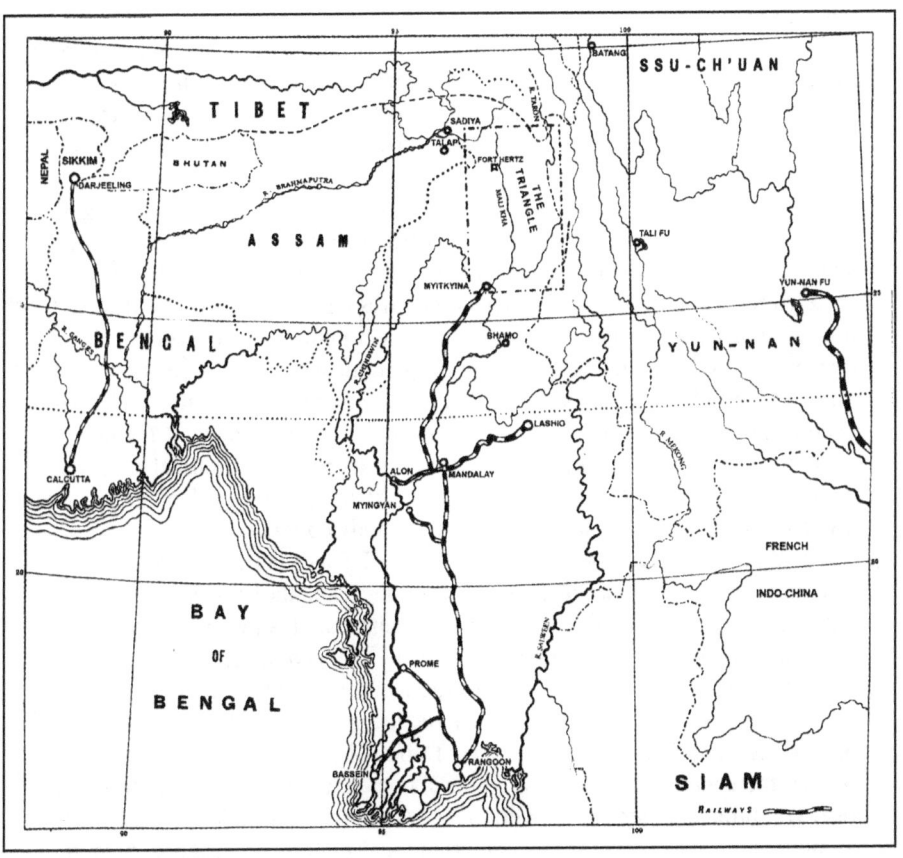

Map II. MAP SHOWING THE RELATIVE POSITION OF THE TRIANGLE TO NEIGHBOURING STATES AND COUNTRIES.
It is situated between long. 95 and 100, and lat. 25 and 30, and is indicated thus: –·–·–·–·–

it was rightly adamant as regards the Hkamti plain: Great Britain could not tolerate a growing Power like China, whose policy has ever been a source of friction on the Burma frontier, to establish herself in the heart of the Burmese hinterland. We shall see adequate reason for this in the sequel.

Hence, though the question was not acute, there was a potential menace, and the time had come to act.

Now there are still left in Burma a group of men who in the old days of thirty years ago were amongst the heroes of the annexation[3]—men fresh to the country, full of enthusiasm, and of a most indomitable energy. They are older men now, though their enthusiasm has never been dimmed by fever, disappointment, or official red tape.

Amongst this band of pioneers who as young men had spent days and nights in the saddle, eating as they rode, sleeping where they dropped, callous to hidden death in the jungle, which threatened them all the time while rounding up the scattered remnants of King Theebaw's army, was a man named Hertz, destined to make a name for himself on the roll of Indian fame. The survivors of those great days who are still in Burma are men in prominent positions—you find them scattered throughout the country, in Rangoon, Moulmein, Mandalay and elsewhere: and perhaps no one of them has come to the front more than Mr Hertz.

Years before the North-East Frontier became a prominent political question, Hertz had realised that one day in the not distant future a settlement would have to be made with China beyond the Irrawaddy confluence.

Unadministered territory which is to be a buffer state between two civilising powers will remain unadministered only so long as neither power is willing to undertake the responsibility of exploration and pacification. Exploration by Government officials with armed escorts is the thin end of the wedge.

Hertz therefore applied himself to the study of Chinese, and later learnt Kachin; meanwhile he thoroughly mastered the geography of the Burma-Yunnan frontier, and being later posted as Deputy Commissioner at Myitkyina, then on the edge of administered country, he had ample opportunity to study local conditions. When the Government was at last persuaded to extend its administration into the Burmese hinterland and delimit the frontier, it found in Hertz, who had urged action, the right man for the work. For following on Hsai-hu's visit to Hkamti Long in 1906 came a raid on the Lashi village of Hpimaw, on the Salween divide, about 170 miles from Myitkyina as the road goes to-day.

In 1911 came the first expedition to Hpimaw, which was subsequently evacuated, again raided by the Chinese, and permanently occupied by the Indian Government eighteen months later, when the present road and fort were

---

[3] *I.e.* the annexation of Upper Burma, always referred to in Burma simply as 'the annexation'.

built, and the 'Nmai valley, with its tributaries coming down from the Salween divide, claimed as British territory.

In the same year, and again in 1912, expeditions were sent up to Hkamti Long in order to ascertain the extent of Chinese influence there. These columns were led by Mr J.T.O. Barnard, one of the most distinguished frontier officers in Burma. In the dry weather of 1912-1913 occurred the great exploration of the Burmese hinterland by two British columns, one of which marched up the Mali valley to Hkamti, the other up the 'Nmai valley to the Ahkyang; and then it was that a Chinese survey party, sequel to Hsia-hu's efforts, and the Tibetan troubles of 1905-1911, was encountered in the Ahkyang valley and pushed out of the country.

In January, 1914, Hkamti Long was permanently occupied and a part of the hinterland brought under direct administration. Hertz, now honoured with a C.S.I. for his work, was appropriately enough the first Deputy Commissioner of the new district, with headquarters at a post called Putao, from the name of the nearest Shan village, but changed in 1918 to Fort Hertz.[4]

Now in any discussion of frontier politics it is necessary to be quite sure of what is aimed at over a wider field than the immediate frontier.

The Indian Government did not pledge itself to Hertz's policy for the amusement of administering the new country. It would indeed have shrunk from doing so as long as it possibly could, for the initial outlay in establishing a new district is heavy, and its subsequent administration a matter of very heavy permanent expense. Moreover, it is impossible to move on this frontier without considering our future relations with China and Tibet, and so, in ever-growing circles of complicity, with Russia.

As long as the hill tribes behaved themselves and did not interfere with British subjects or administered territory, and as long as no other power had designs on the country, it could well be left to go its own sweet way without guidance or assistance. True, no European was permitted to enter unadministered country; while a native, as soon as he had left his friends, ran the serious risk of being sold into slavery. Still these things did not matter.

But as soon as China hinted that she coveted the Burmese hinterland, and required it as a stepping-stone to Tibet, it was necessary to find out something about it and see if such a state of affairs as seemed to be aimed at could or could not be tolerated.

It was no dog-in-the-manger policy. The Indian Government had always claimed the basin of the Irrawaddy on the ground that as Hkamti Long had been originally subject to the Burmese kings, with the change of government in Burma, Hkamti automatically came under British protection.

---

[4] Fort Hertz is the headquarters of the new district known as Hkamti Long. The latter is the Shan name for the plain, comprising a number of petty Shan states, each under its own *sawbwa* or chief.

This is the crux of the matter—that if we had not occupied Hpimaw and Hkamti the Chinese would have anticipated us there, threatening the rich valley of the Irrawaddy and the plains of Lower Burma. But as it does not seem to be generally understood why the occupation of Hkamti by the Chinese would be detrimental to our interests, nor why we should saddle ourselves with the burden and expense of its administration when, it is argued, it were better left alone, it will be as well to say a few words on this point.

The journey from the Salween valley to the plain of Hkamti is, at any season, an extremely difficult undertaking.

For quite four months in the year the passes are blocked with snow, and it is only in summer, when the rains greatly increase the hardships of the journey, that the passage of the watershed, with passes over 12,000 feet, can be effected. It is then obvious that, by having the frontier as far east as possible, a considerable tract of country which is impassable for troops is interposed between China and the nearest habitable part of the Burmese hinterland.

Why then surrender this advantage by allowing the Chinese to occupy Hkamti Long, by which means the entire mountain barrier is at once negatived? For if the Chinese are in possession of the Hkamti plain they can concentrate there, and it does not signify how long it takes them to cross the intervening country in small detachments. In the meantime they are enabled to make the best of the country from the Salween valley to Hkamti, selecting the best route, which is undoubtedly one via the Ahkyang valley, and keeping up some sort of communications.

"But," say many people, "what does it matter if the Chinese do occupy Hkamti? They can't hurt us, and by occupying it we only put ourselves to enormous expense and trouble for nothing."

But we must consider what it may mean fifty years hence. At present neither Myitkyina nor Assam, especially the latter, is easily reached from Hkamti, the country is sparsely populated, and those in possession are to some extent isolated.

On the other hand, Hkamti can support a population ten times as great as it does at present, and a good road from Hertz to Myitkyina presents no insuperable engineering difficulties, as is shown by the success with which the P.W.D. and Pioneers are now pushing on operations.[5]

Suppose, then, Hkamti occupied by a large Chinese community, a good mule-road built to Myitkyina and communication established with the Salween valley, this would constitute a real menace to Upper Burma, already crowded with Chinese; and with Hpimaw also in their hands they would be in a position to advance into the Irrawaddy valley by several routes. This, however, is not the most serous danger.

---

[5] The road has been finished long since this was written.

It is not to be forgotten that before the annexation of Upper Burma the Chinese endeavoured to frustrate any attempt by the British to open up communications between Burma and China, by inciting the hill tribes, just as they subsequently attempted to thwart direct communication between India and Lhasa. Ever since the annexation the hill tribes have been a constant source of anxiety on this frontier. The Chinese revel in diplomatic intrigue and are the worst possible frontier neighbours.

Their methods are indirect. If then they occupied the Hkamti plain in force, they might easily, as they well know how, inflame the Kachins against us, using them as a convenient catspaw to harass the northern frontier. Further, with China controlling the whole of this great plain, all hope of opening up direct communication between Burma, the Zayul valley and south-eastern Tibet on the one hand, and between Burma, Assam and Hkamti via the Hukong valley on the other, would come to an end; and as this route via the Diphuk La is probably the only one by which communication between the Burmese hinterland and Tibet can be established, that dream too would have to be given up.

China, moreover, would have driven a big wedge into the Burmese hinterland, cutting it off from Tibet, threatening Upper Burma and threatening Assam. She would leave behind her the greatest obstacles to any attack on Burma from the north-east, and stultify the great advantage which would otherwise accrue to us from acting on internal lines of communication in case of hostilities on this frontier.

At some future date China will be more formidable than she is at present, and though I do not suggest that China will ever threaten seriously an invasion of India, yet the history of the past thirty years has shown that she can be a very uncongenial neighbour. The western provincial governments have so very clearly shown how they wish to establish themselves in the Burmese hinterland that the Indian Government is wise in anticipating the event, since, whatever the expense now, to turn them out ten years hence, if it were at all feasible, would be a most costly proceeding.

That the Kachins would require little encouragement to worry the people of the plains, especially if they received a substantial backing from the north, cannot be doubted. Some of the clans are independent and truculent, and though it would perhaps be flattery to call them warlike, still, like most hill-men, they can be a serious nuisance on occasion. As recently as January, 1915, the Kachins to the north-west of Myitkyina, occupying unadministered territory, raided the peaceful tribes and stoutly resisted the British punitive expedition. Most of the Kachin tribes probably do not love the British Raj; they dislike paying taxes and at present no doubt neither realise nor appreciate the uses to which those taxes are put.

It can then be readily understood that if the Chinese got amongst them and represented to them that under British rule they would lose their liberty, they might become a formidable menace to our rule in Upper Burma, surrounding British territory as they do on three sides. For this reason alone it is above all things necessary to keep the Chinese out of Hkamti and stand between them and the Kachins.

Raiding parties into the hinterland need not be considered: in the end they can only defeat their own object by forcing the tribesmen to seek the protection of Government. Invasion, on the other hand, is a formidable undertaking, and an army of conquest is useless unless two conditions are fulfilled: (1) that it can be rapidly transported to the point where it is most required and (2) kept there.

As for any army the Chinese could assemble on the North-East Frontier without a single mile of railway within 300 miles of that frontier, and roads so bad as to be almost impassable for mules in summer, no rapid concentration at a selected point could conceivably be effected; and once over the frontier, their base behind them, as many marches as the army went forward it would have to retire, unless it were certain that Hkamti could be reached, and taken, in a given time. To effect a surprise would be impossible, and any such expedition would probably perish in the jungles.

As regards keeping an army in the Burmese hinterland, all supplies would need to be transported there, and the country could not supply the transport. Even the fortified posts in the Salween valley are supplied with meat and other necessaries from the garrison cities of western Yun-nan.

That the Chinese were not already established in Hkamti by 1914 was their own fault; they had spied out the land in 1906. But there is no continuity in China's foreign policy, and the central government is in the habit of leaving provincial governments in the lurch when through failure to succeed in any enterprise they find themselves entangled with a foreign government. This saves her much temporary inconvenience, but may introduce embarrassments later.

Up to 1912 no steps had been taken by the Yun-nan Government for the occupation of Hkamti; the Chinese survey parties which entered the hinterland that winter were chiefly engaged in seeking a road to Tibet, and their numbers were in any case far too few to occupy territory. They were easily dispersed by the British expedition, and all Chinese pretensions to the hinterland, beyond the still disputed Taron valley, disappeared.[6]

It being conceded that it is necessary to keep the Chinese out of the hinterland, the next thing to consider is the best way to do it. Would it be better to occupy the Hkamti plain, or to defend what we claim as the frontier— namely, the Salween divide from latitude 26° N almost to the sources of the Irrawaddy?

The southernmost pass leading from the Salween directly into the Irrawaddy basin—namely, the Hpimaw Pass—had been frequently crossed by Chinese

---

[6] Since this was written the British frontier line has been selected, leaving the Taron to the Chinese, and, in the north, to the Tibetans.

troops and the hill country invaded. Would it be best to extend the road northwards from Hpimaw along the frontier, erecting more forts where necessary, or leave the Hpimaw fort to mark the limit of our advance along the frontier, and occupy Hkamti?

Now I have briefly described my journey northwards from Hpimaw to beyond the Ahkyang confluence, and two things stand out prominently in my memory: (1) the enormous difficulty and expense of carrying a road over the Wulaw Pass and up the 'Nmai hka valley, a route which seems to me to present far greater difficulties than that up the Mali valley from Myitkyina to Fort Hertz (2) the extraordinary wildness and sparse population of the mountains and valleys between the 'Nmai valley and the magnificent barrier of the Salween divide. To carry the Hpimaw road east of the 'Nmai valley, whether the route is more practicable or not, is impossible without vast expenditure, because no labour or supplies are available.

But what advantage is gained by protecting the immediate frontier? We should simply sacrifice all the advantages of maintaining a strip of almost uninhabited and uninhabitable country between the frontier and a less advanced base, without covering Hkamti, which would still be open to invasion from the north via the Zayul valley and Diphuk La if south-east Tibet was in the hands of the Chinese as it was in 1911. By holding Hkamti itself, apart from its economic advantages, we do not imperil the frontier territory in the slightest degree, since the Chinese would never settle in the hinterland except on the paddy-land of Hkamti; while to cross this strip would be for the Chinese to risk everything to meet exactly as strong opposition there as they would meet with if they crossed the frontier 200 miles farther south in the neighbourhood of Myitkyina or Bhamo.

To hold Hkamti, and not the frontier, is to treble the distance between the Chinese military cities of north-western Yun-nan and their first objective in case of an invasion of Burma from the north-east. Any force striking at Burma from the north or north-east must pass through Hkamti. It is the only place an invading force would dare to halt at. Therefore Hkamti Long is the strategic key to the entire frontier.

The defensive position to be thoroughly effective must be as near as possible to both Upper Burma and Assam, so that it can be rapidly reinforced from either direction. The only places fulfilling these conditions are the Hukong valley and Hkamti Long.

The 'Nmai valley is out of the question. Not only is no settlement of it possible—half the advantage of working on internal lines is lost if the base is pushed so far forward in a country devoid of natural means of communication.

Quite apart from the economic advantages of holding the plain, with its paddy-land, its comparative ease of access from Myitkyina, and its control of the routes into Assam, it is of very great advantage to the tranquillity of the Burmese hinterland. As long as there was a possibility of acquiring the plain the Chinese along the frontier were restless. Here was splendid paddy-land, a halting-place on the road to the upper Brahmaputra (Tsanpo) valley and Lhasa, as they thought, and no one in possession. Why should they not acquire it and extend the borders of Yun-nan westwards, so as to embrace the whole of the source streams of the Irrawaddy?

Now that the plain is lost to them they will no longer bother about it. Frontier raiding will become profitless, and the pedlars will come peacefully as of old over the passes selling clothes, cotton yarn and salt to the natives.

I have said above that no advance on Myitkyina from the north-east is possible without first crossing Hkamti, but this is perhaps open to objection. There is still the 'Nmai hka valley, and by entering the country via the comparatively well-populated Ahkyang valley or down the Lading valley, both of which routes have been in the past, and are still, used by Chinese traders, it might be thought that in the event of a simultaneous attack along the Burma frontier a considerable diversion could be created from the north-east.

However, setting aside the improbability of any such combined attack over the widely separated passes which present all degrees of difficulty, no force capable of creating a considerable diversion could be marched down the 'Nmai valley at one time. The posts north of Myitkyina at the lower end of the 'Nmai valley are strong enough to cope with any raiding expedition that could approach Upper Burma from this direction, and it does not seem necessary at present to watch the valleys by which the Chinese might enter the hinterland—namely, the Laking, Mekh and Ahkyang. But so long as such a rallying-point as Hkamti were not occupied by us, it would be necessary to watch every route by which the Chinese could reach it, and this would imply a considerable system of communications in a country less adapted to road-making than is the Mali valley. Whereas by occupying Hkamti the very difficulties which would make it so inconvenient for us to hold the frontier would deter the Chinese from crossing into our territory.

As for local raids, it is scarcely worth while to consider them. North of the Hpimaw hill tracts there is nothing worth raiding and the numbers able to embark on such a profitless undertaking would necessarily be so few that the local tribesmen would be sufficiently strong to resist them.

Having seen something of the North-East Frontier both on the Chinese side (the Salween valley) and in British territory, I feel certain that, so long as we hold Hkamti, aggression from the north-east cannot possibly succeed, nor is an attack from that direction likely. The Salween valley itself is a formidable barrier separating the possible points of Chinese concentration, in western Yun-nan, from the mountainous frontier, and though there are numerous passes into the Burmese hinterland, the routes are so long and difficult that news of the approach of even a small raiding party would be known in Hkamti long before anything useful could be accomplished.

There is another circumstance which must soon bring the North-East

Frontier into prominence. The Burmese hinterland is the link between India and China.

My personal experience of the country leads me to believe that no southern trans-Asiatic railway will ever be built in this region—the physical barriers on the China side are too enormous; nevertheless, with the development of mechanical transport, roads might be built across the North-East Frontier.

The main routes through Asia were marked out in the long past, and, except where they have been obliterated by the gradual desiccation of Central Asia are the same now as they were many centuries ago. Such do not change, for the great centres of population do not change except slowly, and physical barriers remain where they have always been; even when railways replace roads, they follow those roads.

It is sea transport that has diverted attention from the trade routes of interior Asia. Since the Portuguese and the Dutch, the French and the English came to Asia by sea, the land routes, always running from east to west across the continent, skirting the deserts and following the great longitudinal valleys, have not been approached from north or south.

Now the perfection of mechanical land transport may see a return to the great trans-continental roads.

They were wise, those old autocrats. They grasped right principles and built on the grand scale. The Great Wall of China may have fallen into disuse under altered conditions of war, but not the Grand Canal. Peace conditions have not changed so much even after two thousand years, and the Grand Canal is indeed to be restored.

We cannot divert trade in Asia while men live where they do live, migrate as they do migrate, while deserts and mountain ranges and rivers are where they are—it still flows along accustomed routes, and will continue to do so when the pyramids lie in the dust.

We can supplement it, increase it by improving communications, but we cannot stop it. Trade routes are not abandoned till nature renders them impassable.

Thus it is our endeavour to study the main channels of trade, and to ease all friction, that it may flow easily and naturally.

Every new means of transport, every short-cut to the markets of the world, must be employed, not in a selfish attempt to snatch profits, but to benefit all.

And history shows that this is so—in profiting ourselves we profit others. Our policy in Asia has always been to open and to keep open trade routes for all. We spent lacs of rupees and valuable lives—I need instance only that of Margary—to reopen the Bhamo–Tali-fu trade route, since when both Burma and Yun-nan have reaped prosperity as a direct result. The story of that effort is not very creditable to the Indian governments concerned, but in the end the work of the pioneers—Margary, Sladen, Clement Williams and others—was crowned with success, and results have amply justified it.

The history of our attempts to open up direct communication between

India and Tibet, or between India and China, is not dissimilar, except in this respect—that there never has been such communication in the past. The way from Central Asia to India has always been by the North-West Frontier.

We may confidently believe, therefore, that if such a route would have served any useful purpose in the past, it would have been found and used by the Tibetans or by the Chinese.

Before sea trade was developed, such a road led nowhere. It was a blind alley, leading only to the sea. And there were bad lands to cross—it was not worth it.

Now it is different. The great trade routes of Asia are still there as of yore; some of them lie only just beyond the North-East Frontier, to north and east, linking up the richest province in China with the richest part of Tibet. Caravans from half a continent still ebb and flow along them. And in the south the sea-borne trade from the ends of the earth plies patiently, still seeking its way slowly but surely to the heart of Asia. Between them lies the Burmese hinterland, across which we must stride to the open spaces beyond. With the railhead at Myitkyina, only 300 miles from the Tibetan frontier, and a good mule-road already constructed for 200 miles, to Hkamti Long, it would be comparatively easy to extend it so as to link up Burma with the richest provinces of Tibet.

Thus our road would not be useless, our past efforts to open up direct communication with Tibet not wasted. For history proves that the great trade routes are as eternal as the Himalaya. Just out of reach, beyond our frontier, the flood trade rolls on past India. The proposed route, tapping this great stream, will revive it, nourish it, swell it and share its new-born prosperity.

In this way too a land connection between Burma and Assam of strategic value in improving the internal lines of communication would be assured. From Rima, in the Zayul valley, there would be a choice of routes: (1) down the Zayul valley to Assam railway, a distance of about 150 miles; (2) over the Diphuk La to Hkamti Long, whence Burma could be reached via the Hukong valley, or by following the present road, down the Mali valley. By this last route Rima is about 300 miles from railhead.

Thus our policy will be to improve existing communications and open up direct access to the interior by the shortest possible route.

It must not be forgotten that it would not prove a very difficult feat to carry a railway up the Mekong valley, the strategic value of which would be to the Chinese considerable.

From the middle Mekong the railway might be carried across to Tali-fu, thus missing the formidable mountain range between this river and the Yang-tze, while the great range between the Mekong and the Salween would be crossed far to the north, where both rivers flow from the north-west.

As to the proposed southern trans-Asiatic railway, it is certain it will never cross the Burmese hinterland. Should it ever be built, it must run north of the Irrawaddy triangle, from the Tsanpo valley to the Salween valley, entering Yun-nan by the Mekong valley.

APPENDIX I
SYNOPSIS OF THE PRINCIPAL TRIBES, NORTH-EAST FRONTIER

Common English Name	As called by the tribe itself	Chinese	Kachin	Maru	Lashi	Lisu	Shan	Nung	Principal Present Home
Kachin	Ching-paw	Shab-t'ou, or Yêh-jên[1]	—	P'u-man (?)	P'ok	—	Hkang	—	Mali valley, Hukong valley and trans-Mali country
Maru	Lawg-vaw	Lan-su	Ma-ru	—	Lang	La-si	Ma-lu	—	'Nmai hka and tributaries up to lat. 27° 30'
Lashi	Le-chi	Ch'a-shan	La-shi	La-si	—	—	—	—	Htawgaw Hills and Ngawchang hka
Lisu, or Yawyin	Li-su	Li-so, or Yêh-jên[1]	Yew-yen	La-si	La-si	—	Chenung[2]	—	Salween valley, Salween-Irrawaddy divide, tributaries of the 'Nmai hka
Shan, or Tai	Hkamti[3]	Pai-i	Sam, or Hsam	Sen	Sam	—	—	—	Plain of Hkamti Long
Nung	Taron (Tourong)	Kiu-tzu	Nung	—	—	—	Hkunung[4]	—	Taron and valleys to the west, north of lat. 27° 30' -

[1] The words Yêh-jên mean "wild man" and are commonly applied to any of the hill tribes. The word Yawyin is clearly a corruption of it.

[2] The Shans have confused the Lisu with the Nung using the same name for both.

[3] The Shans were once a great race, but have become split up into a number of isolated bodies, of whom the Hkamti Shans are one. The only considerable homogeneous body of Shans now are the Siamese. The word "Shan" is the Burmese name for them. The Hkamti Shans call themselves simply Hkamti.

[4] Hkunung means "slave Nung".

APPENDIX II

The following list includes some of the more interesting plants which I collected in the Htawgaw Hills in 1914 and 1919; others are mentioned in the course of the narrative. Those printed in heavy type are new species; those marked with an asterisk are in cultivation in England raised from my seeds. The numbers refer to my catalogues.

The identifications are by Sir Isaac Bayley Balfour, F.R.S., and Mr W.W. Smith, M.A., to whom I am indebted.

3224.	Abelia sp. (undetermined).
1707.	Acanthopanax evodiæfolius, Franch. var. ferrugineus, W. W. Sm. var. nov.
1963.	Acanthopanax trifoliatus, Schneider.
1414.	**Acer Wardii**, W. W. Sm.
3575.	Aconitum sp. (undetermined).
1945.	Æitiginetia indica, Roxb.
200.	**Agapetes Wardii**, W.W. Sm.
3428.	Allium sp. (undetermined).
3310.	Androsace sp. (undetermined).
3171.	Androsace Henryi (?).
1975.	Apios carnea, Benth.
3590.	Arenaria pogonantha.
1660.	Beesia cordata, B. fil. et W. W. Sm. gen. nov. Ranunculacearum.
1670.	Bletilla hyacinthina, Reich, f.
1867.	Buddleia limitanea, W. W. Sm.
3314.	Buddleia sp. (undetermined).
3697.	Campanula colorata.
1788.⎫ 3366.⎭	**Cassiope myosuroides**, W. W. Sm.
3311.	**Cassiope palpebrata**, (?) W. W. Sm.
1824.	**Chirita umbricola**, W. W. Sm.
1733.	Circæ alpina, Linn.
3084.	Clintonia sp. (undetermined).
1698.	Clitoria Mariana, Linn.
3491.	Codonopsis sp. (undetermined).
1569.	Cœlogyne corymbosa, Lindl.
1708.	**Corydalis saltatoria**, W. W. Sm.
3363.	Cotoneaster rotundifolia.
1783.⎫ 3360.⎭	**Cremanthodium gracillimum**, W. W. Sm.

1796.	**Cremanthodium Wardii**, W. W. Sm.
3361.	
*3409.	Cremanthodium sp. (undetermined).
3478.	Cymbidium, sp. (undetermined).
1643.	Cypripedium bracteatum, Rolfe.
2003.	**Daedalacanthus Wardii**, W. W. Sm.
*	Dendrobium sp. (undetermined).
1599.	Dipentodon sinicus, Dunn.
1526.	Disporum pullum, Salisb.
1596.	Drosera peltata, Sm.
3122.	Enkianthus sp. (undetermined).
*3045.	Enkianthus sp. (undetermined).
*3122.	Enkianthus deflexus (?).
1667.	Epipactis Royleana, Lindl.
1543.	**Euonymus Wardii**, W. W. Sm.
1691.	Gaultheria trichophylla, Royle.
1613.	Gaultheria fragrantissima, Wall.
1590.	Gaultheria Griffithiana, Wight.
*3062.	Gaultheria sp. (undetermined).
1840.	Gaultheria laxiflora, Diels (new to Burma).
1879.	Goodyera Schlechtendaliana, Reichb. f.
1982.	Gynura angulosa, DC.
*3644.	Hedychium sp. (undetermined).
1662.	Herminium angustifolium, Lindl.
1542.	**Hydrangea subferruginea**, W. W. Sm.
1592.	Hydrangea yunnanensis, Rehder.
1853.	Hydrangea aspera, D. Don.
1576.	Illicium yunnanense, Franch.
*3386.	Iris sp. (undetermined).
1043.	**Lagotis Wardii**, W. W. Sm.
3683.	Leptocodon gracile.
1894.	**Lysionotus gracilis**, W. W. Sm.
1895.	**Lysionotus Wardii**, W. W. Sm.
*3427.	Lilium Thompsonianum.
*3261.	Lilium Wallichianum.
*3446.	Lloydia sp. (undetermined).
1979.	Limnophila hirsuta, Benth.
1980.	Limnophila sessiliflora, Blume.
3376.	Listera sp. (undetermined).
3277.	Lonicera sp. (undetermined).
3698.	Magnolia sp. (undetermined).
*3709.	Magnolia sp. (undetermined).
*3281.	Meconopsis Wallichii.
1504.	Microglossa volubilis, DC.

1769.	Microstylis muscifera, Ridley.
1624.	Mimulas nepalensis, Benth.
*3100.	Mimulus sp. (undetermined).
1712.	Millettia cinerea, Benth.
2005.	Mucuna pruriens, DC.
*3268.	Nomocharis pardanthina, (?) B. fil.
1862.	Oberonia myriantha, Lindl.
1865.	Oxyspora serrata, Diels.
3286.	Parnassia sp. (undetermined).
3282.	Philadephus sp. (undetermined).
*3394.	Polygonum Griffithii.
1602.	Polygonum runcinatum, Ham.
1714.	Polygonum microcephalum, D. Don.
1854.	Polygonum molle, Don.
1937.	Polygonum chinense, Linn.
1940.	Polygonum orientale, Linn.
1973.	Polygonum hydropiper, Linn.
1983.	Polygonam perfoliatum, Linn.
*3453.	Polygonum sp. (undetermined).
3393.	Polygonum Forrestii.
1688. } *3093. }	Primula praticola, Craib.
*1632.	Primula seclusa.
*3094.	Primula calliantha (?).
*3389.	Primula involucrata (?).
3186.	Primula Delavayi (?).
1644.	**Primula fragilis**, B. fil et Ward.
1805.	**Primula coryphaea**, B. fil et Ward.
1784.	**Primula sciophila**, B. fil et Ward.
1634.	Primula Beesiana.
1635.	Primula, helodoxa.
3407.	Primula serratifolia.
*3656.	Primula sp. (undetermined).
3092.	Primula euosma (?).
3110.	Primula sp. (undetermined).
3150.	Primula sp. (undetermined).
1572.	Primula sonchifolia.
	Primula sp. (undetermined).
	Primula limnoica.
	Primula Listeri.
1758.	Pueraria Wallichii, DC.
1950.	Pueraria Thunbergiana, Benth.
*3158.	Pyrus sp.
1851.	**Rhododendron agapetum**, Balf. fil. et Ward.

Appendix II

*1628.	**Rhododendron megacalyx**, Balf. fil. et Ward.
*3101.	Rhododendron arizelum, Balf. fil. et Forrest.
1817. 1757. }	Rhododendron crassum, Franch.
1538.	**Rhododendron dendricola**, Hutchinson.
*3392.	Rhododendron dicranthum (?).
1778. *3301. }	**Rhododendron euchroum**, Balf. fil. et Ward.
	Rhododendron erigoynium, Balf. fil.
1596.	**Rhododendron facetum**, Balf. fil. et Ward.
3042.	Rhododendron habrotrychum, Balf. fil. et W. W. Sm.
*3267.	**Rhododendron herpesticum**, Balf. fil. et Ward.
1567.	Rhododendron mallotum.
1791.	**Rhododendron nmaiense**, Balf. fil. et Ward.
1906.	**Rhododendron operinum**, Balf. fil. et Ward.
1565.	**Rhododendron regale**, Balf. fil. et Ward.
*3016.	Rhododendron siderium, Balf. fil.
1629.	**Rhododendron sciaphilum**, Balf. fil. et Ward.
3316.	Rhododendron sino-grande, Balf. fil. et W. W. Sm.
*3095.	Rhododendron tapeinum, Balf. fil. et Farrer.
1566.	Rhododendron tanastylum, Balf. fil.
1568.	Rhododendron zaleucum, Balf. fil. et W. W. Sm.
*3001-D.	Rhododendron sp. (undetermined).
*3040. 3097. 3305. }	Rhododendron sp. (undetermined).
3300.	Rhododendron sp. (undetermined).
3301.	Rhododendron sp. (undetermined).
*3302. *3303. 3391. }	Rhododendron sp. (undetermined).
*3304.	Rhododendron sp. (undetermined).
f 3155. *3189. 3365. }	Rhododendron sp. (undetermined).
*3408. 3721. }	Rhododendron sp. (undetermined).
3722.	Rhododendron sp. (undetermined).
3527.	Rhynchoglossum obliquum.
3006.	Rosa bracteata (?).
3072.	Rosa sericea.
3401.	**Rosa** sp. (undetermined).
*3199.	Roscœa sp. (undetermined).
1695.	Rubus loropetalus, Franch (new to Burma).
1955.	**Sabia Wardii**, W. W. Sm.

1870.	Satyrium nepalense, Don.
1618. *3065	} Schizandra grandiflora, H. f. and T.
1693.	Scrophularia Delavayi, Franch.
*3123.	Sorbus sp. (? undetermined).
1848. 1799. 3307.	} Spathoglottis pubescens. **Spiræa Wardii**, W. W. Sm.
3363.	Spiræa bella.
1735.	Spiranthes australls.
1775.	**Sporoxeia sciadophila**, W. W. Sm. gen. nov. Melastomacearum.
1749.	Streptopus amplexifolius.
3265.	Streptopus sp. (undetermined).
1911.	**Strobilanthes oresbius**, W. W. Sm.
1912.	**Strobilanthes Wardii**, W. W. Sm.
1896.	**Strobilanthes stramineus**, W. W. Sm.
2000.	**Strobilanthes arenicolus**, W. W. Sm.
1857.	**Thalictrum semiscandens**, W. W. Sm.
*3422.	Thalictrum sp. (undetermined).
*3001-A.	Thalictrum sp. (undetermined).
1760.	Tofieldia yunnanensis, Franch.
1514.	Torenia peduncularis, Benth.
1611.	**Tovaria finitima**, W. W. Sm.
1811.	**Tovaria Wardii**, W. W. Sm.
1705.	Tricyrtis macropoda, Miq.
1718. 3099. 1620.	} Tripterygium Forrestii, Loes. **Viburnum Wardii**, W. W. Sm.
1658.	**Viburnum erubescens**, W. W. Sm.
1716.	Viburnum cylindricum, Ham.
1719.	Viburnum fœtidum, Wall.

INDEX

A
Animals and birds—
  animal life, absence of 35; in the jungle 145
  baboon, pig tailed 88, 98, 108, 126
  baboons, forest alive with 4
  bamboo partridge 25, 36
  barking deer 15, 25, 138
  bear 25, 70, 72, 96
  birds, persecution of, by natives 36
  buffalo 45, 122, 125, 130, 133, 136, 137, 141, 142, 144
  Chinese blood pheasant 44
  fowls, destroyed by vermin 20
  game on the North-East Frontier 25, 138
  gibbons 109, 122, 131
  harvest mouse 87, 88
  jays 13
  jungle fowl 4, 124, 138
  jungle rats 20
  kingfisher 105, 145
  mithan 72, 74, 87, 122
  monkeys 4, 56, 57, 72, 81, 88, 93, 95, 96, 98, 107, 108, 109, 113, 114, 115, 117, 145
  Sclater's Monal 44
  serow 25, 70, 72
  shrew, a new 54
  snakes 11, 24, 36, 75, 83, 108, 143
  takin 45, 70, 72, 138; distribution of, 46
  voles 35, 64
  water-shrew 68
  woodpecker 145

B
Barnard, Mr J.T.O. 125, 126, 128, 129, 135, 149, 161
barter, Chinese love of 26
Brooks, Dr 129
Buddhism 135, 136, 143, 144
Burd, Captain 129
burial customs in China 58, 59

C
cane bridges 30, 58, 59, 71, 73, 74, 75, 76, 83, 85, 89, 99, 132; structure of 8

Chinese, migration of 38
Chinese wine 28
coffin plank industry 24, 58, 62
Conry, Captain 119, 122
Cooper, Mr T.T. 124, 135
Cultivation—
  buckwheat 20, 31, 63, 70, 81, 87, 94
  Capsicum 98
  cotton 76, 81, 99, 145, 152
  cucumber 57, 58, 145
  hill-side cultivation: see *taungya*
  indigo 29, 81
  Job's tears 139
  maize 20, 21, 31, 56, 58, 59, 62, 63, 70, 81, 95, 96, 99, 114, 115, 145
  millet 58, 94
  mountain rice 20, 81, 145
  pumpkins 87, 98, 145
  rice cultivation 8, 9, 17, 30, 56, 128
  taungya 20, 29, 31, 56, 57, 62, 63, 81, 87, 94, 99, 145, 146, 152; difficulties of 32; preparation of 21
  tobacco 58, 70, 87, 98, 145
  village cultivation 130, 131, 140, 142, 145, 152
  yams 98, 151

D
Don Juan, a Chinese 18, 19

E
elephants as transport 139, 140, 143, 145, 151
English scenery in Burma 133

F
fever 15, 22, 31, 32, 33, 35, 37, 52, 54, 129, 157, 160
fish drive 99
fish traps 61, 74
Floras—
  alpine flowers 41, 42, 44, 45, 46;
  alpine meadows 12, 13, 24, 54, 66, 67, 117
  bamboo forest 35, 69
  Chinese flora 73; relation to Himalayan 42

conifer forest 11, 24, 35, 58, 64, 68
dwarf shrubs 44
forest undergrowth 12, 22, 32, 36
Indo-Malayan flora 73, 147
limestone peak, flora of a 25, 26, 53
Mekong-Salween divide, flora of 42
monsoon forest 3, 4, 5, 73, 141, 146, 147
North-East Frontier flora, relationships of 41, 42, 147; route followed by 42; where derived from 42, 147
temperate rain forest 11, 12, 13, 22, 23, 35, 54, 69
flowers, Gurkhas' fondness for 52
forest fires 4
frontier forts, construction and use of 19, 51, 52

G
geology of the Mali valley 141, 146, 151
gold dredgers 156

H
heavy rains, effect of 28
Hertz, Mr W.A. 9, 114, 125, 129, 139, 160, 161

I
Insects, etc.—
  bees 12, 69, 107, 113
  bugs, edible 142, 143
  butterflies 58, 73, 82, 86, 95, 107, 123; Dalchina 91; leaf-butterfly 91; Cyrestis 91; Leptocircus 92; a curious assemblage of 91
  butterfly, a huge 53, 54
  caterpillars, curious behaviour of 39
  cicadas 74, 81, 112, 117, 118
  flies: blood-blister 21, 49; fire-flies 14, 44, 49, 131; horse-flies 21, 117; house 25, 107; sand-flies 21, 26, 40, 49, 61, 67, 69, 75, 105, 112, 114, 117, 118, 124, 126, 138
  land leeches, description of 123, 124
  leeches 23, 25, 52, 69, 99, 118, 125, 138

  mimicry, a case of 22, 91, 108
  mosquitoes 38, 61, 86, 105, 112, 113
  red ants 86
  stick-insect 52, 60, 117
  ticks 25, 138
iron mines 146, 150

J
jungle shelter 64, 69, 112, 114

L
Langley, Mr 139
Lao-niu 3, 33, 55
Leonard, Mr P.M.R. 6, 90, 106, 116, 138, 139, 152

M
mahseer fishing 5, 105, 138, 139
Ming-kuan 24, 27
monkey scares 56, 57, 81
moon, eclipse of 84
Mountains—
  Hpimaw hills 19, 36, 79, 155, 166
  Imaw Bum 11, 29, 38, 39, 40, 41, 42, 43, 44, 60, 62, 67
  Laksang Bum 29, 48, 53
  Lawkhaung ridge 5, 7, 73
  Noi Matoi 131, 137
  North-East Frontier, mountain ranges of 1
  Mekong-Salween divide 66
  Salween-Irrawaddy divide 3, 60

N
nat trees 123, 140
nats 71, 77, 97, 123, 136, 140
North-East Frontier, delimitation of 1, 164; recent events on 1, 149; trade on 70, 166; transport on the 55

O
opium 15, 70, 133, 136, 145, 155, 156

P
pagodas, Shan 138, 139
Passes—
  Chimili 60
  Feng-shui-ling 9, 20, 21, 23, 24, 35, 59, 66

Hpare 7, 8
Hpimaw 9, 10, 13, 35, 53, 54, 165
Lagwi 7, 8
Lakhe 72
Panwa 5
Shing-rup-kyet 115
Wulaw 58, 60, 63, 65, 71, 82, 105, 158, 165
phallic worship 83, 148
phosphorescent wood 37
Places and Posts—
 Assam 2, 8, 42, 46, 54, 55, 120, 124, 133, 134, 135, 138, 139, 140, 144, 147, 149, 150, 158, 161, 163, 165, 166, 168
 Bhamo 2, 18, 136, 149, 157, 165
 Black Rock 9, 61
 Fort Hertz 79, 83, 94, 97, 120, 122, 123, 125, 126, 128, 130, 131, 138, 139, 147, 161, 165
 Hpimaw 79, 82, 93; arrival at 10; expedition to 9, 160; departure from 55; Fort 3, 4, 7, 8, 11, 15, 19, 20, 24, 38, 48, 50, 52, 54; garden at 20; occupation of 10, 52; road to 8; supplies at 20; valley 9, 14, 17, 20, 29, 47, 56; village 10, 15, 50, 51
 Htawgaw 7, 8, 14, 51, 158, 170
 Kawnglu 114, 119, 120, 125, 126
 Lawkhaung post 5, 158
 Laza 147, 148
 Li-kiang 3, 26, 27, 50, 63, 157
 Lumpung 8
 Myitkyina 1, 2, 3, 48, 54, 58, 81, 83, 115, 120, 129, 134, 136, 138, 139, 147, 153, 154, 155, 156, 157, 158, 160, 161, 163, 165, 166, 168
 'Nsop post 154
 Peopat 5
 Putao 130, 134, 136, 138, 161
 Sadon 3
 Seniku post 3
 Tawlang 81
 T'eng-yueh 3, 18, 19, 24, 58, 59, 63, 64
 Tibet 1, 13, 46, 55, 69, 83, 97, 113, 120, 131, 133, 137, 138, 149, 158, 161, 163, 164, 165, 168
 Waingmaw 2, 3
 Wauhsaung 3

Yun-nan 1, 3, 13, 16, 18, 20, 21, 24, 26, 38, 41, 46, 50, 52, 54, 58, 59, 64, 68, 70, 73, 81, 83, 89, 33, 134, 137, 145, 153, 158, 164, 165, 166, 167, 168
poisoned honey 39
Policy—
 Burmese hinterland, Chinese claims to 158, 161, 161, 166
 Indian Government and the Burmese hinterland 161
 North-East Frontier, natural defences of the 161, 164, 165, 166, 167
 menace to Burma and Assam 163, 164
 railways, possibility of 167, 168
Pottinger, Captain 81, 158

R
rat traps 70
Rivers—
 Ahkyang 54, 95, 99, 104, 105, 112, 122, 126, 165; expedition to 115, 161
 Chipwi hka 5, 6, 7, 14
 Daru hka 153
 Hpawte 60
 Irrawaddy 1, 2, 18, 25, 60, 76, 77, 115, 128, 130, 133, 134, 137, 152, 158; confluence of 156, 158, 160; navigation on 2, 156; sources of 2, 133, 154, 164, 166
 Laking hka 54, 71, 72, 76, 77, 81, 89, 95, 158
 Mali hka 2, 6, 46, 84, 115, 126, 128, 130, 137, 138, 140, 141, 144, 146, 151, 154, 156, 158
 Mekh rame 54, 81, 84, 85, 86, 89, 92, 94, 97, 99
 Mekong 2, 13, 41, 58, 72, 85, 168
 Nam Lang 140
 Nam Palak 130, 131, 133, 140
 Nam Tisang 118, 122, 123, 125
 Nam Yak 141
 Namre rame 89, 99, 100, 101
 Ngawchang hka 3, 7, 8, 9, 14, 29, 30, 39, 48, 56, 58, 59, 60, 61
 Ngawchang hka 5, 8, 11, 16, 31, 32, 39, 49

'Nmai hka 1, 2, 3, 4, 5, 7, 76, 82, 83, 84, 85, 86, 89, 93, 95, 97, 99, 100, 101, 104, 105, 115, 128, 144, 147, 151, 156, 158; farewell to 115
'Nsop-zup 2
Salween 2, 13, 25, 42, 60, 72, 93, 168
Shang wang 118
Shingaw hka 4
Shweli 24, 25
Ta hka 125
Tammu hka 5
Ti hka 126
Tumpang hka 4
Wot hka 142
rope bridge 74, 113

S
slavery, abolition of 134
storm, a destructive 102

T
terrier pup, adventures of 79, 85, 108, 109, 124, 126
thunderstorm 5, 74, 76, 81, 86, 98
trade routes in Asia 166, 167
Trees and plants—
  Acer 12, 170
  Aeschynanthus 61
  Ailanthus 107
  alders 7, 8, 31, 53, 61, 73, 104, 105
  Allium 66, 170
  Alnus nepalensis 56, 107
  Alocasia 82
  Amorphophallus 61, 75
  Androsace 42, 170
  Androsace axillaris 25
  Anemone vitifolia 31
  Aristolochia 24, 147
  Aroid 107
  Astilbe 54, 68
  azalea 112
  balsams 14, 21, 32, 36, 40, 54, 60, 61, 68, 73, 117, 123
  bamboos, magnificient 125
  banana 79, 100, 112, 114, 125, 130, 142, 146
  Bauhinia 29, 146, 147
  Beesia cordata 23, 170
  begonias 30, 49, 92, 107, 117, 141, 147

  birch 68, 105, 107
  Borassus 123
  bracken 7, 13, 14, 21, 31, 48, 49, 50, 53, 68
  broomrape 46 bryony 48
  Bucklandia 12, 35
  buckthorn 23
  Buddleia limitanea 54, 170
  bugle 21
  Cassiope 41, 42, 46, 170
  Castanopsis 107
  castor-oil plant 151
  cherry 44, 68
  Chirita 60, 75, 82, 92, 97, 170
  clematis 12, 22
  club-mosses 74
  Codonopsis 23, 54, 170
  coffin plank tree 58, 59
  Colocasia 60, 92
  conifer forest: see Floras
  convolvulus 92, 123, 133
  Coptis teeta 70
  Corydalis 36, 68, 170
  Corydalis saltatoria 36, 170
  Cotoneaster 26, 29, 170
  cotton grass 48, 49
  Cremanthodium 41, 42, 46, 66, 171
  cuckoo-pint *(Arisxma)* 12, 22
  Curcuma 3
  currant 68
  Cynoglossum 54
  cypress 59
  Cypripedium 26, 53, 171
  Cypripedium arietinum 53
  Dendrobium 9, 60, 146, 171
  Deutzia 22
  Diapensia himalayica 42
  Didissandra 49
  Englehardtia 112
  Enkianthus 171
  Epilobium 54
  ferns 12, 22, 23, 30, 31, 32, 41, 49, 60, 74, 82, 92, 97, 107; bird's-nest 75, 123
  Ficus cunea 75
  Ficus elastica 153
  fig-trees 5, 73, 75, 123, 131, 144, 146
  fir-trees 40, 65, 66, 74
  flowers, a paradise of 23
  forget-me-not 30

INDEX

geranium 13, 54
Gleichenia liniaris 60
Globba 60, 147
grass-of-Parnassus 66
Hamamelis 53
Hedychium 14, 147, 171
Hibiscus 108
holly 23
honeysuckle 12, 23
Hydrangea 13, 171
Hypericum patulum 8
Impatiens 92, 97, 107, 115, 117
irises 10, 15, 22, 32, 59, 171
jasmine 26
juniper 44, 58
larkspur 66
Leptocodon 171
Liliaceae 41
lilies 14, 22, 23, 30, 31, 48, 53, 68
Lilium giganteum 23; nepalense 14, 53, 174; Thompsonianum 66, 171; Wallichianum 12, 14, 171
louseworts 66
Luculia gratissima 22
Lygodium (climbing fern) 30, 58
magnolias 7, 12, 35, 64
maple 68
marrows 81, 140
meadow-rue 23, 31, 48, 54, 66, 68
Meconopsis Wallichii 67, 171
Melastoma 82, 107
Mimulus nepalensis 21
monkey-flower (Mimulus) 21, 54, 68
monkshood 66
Mucuna 76, 172
mulberry 153, 156
Nipa 123
Nomocharis 13, 44, 66, 172
oak -trees 7, 8, 12, 23, 29, 35, 53, 56, 64, 102, 107, 117, 146
orchids 3, 9, 22, 23, 31, 32, 44, 46, 53, 60, 82, 146; butterfly (Calanthe) 12; remarkable numbers of 8, 9
Osmunda regalis 14
palms 5, 57, 74, 82, 107, 123, 125, 130, 131, 133, 146
peach-trees 70
Pedicularis, 40, 54
Pieris 7, 12

pine-trees 7, 8, 9, 31, 63, 56, 73, 86
Piper 107
Podophyllum Emodi 41
Polygonum 30, 46, 54, 58, 69, 107, 108, 172
poplar 53, 107
poppywort 67
Primula 42, 45, 53, 172
Primula Beesiana 23, 172; coryphaei 45; Delavayi, 66; fragilis, 25, 172; melodoxa 23, 172; limnoica 12, 172; obconica 7; sciophila 42, 45, 172;seclusa 22, 53; sonchifolia 13, 23, 172
Pseudotsuga 24
Pyrus 8, 46, 112, 172
raspberries 11, 15, 22, 40, 68
Rheum 66
rhododendron agapetum 49, 53; an epiphytic 7, 22; crassum 46; indicum 8, 75, 112; megacalyx 22, 172; nmaiense 45, 173; sino-grande 24, 173
rhododendrons 12, 13, 22, 23, 35, 40, 41, 44, 45, 46, 49, 52, 53, 54, 59, 65, 66, 73, 93; dwarf 45, 46; size of 41
Rodgersia 54
rose 23, 44, 140
rowan 68
royal fern 14, 54
rubber-tree 153
Sagittaria 15
sago palms 73, 77, 81, 102, 130, 146, 151
Saxifraga purpurascens 46
saxifrages 36, 41, 66, 68
Schima 12
Schizandra 12
screw pines 107, 117, 140, 146
Selaginella 32, 92, 97
Senecio 66
spiraea 44
stitchwort 66
strawberries 25
Strobilanthes 60, 66, 69, 81, 174
sundew 14
Thunbergia grandiflora 142, 146
Torenia 93, 174
Tradescantia 15
tree ferns 73, 107, 146

Umbelliferae 66
walnut-trees 57, 81, 115, 153
wayfaring-tree 23
Weigelia 26
willow 13, 44, 46
willow-herb (Epilobium) 14
Zingiberaceae 53, 147
Tribes—
　Chingpaw 16, 122
　Duleng, dress of 122, 123
　Hkamti Shans, decline of 149
　Kachin burial customs 143; customs 150; rafts 2
　Kachins 15, 19, 104; dress of 143; independence of 150; religion of 140; silk weaving 153; truculence of 143, 149
　Lashi intrigue 50, 51; savageness 17
　Lashis 8, 16, 17, 19, 20, 23, 26, 31, 33, 36, 37, 40, 44, 50, 51, 57, 59, 63, 69, 71, 79, 83, 110, 112, 135; dress of 30, 31, 48, 49; origin of; 15, 16, 17, 134; relationships of 15
　Lisu huts, situation of 109
　Lisus 7, 71, 89, 104, 107, 109, 110, 111, 113, 114, 115; hua 110
　Marus 7, 15, 16, 69, 70, 71, 72, 78, 79, 80, 82, 83, 85, 89, 104, 137, 151, 152
　Maru courtship 79, 87; customs 76, 77, 78, 83, 85, 87, 96, 104; graves 83, 143; hut, structure of 76, 77, 83; method of carrying loads 83; villages, situation of 5
　Maru, dress of 70, 71, 72, 78, 79, 81; home of 5, 89; origin of 135
　Minchia 21, 26
　Naingvaws 78, 83, 158
　Nungs 16, 137, 139, 142, 151, 154
　Shans 1, 5, 13, 16, 17; history of 16, 134, 149; huts 137;relations of, with Great Britain 149; religion of 135
　Shapa Lisu 65, 70
　Singphos 137
　Tai, tragic history of 133, 134
　Tribal names, origin of 16
　Tribes, distribution of 16, 17
　　Chinese names for different 16
　Yawyins 8, 16, 17, 24, 31, 57, 63, 64, 69, 71, 83, 96, 97, 110; Chinese influence on 110; dress of 63
　T'ung-ch'ien 3, 30, 41, 44, 50, 55, 58, 59, 69, 79, 95, 112, 157

V
village of the dead, a 47

W
water from bamboos 32

ABOUT THE AUTHOR

Frank Kingdon-Ward (1885–1958), OBE, the son of a leading British research botanist and University of Cambridge professor, graduated with honours from Cambridge in Natural Sciences, in 1906, and subsequently accepted a teaching position in Shanghai. In 1909, he broke this contract to travel across central and western China; while the expedition was not specifically botanical in purpose, Kingdon-Ward assembled a small collection of plant samples enroute, which were subsequently presented to the Botany School of Cambridge.

In 1911, he was engaged by the horticultural firm of Bees Ltd. of Liverpool, to collect botanical specimens in Yunnan, an assignment which began for Kingdon-Ward a lifelong career as a professional explorer and plant collector.

In all Kingdon-Ward made a total of twenty-two expeditions, spanning a period of some forty-five years, in western China, northern Burma, Assam and south- eastern Tibet; much of this travel involved extreme hardship, and was undertaken at great risk to his health and personal safety. On all of his travels, Kingdon-Ward not only collected rare and valuable plants, but also surveyed and mapped previously uncharted territories.

During WWI, Kingdon-Ward served in the Indian Army, achieving the rank of captain. He was in Burma when Japanese forces invaded that country in WWII, but with his intimate knowledge of the terrain, he was successful to evade capture and enter India, where he was subsequently engaged to instruct British forces on techniques for jungle survival.

But it was Kingdon-Ward's contribution to botany which remains his foremost legacy, as the plant genera *Kingdon-wardia*, and *Wardaster*, and the wealth of previously unknown plant species now bearing the suffixes *wardii* and *kingdonwardii* attest. In the course of his long and productive career, Kingdon-Ward received honours for his botanical contributions from many learned societies, including the Royal Geographic Society, the Royal Horticultural Society, the Linnean Society of London and the Royal Central Asian Society, among others.

Frank Kingdon-Ward was also a prolific writer, describing his travels in 25 books, as well as in over 700 articles in both scholarly and popular botanical journals. In addition to the present volume, Orchid Press has published the following titles, long out of print:

> *A Plant Hunter in Tibet* (first published 1934)
> *Burma's Icy Mountains* (first published 1949)
> *Return to the Irrawaddy* (first published 1956)

www.ingramcontent.com/pod-product-compliance
Lightning Source LLC
Chambersburg PA
CBHW020849160426
43192CB00007B/844